T0322650

"If there's a soul adrift—physically or spiritually—in the Gem State, chances are good he sprang from the fertile pen of Samuel D. Hunter."

—*PLAYBILL*

"*A Great Wilderness* is meant to challenge, and most will leave the theater with a somber and agonizing sense of unfairness."

—SARAH BRINK, *VANGUARD SEATTLE*

"Hunter hears Middle America's quiet desperation, the low moan of people who have lost their connection to the past, to loved ones, to the lives they thought they'd lead. Many of them are living on the margins, losing ground. These are the inhabitants of his resonant, often ruefully funny plays. Hunter . . . writes with preternatural insight into people of all ages and wildly differing circumstances."

—DARYL H. MILLER, *LOS ANGELES TIMES*

"Hunter is an important new voice in the American theater."

—CHARLES McNULTY, *LOS ANGELES TIMES*

"Hunter tunes into a high frequency of empathy for isolated social-fringe dwellers."

—MISHA BERSON, *SEATTLE TIMES*

Five Plays

Five Plays

Samuel D. Hunter

THEATRE COMMUNICATIONS GROUP
NEW YORK
2016

The publication of *Five Plays* by Samuel D. Hunter, through TCG's Book Program, is made possible in part by the New York State Council on the Arts with the support of Governor Andrew Cuomo and the New York State Legislature.

This publication was supported by the Vilcek Foundation, dedicated to fostering appreciation of the arts and sciences.

TCG books are exclusively distributed to the book trade by Consortium Book Sales and Distribution.

Library of Congress Control Numbers:
2016039888 (print) / 2016045850 (ebook)
ISBN 978-1-55936-501-7 (softcover) / ISBN 978-1-55936-837-7 (ebook)
A catalog record for this book is available from the Library of Congress.

Book design and composition by Lisa Govan
Cover design by Carol Devine Carson

First Edition, November 2016

For John

Contents

Pocatello

Production History

Pocatello received its world premiere at Playwrights Horizons (Tim Sanford, Artistic Director; Leslie Marcus, Managing Director) on December 15, 2014. It was directed by Davis McCallum. The set design was by Lauren Helpern, the costume design was by Jessica Pabst, the lighting design was by Eric Southern, and the sound design was by Matt Tierney; the production stage manager was Lisa Ann Chernoff. The cast was:

EDDIE	T.R. Knight
MAX	Cameron Scoggins
ISABELLE	Elvy Yost
TROY	Danny Wolohan
DORIS	Brenda Wehle
NICK	Brian Hutchison
KELLY	Crystal Finn
COLE	Jonathan Hogan
TAMMY	Jessica Dickey
BECKY	Leah Karpel

Pocatello was originally developed under the title *When You're Here* with support of Geva Theatre Center (Mark Cuddy, Artistic Director), Philadelphia Theater Company (Sara Garonzik, Producing Artistic Director) and Williamstown Theatre Festival (Jenny Gerston, Artistic Director), where it was presented as a workshop on August 14, 2011. It was directed by Portia Krieger. The set design was by Jarrod Bray, the costume design was by Bridget Gavlin, the lighting design was by Steven Maturno, and the sound design was by Charles Coes; the production stage manager was Stephen Milosevich. The cast was:

EDDIE	Harry Ford
MAX	Matthew Nuernberger
ISABELLE	Claire Siebers
TROY	Peter Albrink
DORIS	Vella Lovell
NICK	Kevin Reed
KELLY	Phillipa Soo
COLE	Michael Shaw
TAMMY	Emily Mattheson
BECKY	Crystal Lucas Perry

Characters

EDDIE	Male, early thirties
MAX	Male, early twenties
ISABELLE	Female, twenties
TROY	Male, mid-thirties
DORIS	Female, sixties, Eddie and Nick's mother
NICK	Male, mid to late thirties, Eddie's older brother
KELLY	Female, mid-thirties, Nick's wife
COLE	Male, seventies, Troy's father
TAMMY	Female, late thirties, Troy's wife
BECKY	Female, seventeen, Troy and Tammy's daughter

Setting

The play takes place entirely on the floor of a nationwide Italian restaurant franchise in Pocatello, Idaho. The set should be specific enough that we know exactly what it is but general enough that it could be anywhere in the country. There are several tables in the space, along with bussing stations and an ordering station with a computer. The entire look of the stage should be the American idea of Italianness: wine bottles, paintings of Tuscany, plastic grapes, etc. Two wall-mounted speakers play touristy Italian, pop, or country music at various points in the play.

Notes

Dialogue written in *italics* is emphatic, deliberate; dialogue in ALL CAPS is impulsive, explosive.

A "/" indicates an overlap in dialogue. Whenever a "/" occurs, the following line of dialogue should begin.

Ellipses (. . .) indicate when a character is trailing off, dashes (—) indicate where a character is being cut off, either by another character or themselves.

If desired, an intermission can be taken between scenes four and five.

Scene One

Throughout the scene there is the steady sound of bad pop music playing in the background. Somewhere onstage is a large banner that reads "Famiglia Week."

At one table: Doris, Nick, and Kelly. At another: Cole, Tammy, and Becky. Isabelle is taking Nick's order. The other group have finished their entrées and are about to order dessert.

The scene starts suddenly, like we're being thrown into the middle of something that's been going on for a while.

ISABELLE: —the "Tour of Italy," which is lasagna and / fettuc-
cine—
NICK: There's meat in that?
ISABELLE: The lasagna? Yes.
NICK: / Good.

COLE: Don't make them sing. I don't like it when you make them sing. Didn't like last year.

(Max enters, approaches Tammy, Becky, and Cole.)

TAMMY: / Oh Dad. Grumpy grump!
DORIS: The manicotti, gluten-free pasta please.
MAX: / Everyone finished?

(Max starts clearing dishes.)

ISABELLE: We actually don't have gluten-free pasta right now.
DORIS: You *don't*? You don't have *gluten-free pasta*?

(Eddie enters.)

MAX: / Can I get you guys anything for dessert?
DORIS *(To Eddie)*: Eddie, this girl here is saying / that you don't—
EDDIE: We're out of gluten-free pasta, Mom.
TAMMY: / Well we sort of have a special occasion?
NICK: Just have regular pasta.
MAX: Oh right!
BECKY: / Jesus Christ.
DORIS: *My stomach will / make noise.* Let me just— . . .
TAMMY: You know you can choose to be a happy person, Becky, / you can—
BECKY *(To Tammy)*: There's genocide happening, *right now*.
MAX: Um.
DORIS *(Looking at the menu)*: / Well if you don't have that, I just don't see anything here that I can eat.
BECKY: Children are being *killed*. Women are being *raped*. I am not "choosing" / to be a—
EDDIE *(Looking at the menu)*: / Well what about—? Oh, no.
MAX: Oh, / I don't—

TAMMY: She'll have the tiramisu. You want the tiramisu, right Becky?

BECKY: Stop calling me Becky.

NICK: You really can't / eat the regular pasta?

KELLY *(To Nick)*: Nick, she said she can't have it.

MAX: / O—kay, I'll be right back then.

(Max exits.)

NICK: I'm just saying a little bit won't kill you.

TAMMY: / Thank you.

DORIS: Oh never mind, I'll just have the salad.

EDDIE: Sorry, Mom.

(Eddie exits. Troy enters, crossing the stage. Tammy grabs him on his way over.)

TAMMY: Troy, why haven't you been serving us?

KELLY: / Is there anything you recommend?

TROY: It's not my section.

TAMMY: Did you tell them it was your dad's birthday?

ISABELLE: / Oh I mean it's like all really super good.

TROY: It doesn't work like that.

TAMMY: Becky and I were thinking—

BECKY: / *Oh my God* stop calling me Becky.

KELLY: Oh. I guess then—chicken, then.

TROY: Tammy, let's not start anything today, please?

(Troy exits.)

ISABELLE: Okay, I'll get that right out to you. Can I do anything else for you in the meantime?

NICK: No thanks.

(Isabelle exits.)

9

TAMMY *(To Becky)*: / Why don't you give Grandpa the present you got for him?

DORIS: You didn't have to make such a scene, now I won't get enough to eat.

(Becky takes a small wrapped present out of her bag and gives it to Cole.)

NICK: Oh for God's sake.

KELLY: Mom, I just think that Nick / was trying—

DORIS: Oh honey don't call me that, I told you, I don't like it.

(Cole opens the present.)

BECKY: It's a Chia. It's shaped like a head.

COLE: I don't understand.

TAMMY: Now you have something to take care of!

(Becky pulls out a book, starts reading.)

KELLY *(To Doris)*: So did Nick tell you / the good news?

TAMMY: Will you put that away please?

DORIS: / Good news? Oh my, are you . . . ?

BECKY: No.

NICK: Oh God no, I'm—. / It's a job thing, I got a promotion.

TAMMY: It's Grandpa's birthday.

DORIS: / Oh. Well that's good.

BECKY: Yay.

(Eddie enters, goes to Doris, Nick, and Kelly. Max reenters with a large carafe of rosé wine, goes to Tammy.)

EDDIE: Sorry, guys, one of our deep fryers is being weird, and / our cook doesn't—

DORIS: / We understand.

MAX *(To Cole and Tammy)*: Would you guys like to try a sample?

TAMMY: Oh—sure!

(Max pours Tammy a taste of wine. Eddie sits with Doris, Nick, and Kelly.)

MAX: / Anything free is good, right? Heh. It's a white zinfandel. It's bright and flavorful. How was the food, by the way?

EDDIE: It's just—it's really great to have you guys here. It's been way too long, we're finally all in the same room / together—

COLE: / The meat in my lasagna was strange.

DORIS: How much is the discount?

BECKY: / Well you know ground beef has a ton of feces in it.

EDDIE: Oh, it's—it's fifty percent, it's half off—

COLE *(To Becky)*: / Feces?

NICK: She thinks you can / get it for free.

TAMMY: Okay, Becky.

KELLY *(To Nick)*: Honey.

(Isabelle enters, goes to Eddie.)

DORIS: Well. / He's the manager.

ISABELLE: Eddie, Theo is really freaking out about / the fryer in there—

EDDIE: / Okay, thanks, just a minute.

(Isabelle exits.)

BECKY: I read all about it, there's like a ton of feces in ground beef / because the meat industry doesn't even—

DORIS: Fifty percent is fine, Eddie, thank you.

TAMMY: / *Becky for the love of God.*

EDDIE: I mean I can probably get you some free appetizers if you guys want?

MAX *(Referring to the wine)*: / Do you—want more?

EDDIE: We've got sauces for breadsticks, this mozzarella fondue thingy—

TAMMY: / Yes!

DORIS: Oh I'm sorry that all just sounds so disgusting.

(Isabelle rushes in, waves at Eddie. Max pours Tammy a full glass.)

ISABELLE: *Eddie.*

EDDIE *(To Nick, Kelly, and Doris)*: Lemme just take care of this, and I'll / be right back—

DORIS: Eddie, it's fine.

NICK: Go back to work, buddy, don't worry about it.

(Eddie exits with Isabelle. Max finishes pouring the wine and exits. Tammy notices Nick from across the room.)

TAMMY: Nicky?!

(Nick looks up.)

NICK: Oh, God. Tammy?

(Tammy gets up with her wine, approaching Nick.)

TAMMY: How are you?! It's been forever!

NICK: Yeah, we're just here for a couple days.

TAMMY: Is this your wife?!

KELLY: I'm Kelly.

TAMMY: She's so cute! Nicky, she's so cute!

DORIS: You and Nicky used to date, didn't you?

COLE *(To Becky)*: / What's that you were saying about the feces in the ground beef?

12

DORIS: You were the one with the bangs.

TAMMY: Yes!

DORIS: They were so strange.

TAMMY: / I always admired you for leaving. I doubt Troy and I are ever gonna get outta here. What do you do now?

BECKY *(Pulling out her phone)*: Seriously, the meat industry is horrible, they don't even care. I saw a video on the internet about how they slaughter cows, do you want to see it?

NICK: / I'm in real estate, in Saint Paul.

COLE: Yes.

TAMMY *(Louder than she intends)*: Holy crap! Too bad for me, I could've been— . . . !

(Tammy stops herself, takes a drink of wine.)

It's so good to see you!

(Becky shows a video on her phone to Cole. Troy reenters with some dirty dishes, sees Tammy with the wine, and goes to her.)

TROY: Tammy, what are you doing?

TAMMY: It was—. It's just a sample, he offered me a— . . .

(Short pause. Troy turns away.)

TROY *(To Nick)*: Hi Nicky.

NICK: Hey, Troy.

(Troy exits. Awkward pause.)

TAMMY: Well it's good to see you. She's so pretty.

(Tammy goes back to her table.)

NICK: Anyway, it's not that much more money, but it's a step forward, you know.

DORIS: / Wonderful.

TAMMY *(To Becky)*: What are you doing?

KELLY: / He's very well-liked.

BECKY: He wants to see it.

DORIS: Well of course he is.

BECKY *(Referring to the video)*: And after the knife goes into their throat and they flip around sometimes the cow gets stuck in the / machine and—

TAMMY *(Grabbing the phone)*: / *You're embarrassing us.*

NICK: It's a small company but they've got a great reputation.

DORIS: I'm very impressed.

NICK: Okay, I'm not trying to "impress" you, / I was just talking.

KELLY: / Nick—

DORIS: Nicky please don't read into what I'm saying, I'm truly very impressed.

(Max, Isabelle, and Troy enter, approaching Cole. Isabelle holds a slice of cake with a candle on top. They start singing. Max and Troy aren't that into it; Isabelle is very into it, harmonizing toward the end.)

MAX, ISABELLE, AND TROY *(Singing)*: *Happy birthday / to you, happy birthday to you,* etc.

COLE: What did I say? What did I just tell you?

NICK: / Anyway it's just—a good thing for me.

TAMMY: Oh Dad. Grumpy grump!

DORIS: / Congratulations.

BECKY: Happy birthday Grandpa.

NICK *(Defeated)*: / Thanks.

COLE: I fought in Korea. Stop singing.

(Max, Isabelle, and Troy finish singing. They all applaud.)

14

ISABELLE: *Abbondanza!*

DORIS: / It's so cold in here. Ask Eddie why they keep it so cold?

BECKY: Mom, I'm not eating this.

TAMMY: / Becky you're really pushing it.

NICK: Why do I need to ask him?

KELLY *(To Nick)*: *Honey.*

NICK: / *What?*

TAMMY: Just blow out the candle.

TROY: Blow out the candle, Dad.

BECKY: Maybe he doesn't want to blow out the fucking candle.

(Eddie pops his head in, speaking to Doris, Nick, and Kelly.)

TROY: / *Becky.*

EDDIE: Just give me a minute, I'm so sorry.

NICK: It's fine.

TROY: / Okay, Dad just—. Blow it out.

DORIS: Eddie why is it so cold in here?

BECKY: / I hate this family.

EDDIE: Oh, uh—I don't know?

TAMMY: / Why do you say these things?!

DORIS: Well maybe this is why it's closing. It's too cold / for people to eat—

TAMMY: / Is it too much to ask that your grandfather has a nice—?

EDDIE: *Sh*—Mom—

NICK: Wait what's happening?

TROY: DAD, JUST BLOW OUT THE DAMN CANDLE ALREADY.

(Everyone turns to Cole. Cole looks at the lit candle in front of him, staring at it. There is a very, very long silence during which we only hear music playing in the background. Finally, Cole blows out the candle. Everyone claps halfheartedly.)

15

ISABELLE: Yay! Today you're part of our *famiglia*!

(Isabelle, Max, and Troy all exit.)

NICK: How long do you have?
EDDIE: Um. We really shouldn't—
COLE: / I'm done. I'm going to the car to do my word search.
NICK: What are you gonna do?

(Cole gets up and slowly exits. Troy enters, seeing Cole leave.)

EDDIE: / I don't— . . . I guess I'm not totally sure yet? I'm still working on it—
TAMMY: *Fine*, we're staying here and finishing our desserts. You're seventy-seven for God's sake, you're acting like a child.
DORIS: / I told him there's a new one opening up in Rexburg. He didn't even apply.
BECKY: Maybe he thinks you're acting like a child.
TAMMY: Becky, I swear to God—

(Troy enters.)

BECKY: / *Stop calling me that.*
EDDIE: I don't want to move to Rexburg, I live here.
TROY *(To Tammy)*: What did you say to him?
NICK: / Maybe it'd be good for you.
TAMMY: Oh my God, he's *your* father.

(Troy exits, heading after Cole.)

EDDIE *(To Doris)*: Mom and I'd never see each other.
DORIS: Well.
EDDIE: What? *(Pause)* Mom, what?
DORIS: I'm just saying it might be good for you, that's all.

EDDIE: / But I mean we barely see one another as it is—

BECKY: I don't feel good.

DORIS: / Eddie you're so sensitive.

TAMMY: Just calm down.

EDDIE: / Listen, maybe we could all do Christmas together this
year?

BECKY: I think I need to go the bathroom.

EDDIE: / We could do it here, or we could all go to Saint Paul—

TAMMY: Are you going to make yourself throw up?

DORIS: / Maybe next year, I'm thinking of doing a cruise with
Eileen this Christmas.

TAMMY: I'm not going to let you go to the bathroom if you're
going to make yourself throw up.

NICK: Yeah, we're going to Miami. / We're just sick of the holidays.

BECKY: Mom, I'm really sick.

TAMMY: If you're going to make yourself throw up—

BECKY: / *Mom.*

DORIS: You can afford / another trip after flying all the way out
here?

TAMMY: *Becky sit down right now.*

(Tammy takes Cole's cake, starts eating.)

NICK: I have money, Mom. I have a decent job.

DORIS: That's good, I'm saying that's *good.* Honestly, Nicky.

(Becky throws up on the table.)

TAMMY: *Oh my God, what is wrong with you?!*

(Troy reenters, sees the vomit.)

DORIS: Oh that's going to have a stench.

17

TAMMY: Troy, could you—?

TROY: Is she okay?

TAMMY: / *Troy.*

(Troy quickly exits.)

DORIS: Nicky I can't eat with vomit in the room.

NICK: / Mom, we already ordered.

TAMMY: Get into the car.

DORIS: Eddie, shouldn't someone be cleaning that up?

EDDIE: Oh, uh. Okay . . .

(Eddie quickly exits.)

BECKY: I told you I was sick.

(Eddie quickly exits. Isabelle enters with salad and bread-sticks for Doris, Nick, and Kelly.)

TAMMY: I said get into the car.

BECKY: *God I just hate everything about everything.*

ISABELLE: Here you go! Entrées will be right out.

(Tammy leaves some cash and pulls Becky out of the restaurant. Troy enters with cleaning supplies and starts cleaning up the vomit. Doris gets up.)

DORIS: C'mon.

KELLY *(To Doris)*: Oh, are we—? Are we going somewhere else?

NICK: Mom, the food is coming, we can't / just—

DORIS: They can't expect us to eat food when there's vomit in the room. There's an Applebee's on Ridgemont.

(Nick and Kelly get up.)

NICK: Dear *God*, this is turning into an ordeal.

DORIS: No more histrionics. No one likes a loud person.

(Doris, Nick, and Kelly exit. There is a moment of silence with Troy cleaning up the vomit and the music playing in the background. Eddie reenters with cleaning supplies. He sees Troy cleaning the vomit, then looks to where Doris, Nick, and Kelly were sitting. The food sits untouched at an empty table.)

TROY *(To Eddie)*: Sorry, Becky, she——. She gets sick.

(Eddie doesn't respond. He continues to stare at the food.)

You're the one that wanted the *famiglia* week.

(Pause.)

EDDIE: I just thought it would be nice.

(Troy looks at Eddie.)

TROY: Look none of the other sections saw her throw up, they're /
  not—
EDDIE: It's fine, really, I'm not——. I just can't seem to get anything right this week.
TROY: It's not you, Eddie, it's just——. Look, it was a nice idea.

(Troy pats Eddie on the back, then exits with the cleaning supplies. Silence. Eddie stares at the empty table. Slowly he moves to the table, sitting down. He stares at the food in front of him as the music continues lightly in the background.
  After a moment Nick enters, approaching Eddie.)

NICK: Hey, buddy.

EDDIE: Hey, you—. You guys are leaving?

NICK: I think so? Sorry, you know Mom, she's decided we have to eat somewhere else, so—. *(Short pause)* You—doing okay? Kelly thought that something might be wrong, I wasn't sure / if—

EDDIE: Nah, I'm—. I'm fine.

NICK: Okay. *(Short pause)* Is there any other place in town to eat other than the Applebee's?

EDDIE: Not really.

NICK: What about that place on Alameda? Krista's / Kitchen?

EDDIE: Kathy's Kitchen, closed last year.

NICK: Huh.

EDDIE: Pretty much just fast food other than that now. Or the Old Country Buffet.

NICK: Oof, no thank you. *(Pulling out his wallet)* Here, lemme pay you for the food we / ordered—

EDDIE: Oh, you don't have to / do that—

NICK: Seriously, I'd feel bad.

(Nick hands him some cash. Eddie takes the money.)

And listen, uh—we're actually not gonna see you later if that's okay. Kelly and I are gonna head to Sun Valley for a couple of nights?

EDDIE: Oh. Really?

NICK: Yeah, she's never seen it, so.

(Pause.)

EDDIE: I was sort of hoping we could— . . . My apartment complex has a few grills in the courtyard, I thought I could pick up some meat and / we could—

NICK: Crap—sorry, buddy, we've just been— . . . I promised I'd show it to her this time around, and she— . . . *(Pause)*

Look, Eddie, I'm sorry. Kelly and I were both looking forward to seeing you today, felt like we've barely had a chance to catch up.

EDDIE: *Yeah*, right?

NICK: It's just—I don't know, being back home . . . I feel like once I'm back in Pocatello for more than a couple days, I just get— . . . It's just too much. And this is the only vacation time that we're both going to have for a while, so we just—. And our room at the La Quinta is sorta—not great, the bed / has this—

EDDIE: I mean you guys are welcome to stay at my apartment? I mean it's kinda tight but the futon's pretty comfortable actually—

NICK: Oh nah, we—. We wouldn't want to put you out. *(Pause)* But I mean it really is good seeing you, and we'll swing by the restaurant before we head out. And seriously, don't worry about Mom.

EDDIE: Yeah, she—. I feel like I don't even know how to talk to her anymore.

NICK: Did you *ever* know how to talk to her?

EDDIE: I mean, *yeah*, when I was in high school, it was just / different, it—

NICK: Yeah, well. That was a long time ago.

(Pause.)

EDDIE: Sure.

(Pause.)

NICK: Eddie, you—? You sure you're okay?

(Pause. Eddie looks at Nick.)

EDDIE: No, Nicky, actually I— . . . I'm sort of—in trouble? I don't know what to—. *(Pause)* They're saying I'm gonna have to shut down the restaurant at the end of next week.

(Pause.)

NICK: Wait—*next week?*

EDDIE: They've been warning me for a while now, our profits haven't been—. We're just losing money at this point, and corporate's given me chance after chance—

NICK: And you haven't told your employees yet?

EDDIE: I mean I don't want them to give up, or— . . . I'm still hoping I can save it somehow, or—

NICK: Eddie, you have to tell your staff, if they're all losing their jobs, you have to— . . . *(Pause)* Well, what about Rexburg? Mom said there's one opening up there?

EDDIE: Yeah—

NICK: Maybe it's time to get out of Pocatello, buddy. Kelly and I were downtown earlier, it's looking pretty grim compared to the last time I was here.

EDDIE: Yeah lately it's been—. It's been bad for everyone.

NICK: Exactly, so maybe you should just—leave. Rexburg is fine, right?

EDDIE: Sure, it's—.

(Pause.)

NICK: Or hell, move somewhere else. Boise, or Portland, or— . . . Don't you think you'd be happier somewhere else? I mean you have options, you went to college.

EDDIE: I majored in Pacific Northwest History.

NICK: Yeah, well, you—. *(Pause)* Look, you'll land somewhere. You're a smart guy. And I can help you with your resume if you want, I'd be / happy to—

EDDIE: Nick, I'm feeling sort of—. I'd really appreciate it if you could stick around a few more days?

(Pause.)

NICK: Eddie—

EDDIE: Can't you just change your flight?

NICK: Buddy I really just can't take more time off, this month especially it's / really—

EDDIE: It's just that—I don't really know what to do, I don't / really—

NICK: Kelly has work too, we can't / just—

EDDIE: I could pay to change your plane ticket if you—

NICK *(Aggressive)*: Eddie c'mon, just— . . .

(Max enters, begins to clear the dishes off of a table. Nick stops himself, calms down. Pause. He lowers his voice, moves closer to Eddie.)

(Soft) Eddie, it's just—a restaurant. It's not even yours, it's a *chain* restaurant. I know you've been here a while, but it's—. You just need to find somewhere else, that's all. And for God's sake, *tell your employees.* *(Pause, normal volume)* Look, we'll—. We'll see you in a couple days, and you—. You're gonna be fine. Okay?

(Pause. Max has begun to listen.)

EDDIE: Sure. *(Pause)* Thanks, Nicky.

(Nick starts to exit.)

EDDIE: Bye to Kelly?

NICK: Sure.

(Nick is gone. Eddie stares at the food. Max grabs the last dish, approaches Eddie.)

MAX: You okay?

(Pause.)

EDDIE: Yeah.
MAX: You sure?

(Eddie looks up at him. Isabelle enters.)

ISABELLE: Max that fucking ravioli app has been sitting under the heat lamp for ten fucking stupid minutes.
MAX: *Sorry.* Geez.

(Max exits. Isabelle goes to Eddie.)

ISABELLE: Should I—? You want me to cancel the food?

(Eddie looks at her.)

EDDIE: Yeah, I guess you should.

Scene Two

Later that night.
     Eddie sits at one of the tables with receipts and a deposit bag, counting cash from the day. Isabelle sits with him. Eddie desperately tries to maintain his line of thought.

ISABELLE: Gemini?
EDDIE: No.
ISABELLE: Taurus?

EDDIE: No, Isabelle, I'm—

ISABELLE: Don't tell me! I'm really good at this. Pisces.

EDDIE: No. You were at my birthday, you sang to me.

ISABELLE: Well I don't like know what dates they correspond to, I just do it by feeling. Aries.

EDDIE: No.

(Troy enters.)

TROY: I'm not cleaning the bathrooms anymore. Eddie can't we get people to do this stuff again?

EDDIE: We can't afford cleaning staff right now.

TROY: Make Isabelle do it.

ISABELLE: No way. Scorpio.

EDDIE: / No.

TROY: Or Max.

(Max enters.)

MAX: What am I doing?

TROY: You're cleaning the bathrooms from now on.

MAX: / The fuck I am.

ISABELLE: Sagittarius.

EDDIE: Isabelle—

ISABELLE: I'm right aren't I?!

EDDIE: No.

TROY: Why do I have to do it every time I close?!

EDDIE: Okay, okay, we'll figure out a schedule at staff lunch on Thursday.

ISABELLE: I don't even use our bathrooms, I use the ones in the Men's Warehouse.

TROY: Are they nice?

ISABELLE: They are *so fucking nice*.

MAX: Hey Eddie, table eight left half a carafe.

EDDIE: / Yeah okay.

TROY *(To Isabelle)*: So what's my sign?

(Max exits.)

ISABELLE: Douchebag.

TROY: Nah I think that'd be the guy who dropped you off this morning.

ISABELLE: His name is Alex and he's younger *and* better looking than you, so.

TROY: You're saying *that* guy is better looking than *me*?

ISABELLE *(To Eddie)*: Eddie you've seen Alex, tell him.

(Eddie struggles to add up the receipts while talking.)

EDDIE: Oh I don't know, I just—

ISABELLE: Oh Eddie, I meant to tell you, some of the track lighting over table twelve is broken or something.

TROY: So change the bulbs.

ISABELLE: I'm sorry, was I talking to you?

(Max reenters with a half-full carafe of wine and four glasses. He sets them down and begins to pour everyone a glass.)

TROY: Eddie, can we get rid of the Famiglia Week stuff?

EDDIE: Just—give it a few days.

TROY: I love my family, but I don't need them at work.

ISABELLE: I wanted to kill myself today. Sometimes I'm glad that my parents are dead.

MAX: Jesus.

ISABELLE: I'm just kidding, calm down.

TROY: When I was still working at the paper mill we had a bring-your-daughter-to-work day. Becky almost lost her damn hand.

MAX: Why didn't you guys move after the mill closed? Everyone I knew who worked there is in Boise or Oregon now.

TROY: Tammy didn't want to make Becky switch schools. And so, I'm a fucking waiter.

(Max is about to pour Eddie a glass. Eddie waves him away.)

EDDIE: Oh, no, thanks.

MAX: C'mon buddy, long day.

EDDIE: Maybe—maybe in a bit, I'm just / trying to—

ISABELLE *(To Troy)*: Hey what's with your daughter?

TROY: What the hell is that supposed to mean?

(Max mimes throwing up on the table. Isabelle laughs.)

Very funny, assholes.

EDDIE: GUYS. PLEASE.

(Silence. They stare at Eddie, shocked at the outburst.)

Sorry. I'm—sorry.

(Pause.)

ISABELLE: You okay?

EDDIE: I'm fine, I—. *(Pause)* I lost count, I just—. I got frustrated, I'm sorry.

MAX: I think that's the first time I've ever heard you raise your voice.

EDDIE: Am I a terrible boss now?

TROY: You kidding? My last job at the Best Buy, my supervisor used to pour coffee in my backpack. You can shout once in a while, it's fine.

ISABELLE: Oh my God I worked there three years ago.

TROY: I hated it.

ISABELLE: Yeah I know. *Five percent* employee discount?

(Max tries again to pour Eddie some wine.)

EDDIE: No, really, I'm fine.

MAX: C'mon, it's a special occasion.

TROY: What, you got some new hair gel?

MAX: No, Eddie hired me six months ago today.

EDDIE: Oh. Wow, it's really been that long?

MAX: Yep.

TROY: I've been here *eight years*, you never hear me making a big deal out of it.

MAX: Anyway, Eddie, thanks. This was the only place in town that was willing to hire me.

EDDIE: Oh I don't believe that.

MAX: Seriously. I interviewed *everywhere*, the moment I said anything about drug court, they just fucking—. Anyway thanks for giving me a chance.

EDDIE: Well, we're lucky to have you. Really.

MAX: Thanks. *(Pause)* So, okay—maybe this is totally stupid of me, but—I thought maybe we could all— . . .

(Max reaches into his pocket and pulls out a small bag of weed and a pipe.)

ISABELLE: Hello.

EDDIE: Wait, what / is—?

MAX: It's just pot.

TROY: Six months working here and you want some big party?

EDDIE: Why do you / have that?

MAX: I know it's stupid, but it helps me stay off the other stuff.

EDDIE: That doesn't seem like a good idea to me?

MAX: No, really. They're completely different, this stuff calms me down. Gets my mind off of it. I don't know if I'd be clean without it. Meth is a drug that's all about—

(Max makes gestures to illustrate the idea of "the outside world.")

But pot's all about—

(Max makes gestures to illustrate the idea of "the inner life.")

Totally different.

EDDIE: Look, just—don't bring it to work, okay?

MAX: I won't, sorry. And I never come in to work stoned, I swear. *(Pause)* Does anyone—want some?

ISABELLE: Yes.

EDDIE: Guys, I don't know if—

(Isabelle takes the pipe and bag from Max and starts loading the pipe.)

. . . okay.

TROY: No wonder you're both so damn slow on the floor.

ISABELLE: What, you think this is any worse than wine?

MAX: Eddie, you take the first hit.

EDDIE: No, really I'm—I'm fine.

(Isabelle takes a hit. She and Max pass the pipe back and forth.)

MAX *(To Eddie)*: I have an older brother too. Total dick. Owns some bullshit office supply company in Twin Falls.

EDDIE: Oh.

MAX: We got into a fistfight three Christmases ago. Broke his jaw in two places. I don't spend much time around family nowadays. *(Pause)* Where's he visiting from?

EDDIE: Saint Paul. He's a real estate agent.

MAX: Dick. So is that why you—?

(Max points to the "Familigia Week" sign.)

EDDIE: I—guess. I just thought it would be nice for them. And all of you guys. *(Pause)* I don't know.

MAX: You're a good guy, Eddie.

TROY: All right, gimme that.

(Troy takes the pipe and takes a hit.)

MAX: Having a brother sucks. Two guys forced to live with one another just because they share some bullshit genetic material.

EDDIE: Yeah.

(Silence. Eddie continues to count cash.)

MAX: Does he give you a hard time for being— . . . ?

(Max makes a vague gesture. Troy and Isabelle freeze. Eddie looks at him.)

EDDIE: What?

MAX: You know. *(Pause)* Shit. I'm sorry.

EDDIE: What?

MAX: I'm really bad at this. Please don't be offended, I just assumed you were—. Are you?

(Pause.)

EDDIE: Well I don't exactly . . . I don't go around announcing it or whatever.

MAX *(To Troy)*: But I mean *you* knew, right?

TROY: C'mon, we've known each other for twenty years. None of my business anyway.

30

ISABELLE: Well I think it's *awesome.*

EDDIE: Thank—you. But we don't—. We don't need to keep talking about it.

(Uncomfortable pause.)

MAX: You know I'm bi.

TROY: Oh, Jesus.

EDDIE: You are?

ISABELLE: Bullshit.

MAX: No, really. I don't fall in love with a gender. I fall in love with a person. I'm attracted to people.

(Pause.)

EDDIE *(To Max)*: Have you ever— . . . ?

MAX: Oh, no. I mean not that I wouldn't. I just—. It hasn't come up. *(Pause)* Is your family okay with it?

EDDIE: Oh, we don't—. I mean we're not really a family that— talks? I mean my brother's fine, he doesn't care, but my mom—. I told her years ago, and she—. I don't think it sits very well with her.

ISABELLE: Are you seeing anyone?

EDDIE: No, I—. Not really. I was seeing this one guy in Boise a few years ago, but with the distance, it—. And there's just not much of an opportunity around here, I guess.

ISABELLE: I'm gonna work on that.

EDDIE: Please don't?

MAX: You ever thought about moving away?

EDDIE: Maybe, I don't know. I guess that'd be easier, but—. I just sort of feel connected to this town. It's weird, I feel like moving away would be like *abandoning* it or some- thing, like I'd be—. *(Pause)* Never mind, I'm babbling.

MAX: No, what?

31

(Pause.)

EDDIE: It's like— . . . *(Pause)* My family has been here forever, my great-grandpa's homestead is still standing outside of town. My dad used to take me and my brother out there, and he'd tell us how Great-Grandpa moved up here from Utah, built the house *by himself*, and it was like— . . . I used to know exactly who I was here, I recognized everything here. But lately, it— . . .

(Pause.)

I drive around Pocatello now, and I—. I get lost. So easily. Like I've never even been here before. *(Pause)* Okay now I really am babbling.

TROY: Eddie, I think that is the most I've heard you say, ever.

(Eddie chuckles a bit.)

EDDIE: I'm being stupid.

TROY: No, you're not. You're right, this town is shit nowadays. If we were smarter we'd all get the hell out of here.

(Troy downs his glass of wine.)

All right, am I done?

(Eddie hands Troy a small stack of bills. He glances through it.)

Ouch.

EDDIE: Yeah, bad day.

TROY: Fucking Famiglia Week. They were spending my money anyway.

(Eddie hands identical stacks of bills to Max and Isabelle. Isabelle quickly finishes her wine and gets up, Troy stands up as well.)

ISABELLE: I can't come in tomorrow until four thirty. I'm taking Penelope to the vet.
EDDIE: Okay.
TROY: G'night.
ISABELLE: Bye.
EDDIE: Bye.

(Troy begins to leave, Isabelle follows.)

TROY *(To Isabelle)*: You coming home with me tonight?
ISABELLE: You're disgusting.

(Troy and Isabelle exit.)

MAX: You okay?
EDDIE: Yeah. *(Pause)* Thanks, Max.

(Pause.)

MAX: Are you *sure* you don't want a hit? It's a really mellow strain, it's called Alaskan Thunderfuck but it's not / like—
EDDIE: No, I—. I'm fine.

(Max puts the pipe away, gathers his things, and stands up.)

MAX: I'll see you tomorrow?
EDDIE: Yeah.

(Max exits. Eddie watches him leave.)

Scene Three

The following day, around eleven A.M. The lights are off.

The lights snap on and Eddie enters, keys in hand. He crosses the stage, heading toward the back.

After a moment, Troy enters from another part of the restaurant, obviously having just woken up. He looks to where Eddie exited, then slowly starts to creep toward the exit. Eddie reenters, startled when he sees Troy.

EDDIE: OH—

TROY: I'm sorry. I'm sorry.

EDDIE: What are you / doing?

TROY: I'm sorry, okay, you got me. I—planned on waking up a few hours ago—

EDDIE: You *slept* here?

TROY: Look, I—Tammy and I got into it last night, and I left, and I—didn't feel like shelling out for a hotel. I was gonna leave before you got here, take a shower after Tammy went off to work, and—anyway, just. Sorry. *(Pause)* Look, I don't need to shower, let me just change and I'll—

EDDIE: No, you—go home, take a shower, I'll open, it's okay. *(Pause)* Listen, if this happens again, don't sleep here, just—. You know where I live.

TROY: C'mon.

EDDIE: Seriously. *(Pause)* Are you guys— . . . You doing okay?

TROY: It's fine, it's—whatever. Don't get married. *(Pause)* Yesterday at lunch Tammy decided to have her first drink in four months, and I told her that if she started drinking again then I—. Anyway.

EDDIE: Oh.

TROY: It'll be fine, we've been here before, this isn't the first time she— . . . Hell, we've been together for nineteen years, we're not going anywhere. *(Pause)* We're—fine. I love her, she loves me. We just fight.

(Tammy enters with Becky in tow.)

Woah, / what's—?

TAMMY: I need you to take Becky. Hi, Eddie.

TROY: Wait what?!

TAMMY: Just don't—. It's just for a few hours. She got suspended for the rest of the week. I can get off work but not until three.

TROY *(To Becky)*: What happened?

BECKY: I was just / telling—

TAMMY: *That matters?!*

TROY: Can't you just leave her at home?

TAMMY *(Soft)*: I *told you* Doctor Kendall said we shouldn't leave her alone / when—

BECKY: *I can hear you.*

TROY: Well what am I supposed to do with her?!

TAMMY: I don't know, Troy! Figure it out! I had to get off of work early, you can deal with this.

TROY: Fine, whatever. I was going to go home to take a shower and change clothes, but I guess that's not happening.

TAMMY: You didn't *shower?*

TROY: Did you want me to pay for a hotel? Do you have an extra / fifty bucks?

EDDIE: Listen, Troy—go home, take a shower, change clothes. I can stay with Becky.

(Pause.)

TROY: You sure?

EDDIE: I can open by myself. It's fine, I'll handle it.

(Pause.)

35

TROY: Jesus, Eddie, I'm sorry. Thank you.

TAMMY: Thank you Eddie. *(To Becky)* Don't—just—don't—

(Tammy and Troy exit. Becky and Eddie stand for a moment, unsure of what to do. Finally Becky sits down at a table and pulls a book out of her bag, starts reading.)

EDDIE: Would you—do you want something to eat? Some / soup, or—

BECKY: No.

(Pause.)

EDDIE: Breadsticks?

BECKY: *No.*

EDDIE: Okay, sorry, I—. I'll be, uh.

(Pause. Eddie starts to head back to the kitchen.)

BECKY: Look I'm not trying to be rude but I just think that you're part of the problem.

(Eddie turns to her.)

EDDIE: Oh. What problem?

BECKY: Like "the problem."

EDDIE: Oh, okay. *(Pause)* I still don't think I / understand—

BECKY: I don't want to eat your food because places like this are killing everyone. You're spraying pesticides on our crops and injecting our animals with antibiotics and making people fat and contributing to genocide.

EDDIE: Oh. *(Pause)* I brought some fruit with my lunch?

(Pause.)

BECKY: No. *(Pause)* Thank you.

(Silence. Eddie moves in a little closer.)

EDDIE: You know, Becky, / my—
BECKY: Don't call me that.
EDDIE: Oh. Why shouldn't / I—?
BECKY: I don't want to have a name.

(Pause.)

EDDIE: Really?
BECKY: No one in America deserves a name. And "Becky" is fucking stupid anyway.
EDDIE: So what should I call you?
BECKY: You don't need to call me anything.

(Pause.)

EDDIE: When I was a kid, for a while I started telling people my name was "Randolph."
BECKY: "Randolph"?
EDDIE: Yeah. It's my great-grandpa's name.
BECKY: Sounds like Adolph. Like Hitler.

(Pause.)

EDDIE: Yeah, I—I guess it— . . . *(Pause)* You know, I've known your mom and dad a long time, and they—. They're gonna work this out. *(Pause)* I remember going to your grandpa's hardware store downtown when you were just a toddler, and you were there running up and down the / aisles—
BECKY: I don't care if they get a divorce.
EDDIE: C'mon, don't say that.

BECKY: Maybe they'll get a divorce after this restaurant closes.

(Pause.)

EDDIE: What?

BECKY: I heard you talking to your family yesterday. People think I don't listen but I listen.

(Pause.)

EDDIE: Have you told your / dad?

BECKY: No. Why should I?

(Pause.)

EDDIE: It's not for sure yet that it's shutting down. We've been doing better these past couple nights and I might / be able to—

BECKY: I don't care.

EDDIE: But, I mean—if it does end up shutting down, you guys are gonna be fine, your dad can find work somewhere else—

BECKY: Seriously, *I don't care.* If he loses his job maybe they'll finally get a divorce, it'd probably be best for both of them.

EDDIE: You don't mean that.

(Pause. Becky closes her book.)

BECKY: Excuse me?

EDDIE: I'm just saying, you can't actually mean what you're saying right now.

BECKY: Do you know how many times a day people tell me I *don't* mean the thing I am very clearly saying?

EDDIE: Look, I was seventeen once / too—

BECKY: And do you know how many times a day people try to tell me they know me better than I know myself because they were once my age? *(Pause)* Do you know why I got suspended this morning? I was in history class. We were talking about World War II, and I tried to tell everyone about Nanking. Do you know what that is?

EDDIE: No.

BECKY: Of course you don't. It's a city in China, it was invaded by Japan in 1937 and three hundred thousand people were killed in six weeks. And I pulled out my phone and I typed "Nanking" into Google, and I started showing people pictures. *Real* pictures, stuff that *actually* happened. And the principal said it was "graphic," and I got suspended. For that.

(Pause.)

I go to a school where I get suspended for showing people *true things* from *history* in a *history class.*

(Becky goes back to her book. Silence.)

EDDIE: I shouldn't have said that you don't mean what you're saying. And—it's not fair that people fault you for thinking about things they would rather ignore.

(Becky peers up at him. Pause.)

My dad used to own this little diner here in town. When I was little he had to close it down. He put his whole life into the place, and when it was gone, he just— . . . He used to spend entire days just wandering around town, he'd come home and wouldn't say anything to us. And things just got worse and worse until— . . . And I'd go to my mom and tell her we needed to do something, that we needed to get him help, or—. And she would tell me that *I* didn't know what *I* was saying. And now I'm here telling you the same thing.

(Pause. Becky lowers her book, looking at Eddie.)

BECKY: What happened?

(Pause.)

EDDIE: He killed himself. When I was thirteen, with a shotgun. My brother found him.

(Pause.)

It's sort of hard to know how to live nowadays, isn't it?

(Pause.)

BECKY: Yeah. *(Pause)* Do you have like a banana?

(Pause.)

EDDIE: Yeah, uh—hold on.

(Eddie exits momentarily. Becky puts her book back into her bag. Eddie reenters with his bagged lunch, pulls out a banana and hands it to Becky.)

BECKY: Do you know if it's fair trade?
EDDIE: I—uh, I'm actually not sure.

(Becky looks at Eddie for a moment, rolling her eyes. She considers, then takes the banana.

Becky peels the banana carefully, eating small chunks of it.)

BECKY: My mom sends me to this psychiatrist, Doctor Kendall. The first time I saw him, he just sat there clicking a pen over and over and after like five minutes he tells me I have bulimia. And I'm like, no, I do *not* have bulimia, I don't give a shit if I'm skinny or not. It's just when I eat stuff, all I can think about is where it came from. Like, how the animal was slaughtered, or what third-world country produced the lettuce, how many antibiotics and chemicals have been pumped into it and I just—can't keep it down. So this idiot doctor tells me I'm bulimic, so I need to take antidepressants.

EDDIE: Do they help?

BECKY: I don't take them. Sometimes Mom makes me take one while she watches but I just throw it up.

EDDIE: That's really bad for you.

BECKY: So is taking a pill to forget about what you're actually eating.

(Eddie takes a sandwich out of the bag.)

What kind of meat is in that?

EDDIE: Are you gonna tell me how the animal got slaughtered?

BECKY: Yes.

EDDIE: It's cheese.

BECKY: Not much better.

(They eat for a moment or two.)

Why haven't you told anyone this place is shutting down?

EDDIE: Well, I haven't given up, and I don't want anyone else giving up either. I might be able to save it, the last few nights we've done a lot better—

BECKY: Why would you want to save this restaurant? This restaurant's for idiots.

EDDIE: Yeah, well, it's what we have to work with nowadays.

BECKY: The fucking wine bottles and fake grapes and shit. Only idiots would think this is like real Italy and forget they're in the Best Western parking lot.

EDDIE: I know, I know, but—just about everything else in town has shut down. It sounds dumb, but maybe I can make this place more—permanent.

BECKY: The Applebee's was a Denny's like two years ago. And before that a video store. Places like this barely even exist.

(Pause.)

EDDIE: Yeah.

(Becky puts the half-eaten banana down.)

BECKY: If I left right now would you be cool and tell my parents that I left when you weren't looking or something?

EDDIE: Oh. Uh—where do you wanna go?

BECKY: I don't know, just someplace that's not—here.

(Pause.)

EDDIE: I, uh—. I sort of told your parents I'd watch you—

BECKY: Whatever, I don't care what you tell them.

(Becky starts to leave.)

EDDIE: WAIT—how about—you wanna work here?

(Becky stops, turns to him.)

BECKY: What do you mean?

EDDIE: You're suspended for a few days, right? Why don't you work here? You can do dishes and bus tables.

BECKY: Why would I want to do that?

EDDIE: I'll pay you eight bucks an hour.

(Pause.)

BECKY: Fifteen.

EDDIE: Ten. And no lecturing customers about genocide or where the food came from.

(Pause. Becky moves back in.)

BECKY: The last ten minutes count as work.

EDDIE: Okay, sure. And just—don't tell anyone about the restaurant closing down, all right?

(Becky heads toward the back.)

There are aprons on the door to your right.

BECKY: I'm not wearing an apron.

(Becky exits. Eddie is silent for a moment, then takes out his keys and goes to a switch on the back wall. He inserts a key and turns it. A few more lights come on, and the Italian music begins to play in the background.

He is about to make his way into the back room when one of the speakers begins to crackle a bit. He looks up at it. It continues to make a crackling noise.

He moves a chair below the speaker, stands on it, and hits the speaker a few times. The noise stops.

He gets down and begins to exit. The speaker crackles again. Eddie looks up at it.)

Scene Four

Two days later.

Tammy and Cole sit at a table with food in front of them. Another table is covered with dirty dishes and a half-full bottle of wine. Cole eats a breadstick, Tammy watches. Italian music plays in the background.

COLE: Cardboard and salt.

TAMMY: Oh you're ridiculous. The breadsticks are the best reason to come here, they're delicious.

(Max enters, approaches Tammy and Cole.)

MAX: You guys doing okay?

TAMMY: We're great. How's Becky been the last few days? She's been okay, she's a good worker?

MAX: Uh, sure, she's just been bussing tables.

TAMMY: Is she good at it?

(Pause.)

MAX: . . . Yes.

TAMMY: Good!

MAX: You want anything else, or—?

TAMMY: I'll have another diet.

COLE: Coffee, please.

TAMMY *(To Max)*: Decaf.

COLE: Regular.

TAMMY *(To Max, soft)*: Decaf.

(Eddie enters, setting up a table. Max exits.)

Eddie! I know I already said it but *thank you.* I have no idea how you got that girl to wear an apron.

(Becky enters, wearing an apron, holding a bin for dirty dishes. She clears some plates off the empty table.)

EDDIE: She's a great worker.

(Becky plops some dishes down into the bin. Cole gets up.)

TAMMY: Dad, where are you going?
COLE: I'm not allowed to go to the bathroom by myself?
TAMMY: Don't get snippy, I was just asking.

(Cole makes his way out of the room.)

EDDIE *(To Tammy)*: Enjoy the rest of your lunch.

(Eddie exits. Becky goes to Tammy's table.)

TAMMY: Well this is nice, isn't it! For once you're the one waiting on *me.* Maybe we should try this at home.

(Becky takes Tammy's plate of pasta.)

I'm not finished with that.
BECKY: I don't care.

(Becky exits with the dishes.
Tammy sits for a moment in silence. The bad Italian music plays in the background.
She takes a few bites of a breadstick, then begins to look around the room. She notices a half-empty carafe of wine on another table.

45

She looks at it for a moment, then goes back to eating. She looks at the wine again, and then, eyeing her surroundings, moves toward the other table. She stops, grabs her half-empty coke off her table, then goes to the carafe, pouring the remainder of it into her glass of coke.

Troy enters, unseen by Tammy. She finishes pouring, then turns around, facing Troy.

She looks down at first, ashamed, then thinks better of it, and looks up at him. She defiantly raises the glass to her lips and takes a long drink. Troy stares at her, motionless.

Max enters with Tammy's soda and Cole's coffee. Troy and Tammy continue to stare at one another. Awkward pause.)

MAX *(To Tammy)*: Um. Here's—. Here's the diet.

(Max puts the soda down on Tammy's table.)

TAMMY *(Still looking at Troy)*: Bring me a bottle of the rosé? Thanks.
MAX: Um. Sure.

(Max exits. Silence.)

TROY: I'm taking Becky.
TAMMY: Of course you are.

(Pause.)

TROY: I'm calling County Care, I'll have them come and pick up Dad / and you—
TAMMY: Don't you have some tables to wait on?

(Pause. Troy exits.
Tammy falters, struggling to collect herself.
Cole reenters.)

COLE: Lydia, just take me back to the home.

(Pause. Tammy goes back to her table.)

TAMMY: I'm not Lydia.
COLE: What?

(Pause.)

TAMMY: You just called me Lydia. I'm Tammy.
COLE: I didn't call you Lydia, I'm not an idiot.

(Becky comes out of the kitchen to clear a table, notices the carafe of wine is now empty. She looks at Tammy.
Nick and Kelly enter. Nick goes to Becky.)

NICK: Hey, could you let Eddie know his brother's here?
BECKY: Okay. *(Points to a table)* You can sit there if you like.
NICK: We're fine, thanks.

(Becky exits.)

KELLY: You okay?
NICK: Yeah, I just—. I hate being late to the airport, I don't like worrying / about—
KELLY: We have plenty of time, what are you talking about?

(Eddie reenters.)

EDDIE: Hey! You guys made it, I'm so glad!
NICK: Hey, Eddie.

(Eddie motions to an empty table.)

EDDIE: Here, take a seat.

NICK: Oh, we—. I mean you're busy, we don't want to / bother you—

EDDIE: It's like three thirty, the place is almost empty, it's fine. And I made something special for you guys.

KELLY: I'm hungry.

NICK: Kelly—

KELLY: Well I am! I want to eat something before the flight anyway.

EDDIE: Okay, just—take a seat.

(Eddie moves to the table, pulling out a couple of chairs. Kelly sits.)

NICK: All right, we just—we don't have much time, okay?

EDDIE: This'll be quick?

KELLY: That'd be great.

(Eddie exits.)

We'll be quick.

NICK: We really don't have time for this, we're going / to—

KELLY: Nick. This is important to him, you know that. *(Pause)* Look I know this isn't fun for you, but you can't keep / just—

NICK: You don't really—. Kelly, you don't understand.

(Max enters with the bottle of rosé and a wine glass and pours a glass for Tammy.)

TAMMY: Thank you.

MAX: Sure.

(Pause.)

NICK: I'm sorry, okay? I just—. I don't want to be here.

(Pause. Max finishes pouring, exits.)

KELLY: He's really just *trying*, you know?

NICK: I know he's trying, he's *always* trying.

(Doris enters, sees Nick and Kelly, and approaches their table.)

DORIS: Hello Nick, hello Kelly. I thought you had a flight this afternoon.

NICK: Hey, uh—what's going on?

DORIS: I don't know what you're asking me.

NICK: Eddie told you to come here too?

DORIS: He called me last night, I think he said it was your idea.

NICK: *My* idea?

DORIS: Well I don't know, he just told me to come here and I'm here, I'm just doing what I'm told!

KELLY: We get to see you before we leave, I think this is nice.

DORIS: Sure.

(Isabelle enters, brings them glasses of water.)

ISABELLE: Welcome back, guys! Eddie's really glad to have you all back here.

DORIS: I suppose you're still out of gluten-free pasta.

ISABELLE: Sorry!

DORIS: *Honestly.*

ISABELLE: Can I get you anything else to drink?

KELLY: I'd / like—

NICK: We'd just like to order I think.

(Kelly looks at him.)

ISABELLE: Oh. Actually—Eddie's got something special for you, I just wanted to see if you wanted any wine or pop or / coffee—

NICK: We're not—. We're actually on our way out of town, is this gonna take a while?

ISABELLE: I don't—think / so?

KELLY: I'm fine with water, thank you.

DORIS: Coke, half diet and half real.

ISABELLE: We only have Pepsi?

DORIS: *GAH* this *place*. I'll just have water.

(Isabelle looks at Nick. Pause.)

NICK: Just the food, please.

ISABELLE: Okay! I'll be right back with that.

(Isabelle exits. Tammy finishes her glass of wine, pours another.)

COLE: Lydia, enough.

TAMMY: That is *not my name*.

(Eddie reenters, having changed out of his tie and name tag and into a casual shirt. He joins Nick, Kelly, and Doris at the table.)

EDDIE: Hey, everybody's here! That's great.

KELLY: Oh—you're joining us?

EDDIE: Yeah, it's a slow day anyway.

(Troy enters, goes to Tammy.)

NICK: Eddie, we really don't have time for this, we were just dropping in to say bye. I told you that.

DORIS: / What?

KELLY: Nick.

TROY *(Soft)*: / Tammy, c'mon. I'm calling you a cab and you can—. You can just go home, okay?

50

(Becky enters, setting up tables.)

EDDIE: I just—we haven't all been together in four years, I just thought we could spend a little time together before you head out.

TAMMY *(Soft)*: / I'm doing just fine, Troy. I'm staying right here and finishing my rosé.

DORIS: Eddie I can't stay for very long, I have all these errands before five.

TROY: *Tammy.*

COLE: Okay.

(Becky watches Troy and Tammy. Cole leaves the table, takes a seat away from Troy and Tammy.)

TROY *(Leaning into Tammy)*: / You wanna do this in front of Becky, in front of my dad? You *really* wanna do that?

NICK: Maybe we should forget this then?

EDDIE: It'll be quick, I promise.

KELLY: Nick is cranky because he's been driving all day, it's / fine—

TAMMY: / *Fuck off, Troy.*

NICK: I'm not cranky.

(Troy sits down where Cole had been sitting, staring at Tammy. Tammy continues to drink wine. Becky exits.)

EDDIE: I promise you'll make your flight Nicky, this / won't—

NICK: Call me Nick, okay?

(Pause.)

EDDIE: What?

NICK: My name's Nick. No one calls me Nicky anymore, just call me Nick.

DORIS: Oh please let's not / start something.

EDDIE: Oh, I—I didn't mean to—. I've always called you Nicky.

NICK: Well things fucking change, / I guess.

KELLY: *Nick*—

DORIS: All right, I'm not sitting here if this is the tone this conversation is going to have, I'm not—.

(Tense silence. Max enters, setting up tables.)

EDDIE: Nick—I just want to be your brother. That's it.

(Pause. Doris gets up.)

DORIS: I really just don't have time to eat, I have too much to do—

EDDIE: Mom, *please*. Please, just—stay?

(Doris considers, then sits down. A silence.
Tammy finishes her glass of wine, pours another. Troy stares at her. Isabelle reenters with a large casserole dish. She puts it on the table in front of Nick.)

ISABELLE: Okay, here you go. Let me know if you guys need anything else, okay?

(Kelly looks at the food. Isabelle exits.)

KELLY: Oh, this is— . . . What is this?

(Nick looks at the plate.)

EDDIE *(To Nick and Doris)*: You guys remember?

(Nick looks at the food. Doris looks away. Becky enters with a tub for dirty dishes, passes by Troy and Tammy.)

NICK: Yeah. I do.

EDDIE *(To Kelly)*: Dad used to make this all the time, served it at the diner too.

KELLY: Sorry, what is it?

EDDIE: Oh, it's—Cheese Whiz casserole? It's just broccoli, rice, and a whole bunch of Cheese Whiz, I know that sounds a / little—

NICK: I'm not eating this.

(Pause. Isabelle reenters, goes to the ordering station and types on the computer.)

DORIS: Eddie, this—. This was a foolish thing to do.

(A tense pause.)

EDDIE: Okay, I—. Look, I'm sorry guys, I didn't mean to—. We don't need to talk about the bad stuff, we can just talk about nothing, anything, we can— . . . Look, we used to *work*, you know? *I just don't know why we can't do this anymore, why we can't—*

(Nick suddenly barrels down on Eddie, exploding. Doris and Kelly let out a small scream, the entire restaurant shifts their focus to Nick.)

NICK: *What this fuck is this, Eddie?! What the fuck are you— . . . ?!*

(Nick finally stops himself, having chased Eddie to the center of the restaurant. Everyone stares at him. Pause.
Nick exits to the restroom.
A silence.
Finally, Doris grabs her purse.)

DORIS: This is ridiculous, I just have too much to do today.

(Doris starts to exit. Eddie follows after her.)

EDDIE: Mom, I'm sorry—

DORIS *(Impulsively): Eddie, enough. What is wrong with you?!* *(Going to him, softly)* Please, Eddie, you have to stop doing this to me, you have to stop calling me, just leave me alone! It's not normal for you to be so— . . .

EDDIE: What?

(Pause. Doris looks at him, about to say something. She stops herself, looking up. The entire restaurant is watching her.)

DORIS: This is so embarrassing, people can hear every word we're saying. Go calm down your brother.

(Doris exits. Eddie watches her go.
Nick reenters, taking deep breaths.
Eddie looks at Troy, Isabelle, and Max.)

EDDIE: Could you guys— . . . ?

(Troy, Isabelle, and Max exit. Troy takes Tammy's wine bottle as he leaves. Eddie tentatively goes to Nick.)

I'm sorry, I wasn't trying / to—

NICK: *What did you think was gonna happen? Why would you— . . . ?* *(Pause, calming)* I lost my temper. I shouldn't have done that, I'm sorry. But I don't know what you're doing here, I don't— . . .

(Pause.)

Eddie, you're smart enough to realize that you have a *choice* here. Get out of town, make your own life! Leaving

54

all this shit behind was the best decision I ever made, believe me.

EDDIE: I don't *want* to leave, Nicky, that's what I'm / trying to say—

NICK: Well then I don't know what to say, Eddie, if you just wanna stay in this town and end up like Dad, I don't know what—.

(Pause.)

Look, obviously coming out here was a mistake, I knew it the second I bought the plane tickets that this was a bad idea.

(Nick moves to the exit.)

Look, we have a flight, and—I'll call you, okay?

EDDIE: *Nicky, wait.*

(Nick stops. Pause. He turns to Eddie.)

I don't have anyone? I don't— . . .

(Pause.)

NICK: Buddy, I—.

(Pause.)

I'm not coming back here again. I—can't.

(Pause.)

I'm sorry.

(Nick exits. Pause. Kelly goes to Eddie.)

KELLY: I'm sorry—
EDDIE: Lemme just talk / to him—
KELLY: *Eddie, please, just*— . . .

(Eddie stops.)

This is my fault, if I'd known he'd do *this*, I never would've made him do this trip— . . . *(Pause)* I forced him to come out here because I thought—maybe—he needed this.

(Pause.)

EDDIE: What do you mean?
KELLY: I don't know, I'm not even sure what I thought this would accomplish, I—. We've been talking about having kids for years now, but something's always been in his way, and I thought coming here would— . . . The only way I know how to deal with painful stuff is to talk it to death, but for Nick and your mother, they don't— . . . Obviously they just need to—separate themselves from all of this. Obviously that's what's best for both of them.

(Pause.)

EDDIE: I mean so— . . . So that's it? I don't have a family anymore?
KELLY: Look, we all find ways to move forward. Maybe just— make your way somewhere else, like Nick? You could go anywhere you wanted—
EDDIE: This is what I keep saying—this is my home, it's *their* home. Everyone here, this is all our— . . . But Nick just wants me to—give up on it, but I—
KELLY: Eddie, Nick is just trying to help. Your mom— . . . Look, I don't pretend to understand your mother, I've

56

never understood her. But seeing her keep you at arm's length like this, she obviously just— . . . *(Pause)* I'm just saying, you're trying *so hard*, with your family, with this place, but— . . . Maybe you're not gonna fix all this. Maybe—it's not worth fixing.

(Eddie looks at Kelly. Pause.)

EDDIE: I can't believe that, I— . . . *(Short pause)* It's worth it. I have to believe that.

(Pause. Kelly smiles at him.)

KELLY: Good luck.

(Kelly exits. Eddie watches her go.
Tammy begins to cry softly to herself. Cole looks at her for a second, then slowly walks over to Eddie.)

COLE: She'll be fine. She has emotions when she's drinking wine. The day we were married she bawled into the night.

(Cole pauses, eyeing his surroundings. Tammy continues to cry. Becky enters, looks at Tammy briefly. She goes to Eddie.)

BECKY *(Referring to the dishes)*: You done?

(Cole continues to look around the room. Eddie quickly exits to the kitchen.)

(Calling after him) Hello? Can I take them?

(Eddie is gone. Cole, Becky, and Tammy are left onstage in silence.)

Scene Five

Late at night. The lights are off.

After a moment, Eddie enters from outside. He comes into the restaurant without turning on the lights, looking around the room. Silence.

There's some rustling in the kitchen. Eddie lifts up his head. There's a louder sound, and Eddie bolts up.

EDDIE: Who's there?! *(Pause)* Troy?!

(No response. Another burst of sound from the kitchen.)

I getting out my cell phone right now, I'm calling the—

(Max enters from the kitchen.)

Oh, God.

MAX: Hey, man . . .

EDDIE: What are you—? It's past midnight, what are you doing / here?

MAX: Sorry, I sort of—I made a mess in the kitchen? Sorry.

EDDIE: What do you mean?

MAX: Look I was the last one left closing and I accidentally ran into one of those big jugs of canola oil and I—

EDDIE: Oh.

MAX: I didn't spill the whole thing, it's just—it made a big mess. And it's a bitch to clean up.

EDDIE: Sure.

MAX: What are you doing here so late?

(Pause.)

EDDIE: I just—. Some paperwork.

MAX: It couldn't wait until morning?

(Pause.)

EDDIE: I guess I just didn't feel like being in my apartment right now.

MAX: Oh. *(Pause)* Dude, no offense, but you really should stop inviting your family over here.

EDDIE: Yeah. Well, you don't have to worry.

MAX: Sorry, I just. That was fucked up. Why did he freak out like that?

EDDIE: I don't know, I just—. I made a mistake. *(Pause)* Do you see your family ever?

MAX: Not really. Like I said, I'm not exactly welcome around that house anymore.

EDDIE: So what do you do?

(Pause.)

MAX: What do you mean?

EDDIE: I mean, how do you—? Who do you spend time with?

MAX: Dude I never stop spending time around people. A group home doesn't offer much in the way of privacy.

EDDIE: Oh, sure.

MAX: Believe me, if I could, I'd get as far away from everyone else as possible. Build my own cabin in the woods, all *Walden* and shit. Like your great-grandpa's place, maybe I should just move in there.

EDDIE: Well, it's—you wouldn't want to live there now. Place is barely standing. Windows are all gone, there's a tree that fell a few years ago, caved in part of the roof on the east side.

(Pause.)

MAX: Wait a minute, are you talking about that place on Elm? With the red door?

EDDIE: How do you know that?

MAX: Dude, that's nuts! Me and my friends used to party there!

(Pause.)

EDDIE: Oh.

MAX: God, that's—your family used to own that place?

EDDIE: Yeah. Not for a while now, but yeah.

MAX: That place was *awesome*. We could park behind those trees in the back so the cops didn't know we were there. My friend Chris got his teeth knocked out when he fell out of one of the windows on the second floor. I know people who lost their virginity there.

EDDIE: Oh.

MAX: That's hilarious.

EDDIE: Yeah, it's—. *(Pause)* You still go there?

MAX: Oh no, not for years. *(Pause)* Well, listen, I'm gonna finish up in / the—

EDDIE: We could go there together sometime, maybe.

(Pause.)

MAX: What do you mean?

EDDIE: I mean just—hang out, take some food. It's really nice, it's—. We could do it this weekend.

(Pause.)

MAX: Yeah maybe.

(Uncomfortable silence. Max looks away.)

EDDIE: Look, I'm not trying to——. I just thought we could hang out, have dinner or something. No big deal. *(Pause)* I'm making you uncomfortable.

MAX: No, you're not it's——

(Isabelle enters from out of the kitchen, looking disheveled.)

ISABELLE: Hey.

MAX: Hey, um. Thought you said you were going to leave through the back?

ISABELLE: *It was locked, I waited forever.*

(Another uncomfortable silence.)

MAX: Isabelle was just helping me clean it up, we closed together.

EDDIE: Oh.

(Pause.)

ISABELLE: Look Eddie we're sorry, but he lives in that group home thingy and my roommate is all judgy.

MAX: Oh my God.

ISABELLE: We're all adults! We can talk about this like adults! *(To Eddie)* We've only done it three times, and we won't do it again. And we've never contaminated anything or whatever. We just do it on the floor, missionary, with most of our clothes on. And I never do any of his meth, I swear.

MAX: *Why are you still talking?!*

EDDIE *(To Max)*: Wait—you're on meth? Right now?

(Pause.)

MAX: I'm not like *on* it, I just——. I only do a little bit.

EDDIE: A "little bit"?

MAX: It's not like before, I just do a tiny bit before we— . . . It's just recreational, I'm not using like I did before. Having sex on a little bit is amazing, and I'm not like *addicted* anymore—

EDDIE: Are you hearing yourself? What the hell is wrong with you?

(Uncomfortable silence.)

ISABELLE: Um, okay. I'm gonna—go. *(Exiting, to Eddie)* Sorry? We won't do it again?

(Isabelle exits.)

MAX: I'm gonna go, let's—forget about all of this, okay?

EDDIE: You know, I gave you this job because you told me you were getting clean.

MAX: Jesus, were you listening to me?! I just did a little bit, it's fucking recreational! I'm not like doing it every day! Do I look like a meth head to you?

EDDIE: Max it doesn't matter how much you're doing, what matters is you shouldn't / be—

MAX: JUST BECAUSE I DON'T WANT YOU TO BLOW ME AT YOUR FUCKING GREAT-GRANDPA'S HOUSE DOESN'T MEAN YOU—

(Max catches himself. Eddie looks away, sitting back down at the table.)

Sorry. Fuck. *(Pause)* Look, I—. I won't do it here anymore, okay? And Isabelle and I won't—. We'll just forget about this.

EDDIE *(Still not looking at him)*: Okay.

(Pause.)

MAX: Sorry, okay? I'll—I'll see you tomorrow.

(Max exits. Eddie sits alone.)

Scene Six

Afternoon, between lunch and dinner.

    Tammy stands near one of the empty tables. The other table is covered in dirty dishes. Troy stands, keeping his distance. Country music plays lightly in the background.

    A tense silence.

TROY: We shouldn't be doing this here.

TAMMY: So tell me what hotel you're staying at. *(No response)* We can talk in the parking lot if / you'd rather—

TROY: Tammy, I'm *working*, so I / can't—

TAMMY: Is Becky okay?

(Pause.)

TROY: She's fine.

TAMMY: Did you get a decent—? You aren't at the motor lodge, are you?

TROY: We're fine.

(Pause.)

TAMMY *(Simple, exasperated)*: Come back home, Troy.

(Pause.)

TROY: I told you that if you started drinking / again—

TAMMY: And you only said that so you could—*win* or whatever, be on higher moral ground—

TROY: Tammy I'm in the middle of my shift right now, I'll give you a call later maybe / we can—

TAMMY: *No, I can't do this anymore, I can't*— . . .

(Tammy stops herself, looking at the floor.)

TROY: What?

TAMMY: I can't do this anymore.

TROY: You can't do / what?

TAMMY: This. This *thing*, this same argument, you threatening to run off with Becky, this whole—. How many times have we been here? If we go through this again, I don't know what I'm going to do, I feel like I— . . .

(Eddie enters, unseen by Troy and Tammy.)

We can't do this anymore, we—

(Tammy notices Eddie. Troy turns to him. An uncomfortable silence. Eddie exits.)

TROY: Okay, let's—. Let's please not do this here. And let's both just take this down a notch. Couples go through this kind of / stuff all the—

TAMMY: No, they don't, this isn't— . . . *(Short pause, losing herself a little)* I see myself, I think about who I've turned into, and it's like—I don't even know who I am anymore, I've turned into this *strange* person, this person I don't even *like*, and I—

TROY: Tammy, have you had anything to drink today?

TAMMY: *No, Troy, have you?!* This has *nothing* to do with me drinking. I realize it would be easier for you if it was about me drinking, that would be a lot simpler, but it's not about that, it's—.

(Pause.)

I keep telling myself that eventually I'm going to feel *normal*, but I never feel normal, because *none* of this is normal, our jobs, this town, this isn't—

(Becky enters, they both stop talking suddenly. Becky looks at them for a second, then heads to the table covered in dishes. She starts clearing them off.)

Hi, honey.
BECKY: Hi.

(Pause.)

TAMMY: You doing / okay?
BECKY: You know if you guys are going to fight maybe you could do it in the parking lot or something.
TROY: We're not fighting.
BECKY: You guys don't even know how to *not* fight anymore.

(Becky exits, leaving some of the dishes still on the table. Pause. Tammy stares off into the distance, not looking at Troy.)

TROY: Look, we're—. We're at the Holiday Inn. *(Pause)* Let's please not blow this out of proportion, okay? We've been here before. Just—. Just stay and have some food, I'll see if I can get off early and we'll go talk, and work things out. We always work things out.

(Isabelle enters.)

ISABELLE: Oh, hey. Troy—I thought you had table nine?

TROY: Yeah, I do. Sorry.

(Troy gets up.)

ISABELLE *(To Tammy)*: Would you like anything, or are you just here to talk to Troy?

(Brief pause.)

TAMMY: Yeah, uh. I'll have the soup salad breadsticks thingy. Extra breadsticks.

ISABELLE: You want the Zuppa Siciliana or the Zuppa Toscana?

TAMMY: What?

TROY: Veggies or meatballs.

TAMMY: Meatballs.

ISABELLE: Not a problem.

(Isabelle exits. Pause.)

TROY: Look, I'm sorry, okay?

(Pause. Max enters.)

MAX *(To Troy)*: Buddy they're really looking for you at table nine.

TROY: Okay.

(Troy exits with Max.
Becky enters to get the remaining dishes from the other table. She doesn't look at Tammy.)

BECKY: You guys divorced yet?

TAMMY *(Impulsively)*: You know one day you're gonna wake up and there won't be anyone left in your life that gives a damn about you. Let's see how fucking smart you are then.

(Becky stops, looking at her. Tammy looks down.)

Shit.

(Becky quickly starts to exit.)

Becky, I didn't mean that, I—

(Becky is gone. Isabelle reenters with salad and bread-sticks. She puts them down in front of Tammy.)

ISABELLE: Here you go.

(Pause.)

TAMMY: It's Isabelle, right?
ISABELLE: Yeah.
TAMMY: When you were seventeen did you and your mom hate one another?
ISABELLE: My parents died when I was twelve.
TAMMY: Oh my God I'm so sorry—
ISABELLE: It's okay, it's been forever. Car accident, I was in the back seat. My grandparents raised me, they were okay. They always treated me like I was a fucking princess just because my parents were dead. Oh my God I just said the F-word.
TAMMY: It's okay.
ISABELLE: I got fired from Kmart in high school for swearing. Anyway, don't worry about her, she's okay. You remember being seventeen. You hate everything when you're seventeen.
TAMMY: Actually, I was fine. I liked my life. It's now that I hate everything.

(Tammy grabs a breadstick, starts eating.)

ISABELLE: Well she's just getting it out of the way now, then. *(Pause)* Do you—want me to sit with you for a while?

TAMMY: Oh, you don't have to—
ISABELLE: Seriously, you're my only table. I don't mind.

(Tammy looks at her, smiles.)

TAMMY: Well—okay, yeah.

(Isabelle sits and starts eating salad straight from the bowl.)

ISABELLE: I just think, like, we all have to go through a period in our lives where we think everything is shit. After that everything else feels a little bit better.
TAMMY: Yeah.

(Pause.)

ISABELLE: Look if you're holding something in, let it out. It's the middle of the afternoon, there are barely any people here. Go for it, say what you're feeling.

(Pause.)

TAMMY: I'm just—*so fucking miserable.*
ISABELLE: Fuck yeah!
TAMMY: Jesus. I'm fucking miserable.
ISABELLE: You see? Now there's nowhere to go but up!
TAMMY: I sort of wish they wouldn't come home.

(Pause. Tammy thinks.)

ISABELLE: What?
TAMMY: Troy took Becky last night, they're at the Holiday Inn, and I sort of wish they'd just—*stay there.* I mean I know that's not realistic, but—. They'd be fine. It's nice, there's a pool.

ISABELLE: Oh, wow, I'm not sure I—

TAMMY: And I could just go home, be *alone*, and just—sleep. Get up in the morning. Go to work. Like a—normal person.

(Pause.)

ISABELLE: Oh.

(Eddie enters. Isabelle stands.)

Oh, I—. Sorry, Eddie, I was just—. I'll get back to / the—

EDDIE: No, it's okay. It's Thursday, we have staff lunch, let's just—. Let's get everybody together and eat now. Tammy, you can eat with us.

ISABELLE: No, I'll—really, Eddie, I—

EDDIE: Sit down, eat. You want something else?

ISABELLE: I can give you a hand in / the kitchen—

EDDIE: No, really—stay there. Give me a minute, just— . . .

(Eddie exits. Isabelle and Tammy stare at one another for a moment in silence.)

TAMMY: I was planning on going to South Dakota.

ISABELLE: Oh, cool! What?

TAMMY: My sister Ellie, she lives in South Dakota. On this organic farm, it's so beautiful. I thought that as soon as Becky graduated and moved out of the house, I could make a clean break, move out there, and—.

(Pause.)

But that's never going to happen. We've been together since high school. We don't even know how to be adults apart from one another.

(Pause.)

But maybe—maybe I just need to accept that. I mean maybe we both just need to realize that we aren't gonna be the people we wanted to be, we aren't going to— . . . I mean there are plenty of unhappy people in the world, why should we be the ones who get to be *happy*? Maybe we're just—unhappy people.

(Tammy looks at Isabelle. Pause.)

Does that make sense?

(Tense silence.)

ISABELLE: Yeah, I mean— . . . ? *(Pause)* Actually, I don't know if I'm the one to—

(Eddie reenters with Max, Troy, and Becky.)

MAX: What are we doing?

(Eddie pushes two tables together, creating one large table.)

EDDIE: It's Thursday. We have staff lunch on Thursday.
TROY: Eddie, c'mon—not this week, okay?
EDDIE: The last table just left, we probably won't get anyone else until four thirty, that's an hour from now.
BECKY: I'm not hungry.
MAX: Yeah, Eddie, could we just do staff lunch next / week?
EDDIE: Hey guess what?! I'm your boss!

(Everyone looks at Eddie. Pause.)

Sorry, just—. *(Pause)* It's Thursday, we have staff lunch on Thursday. So just—sit down.

(Confused, everyone awkwardly sits at the large table. Eddie quickly exits.
    Pause. Troy looks at Tammy.)

TROY: Tammy, I don't know what— . . . You wanna just talk later?

(Pause. Tammy looks at Isabelle, then at Troy.)

TAMMY: No, Troy, actually I wanna talk now, I—
ISABELLE: Oh hey Max.

(Pause. Tammy stops herself.)

MAX: Um. Hey.
ISABELLE: So what's going on with you?
MAX: Not—much?
TROY *(To Tammy)*: What / is it?
ISABELLE: How's your band? Tell us about your band!
TAMMY: / Nothing, never mind.
MAX: We broke up like four weeks ago. I told you that.
ISABELLE: Oh that's too bad how'd it happen?!
MAX: Isabelle, what are you doing?

(Eddie reenters with plates, silverware, and a large plastic vat of salad. He puts it all on the table.)

ISABELLE: Eddie you want help?
EDDIE: I'm fine.

(Eddie quickly exits. The speaker begins to crackle as before. Troy looks at it.)

TROY: When did that start?

71

MAX: Couple days ago, you haven't noticed?

TROY: Why aren't we paying to fix these things?

MAX: 'Cause the only customers we have right now are ourselves?

(Pause. A silence in the conversation. Max looks at Becky, nods.)

'Sup.

BECKY: Jesus Christ.

(Eddie enters with a tray of breadsticks.)

TROY: Eddie, we don't need breadsticks, we have the whole dinner / rush—

EDDIE: *We're fine.*

(Eddie quickly exits again.)

BECKY: Are we still getting paid right now?

TROY: Yes, hon, we—

(Tammy starts to get up. Isabelle is increasingly uncomfortable.)

TAMMY: I think— / I think I'm gonna go.

ISABELLE: *Hey Max let's go help Eddie in the kitchen.*

TROY: / Tammy, please just—.

MAX: What's with you?

TROY: Just stay?

(Tammy slowly sits back down. Eddie reenters with a large pot full of soup, carrying it with his bare hands.)

EDDIE: *Ow ow ow ow ow ow ow ow—*

(Eddie plops the soup onto the table.)

Okay. Here we go!

MAX: I'm not hungry.

ISABELLE: Yeah, Eddie, I really don't want anything—

BECKY: Me neither.

EDDIE: Guys, let's just—. Let's just eat something?

(Eddie starts quickly filling bowls with soup.)

It's been a long week, right? We're all tired, we're miserable, but right now? We can all just—have lunch together, / I think we can all manage that.

TROY: Eddie—

MAX: Buddy, calm down—

(Eddie accidentally sloshes some of the soup onto Becky.)

EDDIE: Oh God, I'm sorry Becky—

BECKY: Is there meat in this?

(Short pause.)

EDDIE: *Shit*—

BECKY: There's meat in this!

TAMMY: / Becky, it's okay—

TROY: Honey—

EDDIE: I'm sorry Becky—

BECKY: *It's all over me*—

TROY: / Okay calm down—

ISABELLE: Eddie I think I should probably watch the front in case / someone comes—

TAMMY *(To Becky)*: Honey, it's okay, / just take a deep breath—

EDDIE: I locked up, don't worry about it.

MAX: You *what*?

EDDIE: / It's fine—

BECKY: I'm gonna be sick.

TROY: Becky, you're fine. / Just tell yourself not to throw up and you won't throw up.

ISABELLE: Eddie you can't just close the restaurant—

EDDIE: Why not? / It's my restaurant!

(Eddie continues to serve soup.)

TAMMY: Becky, let's just go home, okay?

TROY: *No, you*—. Tammy I never said that I was going to let you take Becky back / home—

TAMMY: Troy, for God's sake, can / we just skip this part?!

ISABELLE: Eddie, no one wants any lunch, / just stop!

BECKY: I need to go to the bathroom.

(The speaker crackles louder. Max gets up.)

MAX: This is nuts. I'm opening the front.

EDDIE *(To Max)*: No. Stay here.

TAMMY: I'll take Becky home and / she can take a shower—

TROY *(To Tammy)*: You are *not* taking her home—

ISABELLE: / We can't just close in the middle of the day!

BECKY: JESUS WILL YOU TWO STOP TALKING ABOUT ME LIKE I'M NOT HERE?

(Becky takes off her apron, throwing it on the ground.)

TROY: / Great. Here we go.

TAMMY *(To Becky)*: Honey, let's just *go*—

EDDIE: I didn't mean to—I'm sorry—

BECKY: FUCK YOU PEOPLE, FUCK THIS RESTAURANT.

TROY *(Fierce)*: SHUT UP Becky.

TAMMY: / *Troy, stop—*
BECKY *(To Troy)*: I'M GLAD THIS RESTAURANT IS CLOSING.

(Short pause. Everyone stops.)

TROY: What?
BECKY: Eddie said this place is closing, so pretty soon you're
    gonna lose your pathetic / little job—
EDDIE: Okay—
BECKY: —and hopefully you and Mom will *finally* get divorced
    and / I can—
ISABELLE: Wait, hold on—

(The speaker crackles louder.)

TROY *(To Eddie)*: What is she talking about?
EDDIE: / I just—
MAX: Why would you tell / her that, Eddie?
TROY: Eddie, what—? You didn't tell her that, did you?
BECKY: *Yes, he told me—* . . . !

(Becky storms off to the bathroom.)

ISABELLE: Wait, / wait, wait—
MAX: Eddie, what the fuck is going on?!

*(Eddie suddenly attacks the crackling speaker, ripping it out
of the wall with his bare hands and smashing it onto the
ground. The music cuts off. Everyone looks at him. Silence.
Eddie takes deep breaths.)*

EDDIE: I did everything I could, I— . . .

(Pause.)

MAX: Oh my God. When—when is it closing?

(Pause.)

EDDIE: The end of next week.

MAX: / *WHAT?!*

ISABELLE: Oh my God.

TROY: When the fuck were you going to tell us this?!

MAX: Eddie, this is the only place in town that'll hire me, / the drug court says I have to hold down a job!

EDDIE: I wanted to tell you guys—

TROY: *So why didn't you?!*

EDDIE: I thought maybe I could keep us afloat for a while, I've been putting some money from my savings into the cash drop at the end of the night—

TROY: You've been putting your / *own money* in the cash drop?

ISABELLE: God, this was the one place I could stand to work in this town.

EDDIE: I just thought if we all rallied and showed corporate that we could do better, maybe we / could've—

ISABELLE: Oh just stop it, Eddie. God I'm fucked.

MAX: *You're* fucked?

(Max slams the table. The tray of breadsticks falls to the ground. Silence. Tammy stands.)

TAMMY *(To Troy)*: I'm gonna check on Becky.

TROY: It's okay, you can go home, I can—. Just let her calm down a little.

(Pause.)

TAMMY: Okay.

(Pause. Tammy moves toward the exit.)

76

TROY: Tammy.

(Tammy stops, looks at Troy. Pause.)

We'll see you at home.

(Pause.)

TAMMY: Yeah. Okay.

(Tammy exits.)

ISABELLE: I'm going home too.
EDDIE: Guys—*please*.

(Silence. Troy sits at one of the tables.)

MAX: Isabelle you wanna ride?
ISABELLE: *No.*
MAX: Whatever.

(Max exits. Isabelle looks at Eddie.)

ISABELLE: You know, when you hired me I told you that the Applebee's would pay me thirty cents more an hour. And people drink more there so the tips are a lot better. Now I'm gonna have to go back to the Conoco that my cousin Mandy manages. She calls me "Izzy," I fucking hate her.
EDDIE: I'm really sorry. I should have told you, I— . . .

(Pause.)

ISABELLE: Look—I know it's not your fault. And don't pay attention to Max, he's a fucking moron, he listens to Dave

Matthews. *(Pause)* I always thought you put too much effort into this job, anyway.

EDDIE: Well not enough, I guess.

ISABELLE: You think this place is closing down because you didn't *try* hard enough? Eddie, the only reason to work at places like this is you don't need to care. You just go to work, try to have fun, and go to the lake on the weekends. And if it closes, there's plenty more places to work down the highway. *(Pause)* Anyway. Just mail me my last paycheck, okay? I'm gonna steal some silverware on my way out just so you know.

(Isabelle exits. Troy and Eddie are left alone together. Troy looks at him.)

EDDIE: What about you, you gonna beat me up?

TROY: No, I'm not gonna— . . . Jesus, Eddie, why didn't you just *tell* me?

EDDIE: I just— . . . I thought maybe I could save it.

TROY: Eddie, places like this don't get "saved." *(Pause)* Dammit, were you really putting your own money into the register?

EDDIE: I thought if I could prove that we were making / money—

TROY: That's *crazy*, Eddie, that's—. *(Pause)* I guess the McDonalds is always hiring. God, how did I get here?

(Troy gets up, exiting briefly. He reenters with a carafe of wine and two glasses.)

You want some?

EDDIE: No, I—I'm fine. Should you check on Becky?

TROY: She's okay, just need to let her run out of steam.

(Troy pours himself a large glass of wine, drinks.)

EDDIE: Do you know what you're gonna do?

(Silence.)

TROY: There's a lumber yard outside Seattle, my cousin Jen is always saying she can get me a foreman job. It'd pay three times what I'm making here. Eight years ago when the paper mill closed, she offered me the same job. Tammy would've been totally willing to move, Becky would have been fine with it, she doesn't— . . . I didn't even tell them about it. *(Pause)* When I was little kid I thought all I wanted was to get out of Pocatello. I had the opportunity and I couldn't even do it. Felt like I was going to have a panic attack just thinking about moving out of here. And I still don't know why.

EDDIE: It's your home.

TROY: More like my coffin. *(Takes a long swig of wine)* What about you? What are you gonna do?

(Pause.)

EDDIE: I don't— . . .

(Eddie trails off. Pause.)

TROY: Look, I'm sorry for blowing up, we're not—. It's not about you, we all know that.

(Pause.)

EDDIE: Yeah.

(Isabelle reenters quickly.)

ISABELLE: Troy, you really need to come to the front—

TROY: What?

(Cole enters from behind Isabelle, looking a little gaunt, tired. He stares at Troy for a moment.)

Dad, God. What are you—? What are you doing?

COLE: Hm.

(Cole goes to the speaker on the ground, picks it up, and places it on the table. He moves to the decorative wine bottles, starts arranging them.)

ISABELLE: He was out in the parking lot, I didn't know / what to—

COLE: Go get him, would you?

TROY: What?

COLE: I'm not going to ask twice. I'm tired of doing shelves myself. I don't pay people to smoke on the sidewalk.

TROY: Shit.

EDDIE: Should I call someone?

TROY: No, he's just—. He does this sometimes, wanders off, he's okay. *(To Isabelle)* Thanks, Isabelle, you can— . . .

(Isabelle exits. Troy goes to Cole.)

Dad, c'mon. *(Touching his arm)* We're going home, just—

(Cole pushes him off.)

COLE: Get off, would you?

(Becky enters.)

BECKY: What's going on?

TROY: It's fine, Grandpa's fine.

(Cole knocks over a potted plant. It spills dirt all over the floor.)

80

COLE: *You see what you did?! You're distracting me!*
TROY: OKAY DAD? LOOK AT ME. LOOK AT ME.

(Cole finally looks at him.)

You're not at the store, the store closed twelve years ago. Remember? Look at me.

(Cole looks around. Silence.)

COLE: I don't— . . . *(Long pause)* Glass of water, please.

(Cole sits at a table.)

TROY *(To Eddie)*: Just keep him in here, okay? *(To Cole)* Dad, I'm going to get you some water and make a call, okay? Just—stay here.

(Troy exits. Cole grabs a breadstick and starts eating it. Cole looks at Eddie.)

EDDIE: I'm, uh—. I'm Eddie, I work with your son. I work with Troy.
COLE: Damn paper mill makes the whole town smell like dung. When I was a kid we could actually breathe. *(To Becky)* Tammy, this bread is awful. Would you bring me something else?

(Becky, not exactly knowing what to do, goes to the table and pushes the vat of salad toward Cole. Cole grabs a fork and starts munching on the salad. Becky sits, joining him at the table. Eddie watches.)

Where did Troy run off to?

(Pause.)

BECKY: He'll be back in a second.

COLE: He doesn't sit still for ten seconds, that one. You're good for him. You're his ballast.

(Silence as Cole eats.)

BECKY: Grandpa how did you get here?

COLE: How's that?

BECKY: County Care is like six miles away, how did you get here?

COLE: I don't know what you're asking me. Get me some water, please?

(Becky hands him an untouched glass of water from the table. Cole drinks.)

BECKY: Did you walk all the way here?

COLE: Nothing wrong with it, it's good for you. People drive too much in this town.

BECKY: I told Dad not to put you in that County Care place. That place is terrible. I told him it'd just make you worse. But of course, he doesn't listen to me, he's such an idiot.

(Eddie sits at the table across from them, watching.)

COLE: Well, he's not the brightest. I always tell him, if you don't want to take over the store, be a plumber. There's a simple logic to it. You should have waited longer before having a child with him. I don't mean to sound harsh.

(Pause. Cole continues to eat.)

BECKY: No, it's okay.

COLE: Still in his twenties and he thinks he knows everything. His sister is the same way, she rushes into everything. Marries that idiot straight out of school. He's not good for her, you know, I think he smokes marijuana.

BECKY: They got divorced when I was a kid, Grandpa.

(Cole looks at Becky for a second, becoming a little more lucid. He looks around a bit.)

COLE: Hm.

BECKY: Your store is closed. Dad took it over when I was a kid for like a couple years but he sold it and now it's a Payless Shoes.

COLE: I know that, I'm not an idiot. *(Pause)* Becky. Have some.

(Cole serves Becky a little bit of salad.)

BECKY: I don't—I don't want to eat.

COLE: You're skin and bones.

BECKY: I don't know where it came from.

COLE: What do you mean?

BECKY: It might be full of pesticides and antibiotics. Or it might be made of lettuce grown in some country where people get paid five cents an hour, or tomatoes picked by starving nine-year-olds.

COLE: Hm. That sounds needlessly complicated.

(Becky chuckles despite herself. She picks up a fork, starts picking at the salad a bit. A few moments pass.)

I suppose Troy must be calling County Care to pick me up.

BECKY: Probably. Are you better now? Do you know where you are?

COLE: I've pieced it together.

BECKY: That must be annoying.

COLE: Eh. Lucidity is overrated, remember that.

(Cole continues to eat. Becky looks at him.)

BECKY: I should come and visit you more often.

COLE: It's not the most welcoming place, I don't blame you.

BECKY: Do you hate it?

(Pause.)

COLE: Never really thought much about it, it's just—where I am at the moment.

BECKY: But does that—? Does that make you sad?

COLE: I guess at a certain point you stop worrying about that, you just take things as they come.

(Pause.)

BECKY: I wish I was like that. I hate it here. As soon as I turn eighteen, I'm moving out of this town.

COLE: Oh. You think it's going to be better someplace else?

BECKY: I mean, I don't know? It'll be different, at least.

COLE: Towns aren't much different nowadays, Becky.

(Silence.)

BECKY: Grandpa I just like hate everything about life.

*(Cole looks up at her, stops eating. Pause.
Troy reenters with a glass of water.)*

TROY: Okay, Dad—we're gonna take you home, okay? Some people from where you live are coming / to—

COLE: Don't—. You don't need to talk to me like I'm a child, Troy, I'm—.

(Troy puts the water on the table.)

TROY: They'll be here in a minute, let's just wait outside.

(Cole gets up. He begins to exit with Troy, then stops and turns back to Becky. He goes to her.)

COLE: For the intelligent person, the world is full of idiots. I know that's not very helpful.

(Cole kisses the top of Becky's head, then exits with Troy. Becky and Eddie are left alone. Pause.)

EDDIE: You—okay?

(Pause.)

BECKY: Yeah. *(Pause)* Yeah, I'm fine. *(Pause)* I think I'm gonna walk home tonight. Can I go out the back? Will the alarm go off?

(Pause.)

EDDIE: No, you're okay.
BECKY: Cool.

(Becky pauses, then heads toward the back.)

EDDIE: Do you— . . . ? You really hate everything about life?

(Becky stops, turns to him.)

BECKY: I don't know, I just—. *(Pause)* I guess I just haven't figured out how to be a happy person without being stupid and naive.

(Pause.)

EDDIE: I know the feeling.

(Silence.)

BECKY: Look, thanks for the job, okay? That was cool of you.

(Becky approaches Eddie, her arm outstretched. Awkward pause.)

EDDIE: What—what are you doing?
BECKY: Shake my hand.
EDDIE: What?
BECKY: Let's just shake hands.
EDDIE: Why?
BECKY: Because this is awkward and I don't know what else to do. Jesus.

(They shake hands. Pause.)

Good luck okay?

(Pause.)

EDDIE: Okay.

(Becky smiles at him a bit, then exits.)

Scene Seven

Much later, the middle of the night.

    The room is untouched from before, looking more desolate and decimated than ever. It is mostly dark.

DORIS *(From off)*: Eddie?!

    (After a moment, Doris enters. She is wearing a coat over her pajamas, obviously having been woken up out of bed.

    She enters the space, sees the food, the torn up wall, the broken speaker. She reaches into her purse and takes out a small can of pepper spray.)

Eddie, are you here?!

    (Eddie enters from the kitchen.)

EDDIE: Hi, / Mom—
DORIS: *OH*—Eddie, for God's sake, I almost sprayed this pepper spray right into your face! I really almost just did that!
EDDIE: Sorry, I didn't mean / to—
DORIS: What's happened, what's the emergency?! I'm at my wit's end with you this week, Eddie—what happened in here?! Why is there food everywhere? Have you been drinking?
EDDIE: No, no, / I just—
DORIS: I've *never* been more embarrassed than I was yesterday, you provoking your brother, and everyone looking at us, *are we supposed to be here after hours?* You realize they could take money out of your paycheck for these damages, and you—. *What is the big emergency?!*

    (Eddie exits into the kitchen, Doris continues to talk, calling after him.)

Really, Eddie, I don't have the patience for this, I couldn't even find my glasses so I drove all the way here not knowing if I was going to *kill* someone, and I'm not even legally supposed to drive if I'm not wearing my—

(Eddie enters from the kitchen with a large tray holding a wide array of pasta dishes, all pristinely presented.)

What / is—?

EDDIE: Gluten-free manicotti. Gluten-free fettucine Alfredo. Gluten-free cheese ravioli, gluten-free spaghetti with meatballs . . . And some other stuff. I went to the 24-hour mart for the pasta. *(Pause)* Sit down, Mom.

(Pause.)

DORIS: Wait, you want me to—? This is the emergency?

EDDIE: Sit down.

DORIS: I'm not hungry, Eddie, I— . . . *(Pause)* This is so strange, I don't even know what to / say—

EDDIE: Mom. Please. I spent five hours making all this.

(Doris looks at the food, unsure of what to do. Silence.)

Can we just sit and—be together? We used to be able to do this, when I was in high school, we used to be able to just sit and talk—

DORIS: That was almost twenty years ago, Eddie! You're an adult!

EDDIE: What does being an adult have to do / with—?

DORIS: It was an awful time, and we got through it! *(Quick pause)* Do you just want an apology? Fine, then, Eddie, I am so sorry you had an awful childhood. I'm sorry that Dad was the way he was. / It was a terrible time for all of us.

EDDIE: I don't want an apology—

DORIS: But you don't need to *act out* like this, calling me in the middle of the night! People today are so obsessed their feelings and emotions and talking, talking, talking, people have forgotten how to deal with problems on their own!

EDDIE: *I don't want to talk about problems. I just want to get through all this crap so we can sit down and eat fucking lasagna together!*

DORIS: DON'T USE THAT WORD.

EDDIE: SIT. DOWN.

(Pause. Doris doesn't move.)

Please.

(Doris pauses, then pulls the chair a good distance away from the table and sits. Eddie looks at her.)

What would you like?

DORIS: I told you I'm not hungry.

(Pause.)

EDDIE: Okay.

(Eddie serves himself some lasagna.)

DORIS: This is why you brought me here in the middle of the night?

EDDIE: Yeah, Mom, it is. Because I like you, because I miss what we used to have, I miss just being able to talk to you—

DORIS: Well maybe it wasn't—

(Doris stops herself. Quick pause.)

EDDIE: What?

DORIS: Never mind.

EDDIE: No, seriously, just say it!

DORIS: I said never mind!

EDDIE: Mom, let's please just get it out in the open so we can *move on*, I just / want to—

DORIS: *Maybe it wasn't good for you, what about that?!* I don't know why you have to do this, Nicky has always been so independent, but you have this different way, so sensitive, and—.

(Short pause.)

You have to understand, after Dad—. I had no idea how you and your brother were going to move forward. I thought you would just—collapse in on yourselves. But then you both went to college, you both seemed normal. I thought you had both made it through unscathed. Obviously you hadn't.

(Pause.)

You think it was easy for me, after Dad died? Nicky away at college, I was working at the Blockbuster *and* the Albertson's, seeing those people every day who knew me, who used to eat at the diner—my God, what they must have thought of me. It was always a relief to come home and have dinner with you every night, and we didn't have to talk about Dad or our feelings or—any of it. We could just act like normal human beings. And then you came home that night, and you tell me that you're— . . .

(Pause.)

I realized, it just—wasn't normal for a grown man to spend that much time around his mother.

(Pause.)

EDDIE: Wait—you think it's your fault?

DORIS: Well I don't know, you came out of nowhere and told me this thing, I don't—. I just thought that what with your father gone, and you and I being so close, it wasn't too surprising that you— . . . I was terrified for you. Your life had been difficult enough already, and then living with that in this town . . . And thinking that I had somehow *contributed* to it, I just—. I thought that putting some distance between us would be good for you. I didn't *want* to, I—. Oh I hate talking like this, it's so embarrassing.

(Pause.)

You just seem so troubled. I don't like thinking it's my fault.

(Doris looks away from Eddie. Pause.)

EDDIE: It's not your fault, Mom, it's no one's fault, it's just . . . *(Pause)* I never knew you felt that way.

DORIS: Well. You've always just seemed so unhappy.

(Pause.)

EDDIE: I am unhappy, Mom. But it doesn't have anything to do with—.

(Silence.)

You remember Great-Grandpa's old place?

(Pause. Doris looks at him.)

DORIS: Well, of course I remember it—

EDDIE: I still go there sometimes. And I sit there for a while, and I think about Great-Grandpa. Coming up here from Utah, homesteading, farming the land for the first time, and it's so— . . . For a second or two, I feel like I'm—here. *Here.*

(Pause.)

But then I have to leave because it's not our land anymore, and I get back in my car and I drive back to my apartment complex, and all I can think is—there's the Starbucks. The Walmart. The Burger King. The Wendy's. The Staples. The Kmart. The Best Buy. The McDonalds. The Safeway. The Home Depot. The Olive Garden.

(Silence.)

I don't know where I live anymore, Mom.

(Long silence. Doris looks at him. Finally:)

DORIS: Is the Alfredo lumpy?

(Pause.)

EDDIE: No, I—I just made it.

(Doris slowly moves her chair to the table. Eddie serves her some fettuccine Alfredo. Doris and Eddie begin to eat together.)

DORIS: You know Dorothy and Hugh's son, Donald? He's—like you. Maybe you should meet him.
EDDIE: He is?
DORIS: Yes. I think so. Maybe he just seems it, he's always wearing these pants.

EDDIE: Oh. I haven't seen him for years.

DORIS: Well. Maybe you should— . . . *(Pause)* I ran into them a couple days ago. Dorothy and Hugh, I mean.

EDDIE: Oh yeah?

DORIS: Yes. *(Pause)* They just went to Egypt or something, it's—. *(Pause)* The places they travel to. They showed me pictures. It looks so hot.

EDDIE: Sure.

(Pause.)

DORIS: Their daughter. You remember her?

EDDIE: I think so.

DORIS: What's her name?

EDDIE: Um. Ellen?

DORIS: No that's not it. Anyway, she's doing well. She lives in Montana, I guess she got married last year.

EDDIE: Oh.

(Eddie begins break down a bit, but continues eating.)

DORIS: It sounds like the whole family is doing very well. You know who else moved to Montana, that boy Greg from your class.

EDDIE: What—what was his last name?

DORIS: Oh I knew you'd ask me that, I'm not sure. I think he was in your class. Blonde, sort of skinny?

EDDIE: I'm not sure.

DORIS: I think you'd recognize him. Can you pass me that water?

(Eddie passes her a pitcher of water. She fills her glass.)

He married another girl from your class, but I don't remember her name at all. Anyway they moved to Billings,

I think it was. They're both accountants, I guess. Do you want some?

EDDIE: No, thanks.

(Eddie is desperately holding back tears at this point. Doris notices but doesn't say anything.)

DORIS: His parents go to our church now, they're very nice. They helped me with the bakesale last week.

EDDIE: Oh.

DORIS: It was nice of them. I swear we didn't sell more than two brownies, though, felt sort of like a waste of time. Waste of food, at the least. We ended up giving it to the Meals on Wheels people, I have no idea if they're going to be able to use it. But, you know, it's—. It was nice to . . .

(Eddie is now silently crying. He looks down at his plate. Doris stops eating, looks at him. Silence.)

I'm here, Eddie. All right?

(Pause.)

I'm here.

(Eddie looks up at her. Black.)

END OF PLAY

The Few

The Few received its world premiere at The Old Globe (Barry Edelstein, Artistic Director; Michael Murphy, Managing Director) in San Diego, on October 3, 2013. It was directed by Davis McCallum. The set design was by Dane Laffrey, the costume design was by Jessica Pabst, the lighting design was by Matt Frey, the original music and sound design were by Daniel Kluger, and the dramaturgy was by John M. Baker; the production stage manager was Annette Yé. The cast was:

BRYAN	Michael Laurence
QZ	Eva Kaminsky
MATTHEW	Gideon Glick

The Few received its New York premiere at Rattlestick Playwrights Theater (David Van Asselt, Artistic Director; Brian Long, Managing Director) on May 8, 2014. It was directed by Davis McCallum. The set design was by Dane Laffrey, the costume design was by Jessica Pabst, the lighting design was by Eric Southern, the original music and sound design were by Daniel Kluger, and the dramaturgy was by John M. Baker; the production stage manager was Katharine Whitney. The cast was:

BRYAN	Michael Laurence
QZ	Tasha Lawrence
MATTHEW	Gideon Glick

The Few was developed with support of the Playwrights' Center (Jeremy B. Cohen, Producing Artistic Director), South Coast Repertory (Marc Masterson, Artistic Director), Perry-Mansfield New Works Festival (Andrew Leynse, Artistic Director), Williamstown Theatre Festival (Jenny Gersten, Artistic Director), and JAW West at Portland Center Stage (Rose Riordan, Festival Director).

A "/" indicates an overlap in dialogue. Whenever a "/" appears, the following line of dialogue should begin.

Ellipses (. . .) indicate when a character is trailing off, dashes (—) indicate where a character is being cut off, either by another character or themselves.

There is no intermission.

Scene One

Midday.

QZ sits at one of the desks. Bryan sits across from her, mud splattered over his shirt.

QZ stares at him coldly. In the silence, Bryan pulls out a pack of cigarettes.

QZ: Don't smoke in here.

BRYAN: Since when?

(QZ stares at him. Bryan puts the cigarettes away. A silence between them. QZ grabs a newspaper off of her desk.)

QZ *(Reading)*: "The fact is, when our computers hit midnight in four short months and suddenly their internal clocks think the year is 1900, we don't know what will happen.

Will planes fall out of the sky? Will there be worldwide blackouts? At the very least, we can definitely say that the Y2K bug could quite certainly plunge us into a worldwide depression. But whatever happens, I can only hope that we start to reexamine how much of our daily lives rely on these fallible machines."

(QZ puts the paper down.)

BRYAN: Wow, QZ.
QZ: I know. I know it.
BRYAN: That was / really—
QZ: You see how it sounds like an *actual newspaper* now? You see how it / actually—?
BRYAN: Sure.

(Pause.)

QZ: I've been seeing someone else.
BRYAN: Okay.
QZ: I ran my own personal ad in the paper a while ago, we started writing one another. It's amazing, he's actually better than you in every way imaginable. I mean, there is not a single way in which he is not better than you.
BRYAN: That's—good.
QZ: His letters to me are *amazing*. Poetry. For *me*.

(Silence. She stares at him.)

(Referring to his dirty shirt) How'd that happen?
BRYAN: Oh, it's just—. Happened last night—

(The phone rings.)

I was trying to get a ride on the side of the highway, truck hit a puddle and / I got—

QZ: You *hitchhiked* here? What happened to the Toyota?

(The phone rings again.)

BRYAN: Oh that thing hasn't—. Stopped running about a year after I— . . .

(The phone rings one last time. The answering machine picks up. QZ exits to the back.)

VOICE OF QZ: Hello love seekers! You've reached the message line for *The Few*'s personal ad section. Please leave your name, phone number, location, and your personal ad exactly as you would like it printed. Someone will call you back soon for payment information. Happy hunting!

(QZ reenters. She tosses Bryan a clean flannel shirt. Bryan catches it, changes his shirt. The answering machine beeps.)

MALE VOICE ONE: Hey there. Danny callin' again, QZ has my payment info, Eastern Oregon, 541-235-2950. Looking for lady copilot to navigate end times. Spacious bunker with comfortable bed, running water, tape deck. Can withstand four-megaton blast. Me: over sixty. You: under forty. Let's ride!

(Pause.)

QZ: You're thin.
BRYAN: I am?
QZ: Yeah, you—. Yeah.
BRYAN: I guess I—haven't been taking very good care of myself.

(Pause.)

QZ: Milo died.

BRYAN: Oh, okay. How'd he die?

QZ: Ran out onto the interstate.

BRYAN: Oh, that's—. Did you bury him?

QZ: *Bury* him? How would I get to him? He was in the middle of the interstate. It was awful, too, these trucks just kept driving over him again and again, pretty much spread him evenly from here to mile 436. Didn't rain forever that summer, thank God when it finally did. Washed the stains of him off the road.

(Pause.)

BRYAN: I remember when we got Milo. That little girl was giving away kittens at the rest stop, and you went up to her / and—

QZ: You don't have anywhere else to go?

(Pause.)

BRYAN: No, I just—. Really needed to come back.

(Tense silence. They stare at one another.)

I mean it's—. I mean, it's still my paper.

QZ: Excuse me?

BRYAN: I don't mean—. I'm just saying *legally*, it's still—mine, I still own it. I still own / this trailer—

QZ: This is not the same paper the three of us started here. This is something entirely different. It had to be different, your idea sucked.

BRYAN: C'mon, you believed in it just as much as / we did—

QZ: Well, truckers don't want the long-winded, unreadable crap we were giving them. What they want is to post and respond to personal ads.

BRYAN: You used to tell me that we were saving these guys' lives, you / always—

QZ: Why are you here, Bryan?

(Pause.)

BRYAN: You said yourself, maybe we don't have much time left. God knows what's gonna happen, the millennium and everything. Maybe I just—wanted to come back before the world blows up.

QZ: You think you're funny?

BRYAN: I'm not trying / to be—

QZ: You can take your stuff, it's all boxed up in the back. If you need a place to stay, there's a new Econo Lodge off exit 425. Ask for Trista, tell her you know me, she'll give you a deal.

BRYAN: I was thinking I would just sleep here.

QZ: What?

BRYAN: I'll just sleep here, QZ, in the office. You still have Jim's old army cot?

QZ: *No,* that is not happening, that is not— . . . *(Pause)* You left four years ago without a *word,* without saying anything to me, and now you just want to waltz back in here and—

(Bryan stands.)

BRYAN: Look QZ, to be honest I'm sort of at the end of my rope here, I sort of—. I know it was awful of me to walk outta here, I know it, but— . . . *(Pause)* You're the only person I have left?

(Pause. QZ stares at him. Finally, Bryan turns to the door, grabbing his things.)

I'm sorry, I'll just go, I didn't mean / to—
QZ: No, just— . . .

(Bryan stops. QZ looks at him.)

Cot's still in the closet. Goddammit. *(Pause)* Listen, if you're gonna stay here a few nights then you're going to *work*, okay? We're behind with the layouts, you can finish those and help with the drop-offs. You're not just gonna come back here and sponge off me, *no way*.
BRYAN: That's fine.
QZ: And we're not changing anything about the paper, you're not gonna write for it, you're not gonna start inviting any long-haul guys over here. The paper works now, we're not changing it back to what it used to be.
BRYAN: Okay.

(Pause.)

QZ: We use new programs now. Distribution is a lot more than four years ago. You'll be doing the longer drop-offs. And you'll be paying for your own gas. We go as far as South Dakota now.
BRYAN: Oh neat.
QZ: Shut up.

(QZ grabs a newspaper off her desk, throws it to Bryan.)

Layout's all different, too. Now we lead off with the personal ads. We've got twelve to fifteen pages of personals, only a couple pages of content. Horoscopes and my column, that's it for content. Thirty percent ad coverage in personals, twenty percent in content.

BRYAN: Where do you get the horoscopes?

QZ: I make 'em up.

BRYAN: Okay.

(Pause.)

QZ: Bryan, it's not— . . . It's not the same paper we started here with Jim.

(Pause.)

BRYAN *(Looking at the front page)*: You kept our title.

QZ: It's a shitty title. *The Few?*

BRYAN: But you kept it. *(Looking at the paper)* It looks good.

QZ: Uh-huh.

BRYAN: Formatting's okay. Some of the artwork is pixilated. *(Reading)* You still mix your tenses.

(QZ grabs the paper out of his hand, throwing it back on her desk.)

QZ: There's a few stacks in the Honda that need to be delivered, do that now. The McDonald's off 489, you remember?

BRYAN: Sure.

(Bryan heads toward the door. Just before he's out the door, QZ stands up.)

QZ: Wait.

(Bryan stops.)

Bryan, what are you— . . . ? How long are we gonna do this? *(Pause)* Tell me why you're back here.

(Pause. Bryan turns to QZ.)

Tell me why you're back, Bryan. Right now.

(They stare at one another. An irrationally long silence.)

BRYAN: QZ, I'm—

(The phone rings. Bryan and QZ continue to stare at one another. The phone rings again. And again.)

I'm gonna go do the drop-offs.

(Bryan exits. QZ watches him leave. The phone rings again.)

Scene Two

Later that day.
Matthew sits at one of the desks sorting mail. Bryan enters from outside, stops when he sees Matthew.

MATTHEW: Hi! *(Pause)* QZ said—she said she'd like you to finish the layout for the ads on page seven? If that's— . . . ? *(Pause)* I'm—Matthew?

(Pause. Bryan looks away, slowly making his way inside. He sits at a desk, turns on the computer. He waits for it to start up. Matthew continues sorting letters. Silence.)

I've, uh. I've been working here a few years now? Like since you left, I've been working on the paper since you—. *(Pause)* The distribution, you know. It started to pick up, and QZ needed, uh—she wanted help with—. *(Pause)* It's cool that you're back though! Yeah.

(Pause.)

BRYAN: Well I can take it from here, so. You can go.

(Pause.)

MATTHEW: Wait, what?

BRYAN: Look, things are probably gonna get a little jumpy around
here, so why don't you just—go home for a few days.

MATTHEW: Oh see—this is kind of like—my *job*. Like, this
is how I make money. *(Pause)* Were you and QZ, like,
married?

BRYAN: She tell you that?

MATTHEW: No, she—. I just never really figured out what—.
(Short pause) I've, uh—. I've read a lot of the articles you
used to write. A lot of the articles you and Jim used to
write, I used to read them.

BRYAN: What were you, like five years old?

MATTHEW: I'm nineteen, I was like fifteen. *(Pause, then quickly:)*
So—where have you been all this time?! I think I always
figured you were traveling, like exploring the country or
something, or—. Have you been writing the whole time?
I mean if you have *four years'* worth of writing then that's—
that's amazing, I bet you've / gotta have—

BRYAN: I'm gonna work on the layout for page seven now.

MATTHEW: Oh. Cool, um.

*(Bryan goes back to the computer, pulls out a cigarette,
lights it up. He smokes a bit. Matthew looks at him.)*

Could you—?

BRYAN: I'm working now.

MATTHEW: QZ says people can't smoke in here.

(Pause.)

BRYAN: What?

MATTHEW: Like, she doesn't want people to smoke? She says she doesn't want people smoking in here.

(Pause.)

BRYAN: I own this trailer, I can smoke here if I want.

MATTHEW: The thing is, I'm sort of allergic?

(Pause.)

BRYAN: No you're not.

MATTHEW: No, I really am.

BRYAN: No one's allergic to cigarette smoke.

MATTHEW: No seriously. Cigarettes and some animals, that's what does it. Went to a rodeo when I was a kid, almost died. Went to the emergency room.

(Bryan looks at him for a moment, then takes a puff of his cigarette. He continues to smoke as he works on the computer. Silence as Matthew goes back to his work, defeated. Suddenly Matthew stands up, taking out his wallet. He takes a small newspaper clipping out of his wallet and begins to read, a little nervous.)

(Reading) "You can find us in between Wallace and Mullan, off exit 419, about two miles south of the gas station. If you ask us what our agenda is, we'll tell you that we don't know. If you ask us why we started a newspaper for truckers, we'll tell you it's because we had to. Because after—"

BRYAN: Stop. *(Pause)* Why do you have / that?

MATTHEW: I'm Jim's nephew. *Was* his— . . .

(Pause.)

BRYAN: You're— . . . ?
MATTHEW: Yeah. *(Pause)* I met you, once. At Jim's funeral?

(Silence. Bryan puts out his cigarette.)

And there's actually a nice little memorial near the bridge where it happened, if you've never seen it—it's like this series of crosses, one for Jim, and then a few for the people in the other car, it's really— . . .

(Pause.)

BRYAN: You from Mullan?
MATTHEW: Yeah.
BRYAN: I grew up there.
MATTHEW: Yeah, I know.
BRYAN: You like it?
MATTHEW: It's okay.
BRYAN: I fucking hated it.
MATTHEW: Yeah, well, it's—. I hate it too.
BRYAN: You go to Mullan High?
MATTHEW: Yeah. I fucking hated it.
BRYAN: I thought it was okay.
MATTHEW: Yeah it was okay I guess.

(Pause.)

BRYAN: I started a poetry club with a friend of mine. Used to publish a little book thingie every semester, they still do that?
MATTHEW: Yeah, actually, I—. I used to edit it.
BRYAN: Really?

MATTHEW: Yeah, it's sort of—my thing. Poetry. I mean I'm not like a *poet*, but I like—write poems?

BRYAN: You drive all the way out here every day from Mullan?

MATTHEW: No, I. I sorta live here.

BRYAN: You— . . . ?

MATTHEW: Yeah, the old Airstream next to QZ's trailer, I sort of—. It's okay, sorta hot in the summer, but—. *(Pause)* Look, I know I—. It must be weird to show up and I'm here, and you don't remember me, but—. When I started reading *The Few*, things were pretty bad for me, my stepdad— . . . Anyway, I sorta hated life? But I read your articles, and it was like—. I'd never read anything like that, it—. It was really—important to me. Still is.

(Bryan looks at him.)

BRYAN: Really?

MATTHEW: Yeah, and not just me! Sometimes, when I'm doing drop-offs, I run into some of the truckers who would stop by here during their runs. They see me dropping off copies of the paper, and they come to me and they tell me these stories, how they felt like you and Jim and QZ saved their *lives*, that you—. One guy I met, I think his name was Lance? You remember him?

(Pause.)

BRYAN: Yeah.

MATTHEW: He told me that when his wife died, and he was doing these seven-thousand-mile runs by himself—he felt like you guys were the only family he had. He said he probably wouldn't even be alive anymore if it wasn't for the paper.

BRYAN: It was—something pretty special back then.

MATTHEW: Right! And now that you're here, we can get back to what it used to be! To what it used to do for all these guys. I don't know where you've been, but I bet you've, like— I mean I bet you saw, like, the heart of America, and now—you can write about it. Yeah?

(Bryan looks at him. QZ enters with a stack of mail in her hands and an open envelope.)

QZ: Matty, I need you to call Bruneel Tires, we can't run this ad—the artwork is terrible, you can't even read the copy—
BRYAN: Send him home, QZ.
QZ: What?
BRYAN: We don't need someone else here now, so just—send him home.

(Pause. QZ stares at Bryan.)

MATTHEW: Oh, I—I'm sorry, I didn't mean to—
QZ *(To Matthew)*: I left the backup disk in my trailer on the coffee table. Run up and get it for me? *(Pause)* Matty, just give us a minute. Please.

(Pause. Matthew nods, defeated.)

MATTHEW: Uh—yeah. Okay.

(Matthew gets up and exits.)

QZ: Believe it or not, Bryan, while you've been off doing whatever the hell it is you've been doing, I've had a *life* here, and he's part of it. He's been here for years, he's put more work into this paper than you have. *(Pause)* So just—don't mess with him, okay? He doesn't have anywhere else to go.

113

BRYAN: He doesn't have parents?

QZ: He has an alcoholic stepdad who threatened to kill him after catching him messing around with a boy from his class. You wanna send him home to that?

(The phone rings. Pause.)

When Jim died, he—.

(The phone rings again.)

He didn't have anyone left, so just—.

(The phone rings one last time. The answering machine picks up. QZ turns to her computer. Bryan awkwardly sits at a desk.)

VOICE OF QZ: Hello love seekers! You've reached the message line for *The Few*'s personal ad section. Please leave your name, phone number, location, and your personal ad exactly as you would like it printed. Someone will call you back soon for payment information. Happy hunting!

(The answering machine beeps.)

MALE VOICE TWO: Hello. I'm in Eastern Washington, 509-645-7842. Bradford. I am starting now. Seeking: one Christian lady for one man. I'm not crazy fanatic or using God here. I am a one-man-to-one-lady man. True blue. Looking for healthy relationship through God according to King James Version, not perverted or twisted. No cussers.

(The man hangs up. The answering machine beeps. Pause.)

BRYAN: Do you want me to . . . ?

(Pause.)

QZ: What?

BRYAN: You want that one in this week's issue?

QZ: What?

BRYAN: That ad. The one on the machine.

QZ: That's why we have a machine. Can you stop? I'm trying to do Tetris.

(A silence between them.)

BRYAN: So—what's his name?

(QZ glances at him, keeps playing Tetris.)

QZ: Really? *(Pause)* Rick.

(Pause.)

BRYAN: How long? Have you guys been—?

QZ: Couple years.

BRYAN: Sounds serious.

QZ: It is.

(QZ pauses her game, turns to Bryan.)

He proposed to me.

(Pause.)

BRYAN: Really?

QZ: Yep.

(Pause.)

BRYAN: What'd you say?

(Silence. QZ looks away.)

QZ: Are you—seeing anybody?
BRYAN: Me? Oh, nah. Not since . . .
QZ: Nobody?
BRYAN: Nope.
QZ: Not *one*?
BRYAN: Not one.
QZ: Bullshit.
BRYAN: Seriously.
QZ: Why not?

(Bryan looks at QZ.)

BRYAN: I don't know, it doesn't matter. It's all ephemeral anyway.
QZ: Uh-huh.
BRYAN: It doesn't last.
QZ: I know what ephemeral means, go to hell.

(QZ goes back to her computer. Silence. Bryan approaches her.)

BRYAN: And I guess I just knew—I could never find someone as good as you.

(Pause. QZ looks at him.)

QZ: What the hell am I supposed to say to that?
BRYAN: I'm sorry—
QZ: You left me here *alone*, you realize that?
BRYAN: I know, I'm sorry—
QZ: Two days after *Jim's funeral*, you leave me here and—

(Matthew reenters. Bryan and QZ stop.)

MATTHEW: I, uh. I got the zip drive. *(Pause)* Did you actually need the zip drive?

QZ: Yes, Matty, thank you.

(Pause. Matthew puts the drive on QZ's desk. Bryan sits down at a desk, his head in his hands. QZ turns to her computer, presses play on the answering machine. It rewinds. Matthew cautiously approaches Bryan.)

MATTHEW: That's, um. *(Pause)* It's just. That's sort of my desk. It's sort of my work station?

(Bryan and QZ don't move. The answering machine beeps. QZ types the ads as she listens. Matthew awkwardly finds a folding chair, sets it up in a corner.)

MALE VOICE THREE: Wyoming, uh, Bruce, 307-239-5639. All-American in search of American honey. Like long walks and the second *Harry Potter* book, I-S-O L-T-R. All shapes and sizes welcome, please be under sixty. Serious responses only.

(The answering machine beeps. Then suddenly:)

MATTHEW *(Louder than he intends)*: You guys this is so great!

(Pause. Bryan and QZ don't respond.)

MALE VOICE FOUR: / Bobby, 406-785-6352. Montana, North-west. Fat and proud seeking—

MATTHEW: You know I was thinking—maybe we could invite some people over tonight, some of the truckers that used to come over here. I know some of them still live around here, they—

(QZ hits stop on the answering machine, looks at Matthew.)

I mean not like—. I mean it doesn't have to be about the *paper*, I just thought that people would like to see Bryan, that they'd like to—. *(Pause)* It's just so great you're back.

QZ: What did you tell him?

BRYAN: What?

MATTHEW: I mean I was just thinking / that we could—

QZ: Wait, is *that* why you're back here? You think you can come back here and get me to change the paper?

BRYAN: *I'm not trying / to—*

MATTHEW: I just thought we could let people know that he's back—

QZ: The paper *finally* works, we're not messing with it. We're not inviting anyone over here, we're not doing *anything*.

BRYAN: Yeah, I mean God forbid— . . .

(Pause. QZ looks at Bryan.)

QZ: I'm sorry, what was that?

BRYAN: Nothing.

QZ: No seriously, what?

(Pause. Bryan turns to QZ.)

BRYAN: God forbid we try to do anything for these guys, right? God forbid we actually reach out to them like we used to, God forbid we actually put any energy into / making it—

QZ: Oh so I'm *lazy*, is that what I'm hearing? You left me with twelve grand of debt, which I have *almost* paid off, and you have the *balls* to say that I—

BRYAN: Oh congratulations, QZ, it's making money, very impressive. I seem to remember that when we started this paper, it wasn't about personal ads, it wasn't some stupid get-rich-quick scheme—

QZ: Oh yeah, because I'm so *rich* now.

MATTHEW: Oh crap guys, I didn't mean / to—

BRYAN: I don't even know why you still call it *The Few*, might as well call it *Hot Trucker Monthly* or *Truckerbang* or— . . . *(Short pause)* Fuck it, forget it.

(Pause. Bryan turns away.)

QZ: Fine. Let's do it. Let's invite the old gang over.

(Pause.)

MATTHEW: Wait really?

QZ: Why not? Haven't seen anyone for years. I bet they'd love to see you, right Bryan?

BRYAN: Look, you're right, the paper's fine the way it is, let's / not—

QZ *(To Bryan)*: Why don't you go into town and grab some Carlo Rossi, give everyone a call, we'll have a nice little community forum, just like we used to do with Jim. Right? *(Pause)* Matty I've got this big headache so I'm gonna lie down for a while. Someone enter the rest of the messages.

(QZ exits. Pause. Bryan buries his head in his hands.)

MATTHEW: Look, I know she's just being—. But I really think when she sees everyone, when she remembers—

BRYAN: You know I could really use a few minutes. *(Pause)* Alone.

MATTHEW: Sure, I can—I can go do a few drop-offs, that's—. If you don't mind, we just need to get the messages entered into the—

BRYAN: Okay.

(Pause.)

MATTHEW: So you'll— . . . You'll make some calls? *(Pause)* Bryan, really, when I run into these guys, when I talk to them . . . They need this. They need it back.

(Pause. Bryan nods at him. Matthew smiles, then grabs a key ring and exits. Silence. Bryan stands up, looking around the office. He takes a deep breath. He thinks. Finally, he goes to QZ's computer and presses play on the answering machine. The answering machine beeps. He types the ads as he listens.)

MALE VOICE FOUR: Bobby, 406-785-6352. Montana, Northwest. Fat and proud seeking F. Easygoing and friendly into all sorts of things. Ask any questions nothing offends me. I like sex it is important for me to have that. Thank you for reading.

(The answering machine beeps.)

FEMALE VOICE ONE: It's, uh. Shit, I don't—. *(Pause)* Never mind, sorry.

(The answering machine beeps.)

MALE VOICE FIVE: Okay, Southern Idaho, Billy's the name, 208-345-0375. Here goes. Hey there! Hi there! Whoa there! Billy here looking for a female codriver with at least two years' experience. Intimate relationship not mandatory but welcome! Want to run seven-thousand-plus miles. No druggies or drunks or fatties don't be offended that's just me. Whoa there!

(The answering machine beeps.)

FEMALE VOICE ONE: Okay, uh. It's me, again. Sorry. Cindy, um. Idaho location, 208-347-3497. Cindy. *(Pause)* I don't, um. I've never done one of these before, I. If this doesn't make sense, you can just delete it, I don't know what I'm doing. *(Pause)* So, I'm a woman. Female. I'm forty-seven, and I used to drive an eighteen-wheeler but I had a little accident and I'm on disability now. Should I say things like that? *(Pause)* I just—I think I just want someone who—. Can I start over?

(Bryan sighs, hits delete on the keyboard.)

Okay, female. Forty-seven. Have been single for— . . . Sorry, don't print that, shit. Female, forty-seven. Looking for good person—good man. I have long blonde hair and green eyes, and a few extra pounds truth be told. Please be nonviolent, and with a sense of humor. *(Pause)* I'm looking for—. Honesty.

(Bryan stops typing, listens.)

I mean, I know that people lie, I know that. But I'm looking for someone who is generally honest. When I do stupid things I need someone to say, "Cindy, don't be stupid." But when I do things well, when I'm good at something, I need someone to say, "Cindy, you did that well. You're good at that thing." And I just don't think that's asking too much. I think that I deserve that much. I may not deserve a lot, but— . . . *(Pause, a hint of desperation)* I guess I just feel like I woke up a couple days ago and realized, for heck's sake it's gonna be a *new millennium* in a few months, and what am I even doing? What have I *ever* done? In my whole life, what have I ever— . . . ? *(Pause)*

I'm sorry, just. I'm sorry, I'm wasting your time, I'm sorry. I apologize. You can delete this, please just delete this, I'm—.

(She hangs up. The answering machine beeps, then is silent. Bryan stares forward for a moment, then hits rewind on the answering machine.)

Scene Three

Later that night.

Matthew has set up a few folding chairs. A large pile of old newspapers rests on one of the desks. Bryan enters wearing a backpack and holding two large jugs of Carlo Rossi white zinfandel.

MATTHEW: Hey. *(Pause)* Party time! Heh.

(Bryan makes his way inside, puts the jugs on a desk. He opens one, finds a glass, pours himself some wine. Bryan pours a second glass, hands it to Matthew.)

Oh, I. I don't really.
BRYAN: You allergic to this too?
MATTHEW: Well, yeah.

(Pause.)

BRYAN: What?
MATTHEW: Seriously. The tannins or something. My mom gave me a sip of red wine when I was a kid, my throat closed up.
BRYAN: What else are you allergic to?
MATTHEW: Cigarettes, red wine, some animals. That's it. *(Pause)* Really, that's it.

(Bryan takes his backpack off, takes out a large bottle of bottom-shelf whiskey. He opens the bottle, hands it to Matthew.)

BRYAN: So you're not allergic to this then.
MATTHEW *(Taking the bottle)*: Oh, um. Cool.

(Bryan motions for Matthew to drink from the bottle. Matthew takes a halfhearted swig of the whiskey.)

BRYAN: Good?
MATTHEW: Yeah, it's—. Oak-y.

(Bryan notices the old newspapers sitting in the corner.)

Oh, that's. Those are like, mine. All the way back to the first issue. I thought it would be nice to look through some of them when people get here, or—
BRYAN: Yeah or we could just drink.
MATTHEW: Oh. Okay.

(Bryan sits down, drinking his wine. He takes the whiskey bottle.)

You know, um. I was reading that article that you wrote a few years ago about those motels in Western Montana that you had stayed at when you were still trucking and it—

(Bryan mixes some whiskey in with his wine. Matthew watches him.)

Wow. Is that—should you be doing that?
BRYAN: QZ doesn't drink these anymore? She calls it a "Dirty Rossi." Used to be her favorite.

(Bryan drinks. Matthew watches him for a moment. Then suddenly:)

MATTHEW *(Quickly)*: Anyway, the way you wrote about the trucker you had met at that one motel, the guy from the Philippines whose mother had just died the day before you talked to him? That was the one for me that was like— . . . I didn't even know that writing could make me—. I'm being weird, *anyway* I was thinking that it could be a cool project or whatever to go back to some of those motels and do like a follow-up piece or whatever, and maybe it could also be a way that we could start getting to know more truckers, and—. Here, let me see if I can find it . . .

(Matthew goes to the stack of newspapers and starts rooting through them.)

One of the motels you wrote about closed a couple years ago, but we could find some / other—

BRYAN: Okay look, I'm not—. Shit, I'm not trying to be rude. Please try to understand that I just don't care anymore. I really, really just *don't care.*

(Silence.)

MATTHEW: Why did you come back here?

BRYAN: You know I'd really appreciate the chance to just quietly get drunk if you don't / mind—

MATTHEW: No, seriously. If you don't care about this paper anymore, then why did you come back?

BRYAN: Frankly, kid, it's because I was tired and this is the only shelter I have legal right to anymore. I needed a place to stay, and if I have to pay my way by doing drop-offs and formatting personal ads, then fine.

MATTHEW: Bullshit.

(Pause.)

BRYAN: What was that?

MATTHEW: Bullshit. That's such bullshit, it's— *(Pause)* Look you can act this way all you want, but—you started this thing for a / reason—

BRYAN: You know I gotta say, Matthew, you're starting to get a little irritating. And despite QZ's claim over this place, the fact is I still have the deed so I could have you out on your ass if it fucking pleases me. Okay?

(Silence. Matthew stares at him, hurt. Finally he heads to the door, opening it.)

Sorry. Fuck.

(Matthew stops.)

Sorry.

(Matthew takes a few steps toward Bryan, leaving the door open.)

MATTHEW: Look, you gotta realize—when Jim fell asleep at the wheel, I didn't really have anyone?

BRYAN: I know—

MATTHEW: No, actually, you *don't* know, you—. *(Pause)* When I lost Jim, this paper was the only part of him that I had left. When QZ let me move in, and I started working here, I thought you'd eventually come back, and when you did, I thought—. I don't know, I thought you'd—understand.

(Pause.)

BRYAN: Guess I must be a pretty big disappointment.

MATTHEW: I mean I just don't—. Why did you leave? Was it because of what happened with Jim? Was it—?

BRYAN: This isn't really something I'm eager to get into right now—

MATTHEW: Sorry but I've sort of been keeping your paper alive? For years? If you're ready to give up on it, can you just tell me *why*? Maybe you owe me that? *(Pause)* Please.

BRYAN: Look, when we started this thing, it— . . . *(Pause)* Jim and I started trucking around the same time. We both thought the money'd be good, thought it'd be nice to see the country. For a while it was, but— . . .

(Pause.)

It does something to you, driving that much. Jim and I were both doing runs across the whole country, easily saw forty-eight states between the two of us. After a while— you start to feel like you don't exist. Like you're never in a place long enough to even exist. You stop talking to people at gas stations and truck stops, you start avoiding the restaurants where the waitresses might recognize you, you start sleeping in the back of your cab just so you don't have to talk to a motel clerk. You go to diners and truck stops full of other long-haul guys, and you don't even look at each other.

(Pause.)

One night, Jim and I were both doing runs. I was in Utah, he was in North Carolina or something. He gives me a call, and he says he's at a truck stop—he says that he can't see anyone's faces. He says he's looking at people's faces, try- ing to see them—but he can't see anything.

(Pause.)

That night, I guess—QZ and I decided to do something.

MATTHEW: That's why you started the paper? For Jim?

BRYAN: Wasn't even a paper at first. I quit trucking, sunk the inheritance from my dad into this place. QZ quit her job at the gas station, and we both started spending all our time here. We just thought it could be a place where truckers could just—look at each other, talk. Remind each other that they still existed. QZ called it a "church without God." And it was.

(QZ appears in the open doorway. She smokes, being careful to blow the smoke outside. Bryan and Matthew don't notice her.)

Pretty soon, long-haul guys were stopping by almost every night, just to talk. A lot of the time it was just daily stuff— long-distance marriages, gas prices, that kind of stuff. But every so often there'd be some guy, some trucker from some random corner of some random state who was *amazing*, come in and tell us a story about driving a tanker in the middle of a hurricane, or show us pictures he'd taken of sunrises at McDonald's in forty-three different states. And after a while, the three of us had the idea to just— write it down.

(Pause.)

Jim was still trucking, he'd drop off copies everywhere he could, every truck stop he came across. These little beacons scattered along the interstate, something to— . . . Something to remind us that we still existed.

(Pause.)

QZ: Hey.

(Bryan and Matthew turn to QZ. She comes inside. Pause.)

(To Bryan) You make me one?

(Bryan pours a tumbler half full of wine, half full of whiskey. QZ takes one last puff and throws the cigarette outside. She goes to Bryan, takes the cup.)

Pretty speech, Bryan. Didn't think you had it in you anymore.

(QZ takes a drink.)

BRYAN: Yeah, well.
QZ *(Referring to the wine)*: You got the white zinfandel?
BRYAN: You always drank the white zinfandel.
QZ: People change, Bryan. Tastes evolve. I'm a cabernet sauvignon girl now.
BRYAN: Well then.
MATTHEW: So I don't know when you told everyone to show up, but I thought we / could—
QZ: Yeah, Bryan, when's everyone getting here?

(Pause.)

BRYAN: I don't have anyone's number anymore.
QZ: Oh, really? So you're not feeling ashamed, that wouldn't have anything to do with it?
BRYAN: Can we please / just—
QZ: I don't blame you, I wouldn't wanna face them either. After abandoning everyone like that.
MATTHEW: Wait, so—wait no one else is coming?

(QZ sits down, drinking.)

BRYAN *(To QZ)*: You seen anyone lately?

QZ: Not for a while. People stopped coming over pretty quick after you left.

BRYAN: You ever hear from anyone? Cody or Jessica? Or / Ike—?

QZ: Not for years. Everyone had to grow up, I guess.

(Pause. Bryan looks at her.)

BRYAN: "Grow up"?

QZ: People had to realize this was just cheap group therapy and that they needed to get on with their lives—

BRYAN: C'mon, QZ.

QZ: I think a lot of them only came over here 'cause we'd give 'em free booze.

BRYAN: How can you say that? You loved this place, you had just as much faith in it as / we did—

QZ: And look what all that faith got us, huh?

(QZ drinks. Bryan stares at her. Silence.)

What?

BRYAN: No, it's—nothing.

QZ: No, what?

BRYAN: You're just—different. From four years ago. You look different.

QZ: What the fuck is that supposed to mean?

MATTHEW: Okay so maybe the three of us could just talk? I mean QZ I know you don't want to change the whole paper and that makes / sense but—

QZ: How do I "look different"?

BRYAN: You just look—cynical, I guess. You never used to look so cynical.

(Pause.)

QZ: Well, having the supposed love of your life walk out on you two days after your best friend's funeral? That does tend to recalibrate your worldview a little bit.

MATTHEW: Okay! Maybe new topic?

QZ: Okay, sure. New topic: Why the fuck is Bryan back after four years?

BRYAN: Okay QZ—

QZ: Oh right, he doesn't feel like talking about that right now, he doesn't want to tell us the reason he's back here, he just feels it's appropriate to come back, hold the deed to this place over my head, and then fucking tell me that I / "look cynical"—

BRYAN: I said / OKAY QZ.

QZ: —and try to ruin this paper after I've spent the last four years desperately trying to make it *profitable*, trying to make it into a *decent paper*—

BRYAN: Oh a "decent paper," is that what you've turned it into? Okay, let's see what you're working on for this month.

(Bryan goes to QZ's computer.)

QZ: Get away from my computer, Bryan.

BRYAN: "Al Gore's Anti-Gun Presidential Platform." Nice QZ, real topical. / Well done.

QZ: I said get the fuck away from my / computer Bryan—

BRYAN *(Reading)*: "Gore wants us to believe that the Second Amendment did not exist, he—" *Jesus Christ*, what is it with you and mixing tenses?!

QZ: It's what people are talking about, Bryan, it sells papers—!

BRYAN: FINE. FORGET ABOUT IT, FORGET ABOUT WHAT WE MADE TOGETHER, FORGET IT EVER EXISTED.

(Bryan goes to the stack of papers. He opens one up, rips it up, and throws it on the floor.)

MATTHEW: Wait—those are kind / of like, mine—

BRYAN: You believed in this paper / just as much as I did, you—

(Bryan grabs a clump of papers, crumpling them, throwing them to the floor.)

MATTHEW: / *Please, stop, that's like my personal*—

QZ: You think there would even *be* a paper anymore if it wasn't for me?! We're actually *making money* now, we're almost ready to hire a web designer so we can start a / dating site—

BRYAN: If Jim could see what you've— . . .

(Bryan stops. QZ stares at him. Pause.)

QZ: You wanna talk about Jim?

BRYAN: Don't—

QZ: No seriously, you wanna talk about Jim? Let's talk about Jim.

BRYAN: *Don't.*

QZ: How'd he turn out, Bryan?

(Pause. Bryan looks at her, pleading.)

BRYAN: QZ, / *please*—

QZ: You can preach to this kid all night about our wonderful paper, about faith and all that horseshit, *but you know how it ended, you know what he*—. *(Pause)* Tell him, Bryan. *(Pause)* Tell him.

(Silence. They stare at one another. Finally:)

I'm going to bed.

(QZ exits. Silence.)

MATTHEW: I don't understand, what did—? *(Pause)* What did she mean, tell me what?

(Pause. Bryan looks at Matthew.)

BRYAN: He left a note.

MATTHEW: What?

BRYAN: A suicide note. Jim left a suicide note, here. A few hours before he— . . . *(Pause)* Four words. "can't live anymore sorry." No capital letters, no comma. He writes this note, then he gets in his truck, crosses the median on a bridge in North Dakota and takes out an entire family.

(Pause.)

"can't live anymore sorry"

(Silence.)

MATTHEW: No, I don't—. I don't believe you. They would have— the police would have found out, they would have—

BRYAN: Everyone just assumed he fell asleep, he had been driving all night, and he—. We—decided it was best to not tell anyone.

(Matthew wanders in disbelief for a moment. He looks at the papers on the ground, kicks them in frustration. He looks at Bryan for some response. Bryan doesn't move. Matthew exits, slamming the door behind him.

A few moments pass. Bryan sits down, leans back in his chair, staring at the ceiling. Matthew reenters.)

MATTHEW: I mean, look, you don't have to be like a prophet or something, you don't have to be fucking *Gandhi* to me. But you could—. You don't have to act like a complete dick and treat me like I'm some sort of—, like I'm not even worth your time. And I don't need you to be brilliant, I don't need you to—. *(Pause)* Show it to me.

BRYAN: What?

MATTHEW: Show me the note. The note Jim left, show it to me.

BRYAN: Matthew, I don't / have—

MATTHEW: Then I don't believe you. I don't—. *(Pause)* He did it on *purpose?*

(Silence. Then, in a fit of rage, Matthew grabs a clump of papers and slams them down on a desk—they fly everywhere. The force of the papers hitting the desk accidentally turns on the answering machine. Matthew exits. The answering machine beeps.)

MALE VOICE SIX: It's, uh—. Wait what am I supposed to—? Uh. Trent, I'm in—. Why do you need my phone number? Look don't print my name. Truckers call me Bent Nickel, just print that. No, uh, actually don't print that, just print—. Just print—hot trucker. Print hot trucker seeking—

(Bryan hits stop on the answering machine, then sits down. He stares up at the ceiling, whiskey bottle in hand.)

Scene Four

The next morning.

Bryan, very drunk and unrested, sits in the same position as before, holding the now mostly empty bottle of whiskey. There is a large jug of antifreeze sitting on the desk in front of him. Bryan is staring at it, motionless.

Matthew bursts into the office wearing his backpack. Bryan keeps his eyes on the antifreeze.

Matthew stops, looks at Bryan. He slams the door behind him as hard as he can. Bryan doesn't move.

Matthew goes to his desk, petulantly throwing his backpack on top of it. He looks at Bryan, who still doesn't react.

Matthew finally sits, turning on his computer. He looks around on his desk for a moment.

Silence.

MATTHEW: Where's the red floppy disk?

BRYAN: What?

MATTHEW: The red floppy disk. The one that's always right here, it has the master layout on it. It's important. Where is it?

BRYAN: I don't know.

(Pause.)

MATTHEW: Have you— . . . Did you sleep at all?

BRYAN: Not really.

MATTHEW: What are you doing with our antifreeze? *(No response)* There's a few stacks outside that need to be delivered still. The Denny's off 412, the Conoco off 401. *(Referring to the whiskey bottle)* But I guess I'll have to do them myself, just like every—! Has QZ come in yet?

(Pause.)

BRYAN: You're working?

MATTHEW: Yes, I'm working, because I *have* to. This is how I make money, this is how I *live*. Has QZ come in yet?

BRYAN: No.

(Pause.)

MATTHEW: I bought that disk with my own money, I always leave it *right here*. Are you sure you didn't do something with it?

BRYAN: I don't even know what you're / talking about—

MATTHEW: *A red floppy disk, it's square, and it's red, and / it—*

BRYAN: I heard you, I don't know / where—

MATTHEW: Forget it. Not like I have enough money to buy another / one—

BRYAN: Is that what you're talking about?

(Bryan points to a red floppy disk sitting on the desk next to Matthew.)

MATTHEW: Oh.

(Matthew takes the disk, puts it in his computer.)

It's ten o'clock, where's QZ?

BRYAN: Gone.

MATTHEW: Where?

BRYAN: I don't know.

MATTHEW: Did she say if she was going to be back before noon? I need her / to—

BRYAN: No, but I doubt it.

MATTHEW: Why?

BRYAN: Because she took all her stuff.

(Pause.)

MATTHEW: What do you mean?

BRYAN: It was kind of amazing, around three in the morning she just starts packing up her station wagon. Managed to fit her whole bedroom in there, looked like. I watched her the whole time. She knew I was watching. She acted like she didn't know, but she knew.

(Pause.)

MATTHEW: Wait, what are you—what are you saying?

BRYAN: Allow me to simplify. QZ took her shit. She's gone. Probably for good.

(Matthew pauses for a second, then bolts toward the door, exiting.

A moment of silence.

The phone rings. Bryan doesn't move. The phone continues to ring. Finally, Bryan stands up, wobbling. He goes to the phone, picks it up, then immediately hangs it up. The ringing stops. He sits back down.

Matthew reenters.)

MATTHEW: Oh my God. She's gone.

BRYAN: Yep.

MATTHEW: Where was she going?

BRYAN: I don't know.

MATTHEW: She didn't say anything to you?

(Bryan shakes his head, drinks the whiskey.)

But we—I don't know what to do. I don't know how to . . . We're supposed to have our new issue ready to print by *tomorrow*, if we don't have it everyone's gonna want the money from their ad space back, and we don't even have enough money in the bank right now to pay the electric bill, I don't— . . . *(Pause)* Shit. Oh shit.

(Bryan looks at Matthew. Matthew looks back. The phone begins to ring. Awkward pause.)

What?

(Bryan takes a long drink of whiskey, then grabs the jug of antifreeze.)

BRYAN: I guess Jim found a more dramatic way to do it, but this just seems a lot easier.

MATTHEW: Wait, what?

(Bryan looks at the antifreeze. The answering machine picks up, QZ's greeting is heard.)

VOICE OF QZ: / Hello love seekers! You've reached the message line for *The Few*'s personal ad section. Please leave your name, phone number, location, and your personal ad exactly as you would like it printed. Someone will call you back soon for payment information. Happy hunting!

BRYAN: Antifreeze uses either ethylene glycol or propylene glycol, propylene is poisonous but ethylene is *really fucking poisonous*, so—

MATTHEW: Wait—

BRYAN *(Examining the label)*: And this—here—is ethylene. Perfect.

(The greeting concludes, the answering machine beeps.)

MALE VOICE SEVEN: / Hi it's Kent F., you have all my info. Widowed S-W-M trucker in my early sixties.

BRYAN: I guess it'll probably still take a few hours, but.

MATTHEW: WHAT ARE YOU DOING?! I DON'T KNOW WHAT YOU'RE DOING!

BRYAN: I can do it outside—

(Bryan stumbles toward the door.)

MATTHEW: *Please don't leave me here alone—!*

(Bryan stops, halfway out the door, the antifreeze in one hand, the whiskey in the other. He looks at Matthew.)

MALE VOICE SEVEN: Looking for any woman. Age and body type not important. Please— . . . Please respond. I'm faithful. Please.

(The answering machine beeps. Matthew and Bryan remain motionless, looking at one another. Silence.)

MATTHEW: Could you—not drink that antifreeze? Please? *(Pause)* Look, she's gonna—QZ'll come back, she's probably just—
BRYAN: No she won't. *(Pause)* I proposed to her.
MATTHEW: You—?
BRYAN: The last letter I wrote to QZ, I proposed to her. She didn't answer, so—I came back. To get my answer. And now she's gone, so I suppose that must be a "no."

(Pause.)

MATTHEW: Wait, you—? I thought Rick proposed to her—
BRYAN: If *I* responded to her ad, she never would have written me back, so— . . . So I just—wrote her as Rick.

(Pause. Bryan takes a long drink of the whiskey. He cradles the whiskey and the antifreeze in his arms.)

MATTHEW: Wait, you're—? *You're Rick?*
BRYAN: It was more romantic in my head.
MATTHEW: You've been—?
BRYAN: I told her I wasn't ready to meet her in person, just went through a personal tragedy or whatever, wasn't ready to see anyone . . . That part was true, I guess.

(Bryan downs the rest of the whiskey. The liquor has now gotten to him. He slowly starts to slide down to the ground.)

MATTHEW: That's— . . . That's *awful—*

BRYAN: Yeah.

(Bryan is now on the ground, leaning up against the door. The whiskey bottle rolls out of his hand. He continues to clutch the antifreeze.)

I am—*really* terrible at being a person.

(Matthew goes to him. Bryan's eyes begin to close. Silence.)

MATTHEW: Bryan?!

(Bryan is passed out, the antifreeze still in his arms. Matthew looks down at him.)

Scene Five

That night.

Bryan is in the same position as before—everything is the same except for a large bike lock that seals the front door shut. The antifreeze is no longer in his arms and is nowhere in the space.

Bryan slowly starts to wake up. He is profoundly hungover. He gets up, groaning, searching for water. He goes to a water cooler, looks around for a cup, and when he doesn't find one, he puts his mouth on the spout and drinks for a while.

Matthew enters from the back. He stares at Bryan silently, stiff and intense.

Bryan turns, sees Matthew. Matthew stares at him.

BRYAN: What?

MATTHEW: I locked the door.

(Pause.)

BRYAN: What?
MATTHEW: I padlocked it with my bike lock.
BRYAN: Why?
MATTHEW: 'Cause you're not leaving. I'm not letting you leave.
BRYAN: All right, I'm really not feeling up for this, I'd really just rather—
MATTHEW: Shut up.

(Pause.)

BRYAN: What?
MATTHEW: I said shut up. *Shut up.*

(Pause.)

BRYAN: I have no idea what's happening right now.
MATTHEW: What's happening is—you're gonna sit down and write. You're gonna write an article, we're gonna format the personals, then we're gonna send it to the printers and do all the drop-offs. Okay?
BRYAN: No, we're not going to—. *(Pause)* Look, I know this paper means something to you, but it's done, okay? Just— go home to your family or whatever, just—

(Matthew pulls out a handgun and points it at Bryan.)

What?
MATTHEW: You're not leaving. There's enough food to last us a few days. You're going to *shut up*, and do what I say. We're not missing our deadline this month.

(Pause.)

BRYAN: Matthew, that's a BB gun. It's my old fucking BB gun.

MATTHEW: Yeah but if I shoot you it's *really* going to hurt.

(Matthew pumps the BB gun five or six times. Bryan moves toward Matthew.)

BRYAN: Okay, look. Just give me the key to the bike lock, I'll—

(Matthew shoots Bryan in the thigh. He cries out in pain.)

JESUS CHRIST, that went into my fucking skin, you know that?!

MATTHEW: I KNOW! I'LL DO IT AGAIN.

(Bryan looks at his thigh.)

BRYAN: I'm serious, it went into my skin!

MATTHEW: Fucking A!

(Matthew pumps the BB gun again.)

BRYAN: All right give that to me *right now*—

(Matthew shoots again, this time hitting Bryan in the hand.)

THAT HIT MY FUCKING FINGERNAIL!

MATTHEW: DON'T COME NEAR ME!

(Matthew pumps the gun again, Bryan lunges at him. Matthew easily evades him. Bryan falls into a desk.)

Dude you're not going to be able to catch me. I'm spry.

BRYAN: Look—I am *not* in the mood for this, do you understand? You are going to give me the key to that bike lock, you are going to go home, and—

141

MATTHEW: No, I'm not letting you kill yourself.

BRYAN: What?

MATTHEW: This morning you said you were going to kill yourself. I'm not letting you do that.

BRYAN: I was—. I was just *talking*, I don't know, I—

MATTHEW: You almost drank a jug of *antifreeze*. I'm not letting you kill yourself like Jim, I'm not letting the paper just *die*. I'm in charge now!

(Bryan looks around the room for a minute. He moves toward a printer and picks it up.)

What are you doing?

BRYAN: I'm breaking a window and I'm getting out of here.

MATTHEW: Don't try it.

(Bryan moves toward a window with the printer.)

I SAID DON'T TRY IT!

(Matthew fires the gun at Bryan. It hits him in the eye. Bryan screams in pain, dropping the printer, grabbing his eye.)

OH MY GOD OH MY GOD I'M SORRY I / DIDN'T MEAN TO!

BRYAN: YOU JUST FUCKING *BLINDED* ME—

MATTHEW: SORRY SORRY SORRY / SORRY—!

BRYAN: WHAT IS WRONG WITH YOU?! WHY DO YOU CARE SO MUCH ABOUT THIS FUCKING PAPER?!

MATTHEW: *BECAUSE IT'S ALL THAT I HAVE RIGHT NOW, DON'T YOU SEE THAT?!*

(Silence. Bryan takes his hand off his eye, checking for blood. He finds a reflective surface, tries to examine his eye.)

Did I really hit you right in the eye? Do you need to go to the hospital?

BRYAN: No, it's—. It's just scraped, it's—. Fucking BB is still in there, I can feel it when I move my eye. Jesus.

(Bryan sits down at a desk. Pause.)

MATTHEW: Look, I'm sorry I shot your eye. But I can't—. I can't just like *go home*, my stepdad wouldn't even let me in the front door. And my mom's always on fucking pain pills, so she's not going to—. You can't just come back here and get drunk, chase QZ off, and shut down the paper because you don't care. *I care.*

(Pause.)

BRYAN: Look—I don't know what you expect me to write. I haven't been around for four years, it's not like I can offer anything to—

MATTHEW: I already know what you can write about.

BRYAN: Fantastic.

MATTHEW: The last four years. What you've been doing these past four years.

(Bryan looks away.)

BRYAN: Look, we—our readers are totally different now, no one even knows who I am, no one—

MATTHEW: That doesn't matter. Just give them something honest, you tell them about the last four years. You can tell them about how you've been writing to QZ.

(Pause.)

BRYAN: I told you about that?

MATTHEW: Yeah.

BRYAN: Fantastic.

(Matthew goes to him.)

MATTHEW: Look, I just / think—

BRYAN: Could you put the goddam BB gun / down?!

MATTHEW: Sorry, sorry.

(Matthew puts the BB gun on a desk.)

Look, we can find new readers, build the paper up, once you tell them what you've learned, you know—what you've been doing all this time. Yeah?

(Short pause.)

BRYAN: I was working at a Perkins in Boise.

(Silence.)

MATTHEW: Like—the restaurant?

BRYAN: Yes. The restaurant. I wasn't traveling, I wasn't exploring, I wasn't searching out the fucking heart of America. I was a short-order cook at Perkins. I lived in a motel across the parking lot that smelled *constantly* like burnt hair, and I drank myself to sleep every night. There's your article, stop the fuckin' presses.

(Pause.)

MATTHEW: You left—to work at a Perkins? *(Pause)* You're a *real asshole*, you know that?

BRYAN: Yes, I do know that, actually.

MATTHEW: No, I mean—. I thought you were doing something *important*, I thought you were like *searching* for something, or—

BRYAN *(Turning to Matthew)*: Okay, you wanna know what I've learned? Listen to me. When we started this paper we wanted to connect these guys, help them with their loneliness, blah blah blah, but the reality? The reality is, other people are *bullshit*.

(The phone begins to ring. Matthew and Bryan pay no attention to it. It continues to ring underneath the following:)

Any sense of connection you have with another person is either a complete illusion or chemicals dancing around in your brain. I wasted years of my life trying to convince myself that we're not really alone, trying to convince Jim of that, and where did that get him?

(The answering machine picks up. QZ's greeting is heard.)

VOICE OF QZ: / Hello love seekers! You've reached the message line for *The Few*'s personal ad section. Please leave your name, phone number, location, and your personal ad exactly as you would like it printed. Someone will call you back soon for payment information. Happy hunting!

BRYAN: The sooner you accept the fact that you are completely alone, the sooner you accept that *everyone* is completely alone, the better off you'll be.

(The answering machine beeps.)

MATTHEW: You can't actually believe that.

QZ *(On the machine)*: Hello?

BRYAN: *Believe* that?

QZ *(On the machine)*: Matty, are you—? Someone pick up?

(Bryan stops. Matthew and Bryan stare at the machine.)

Look, I'm—. I'm in the hospital, it's not a big deal, it's not—. I shouldn't have been driving last night after— . . . Anyway I had a little accident, I'm fine, but the car is—. I'm in Missoula, at—I don't remember what the name of the hospital is, it's—. Saint something, or—. Saint Patrick, it's Saint Patrick's, in Missoula. I need someone to come get me. *(Pause)* Please pick up? *(Pause)* Please. Pick up.

(Matthew looks at Bryan. Bryan moves to the phone, picking it up.)

BRYAN: Hi. *(Looking at Matthew)* You— . . . ? Are you okay?

Scene Six

The following morning.

QZ enters, followed by Matthew who holds car keys. QZ has one arm in a sling and a few small bandages on her face.

Matthew hangs up the keys and closes the door. He goes to a computer, turns it on.

MATTHEW: I mean look, they're gonna be pissed, we'll probably lose some ad business, but as long as we get the issue together by this afternoon then I think we're gonna be fine, I think we—

(Matthew looks at the computer. The screen is blank, the computer is unresponsive.)

Are you fucking kidding me?

(QZ stands in the middle of the trailer, looking around, as if for the first time. She looks up. Matthew hits the computer a few times, trying to get it to start up.)

(To the computer) Now, really? You're gonna do this *now*? *(Pause)* Okay, that's— . . . That's okay, it won't look good but I can go to the Kinko's and copy some of the ads from last month, it's not gonna look / right but—

QZ: That water stain is shaped exactly like Alaska.

(Pause.)

MATTHEW: What?

(QZ points up.)

Oh. Okay?

QZ: You see that?

MATTHEW: Yeah?

QZ: When we started this place that water stain was nothing. Like a dot. It was Rhode Island, and now it's fucking Alaska.

(Pause. Matthew goes to QZ's computer.)

MATTHEW: Look I don't know if you've finished your column for this month but if we can sort of throw it / together—

QZ: Matty.

MATTHEW: I can clean it up if you like, if it's not—. I can't find the file, is it— . . . ?

(QZ goes to him.)

If you don't have it finished then maybe we could run something from last year, or maybe we could / just—

QZ: You're fired.

(Pause.)

MATTHEW: What?

QZ: I know it doesn't feel like it, but believe me this is a gift. *(Pause)* You can stay here as long as you like of course, I'm not kicking you out, but / you—

MATTHEW: Wait, you're—? What are you doing?

(Pause.)

QZ: Matty. Don't you want to get out of here? Did you really think that this is where you were gonna spend the rest of your life?

(Matthew stands up, paces a bit. QZ watches him. Pause.)

I know that this paper meant something to you, but it's never going to turn back into what it used to be. I know that the only reason you worked here all this time is because you were hoping that eventually Bryan would come back and the paper / would—

MATTHEW: I worked here because I wanted to. I *wanted* to. *(Pause)* You know, when you first let me move in here, and Bryan had already left, I figured—. I mean I thought you'd just shut the paper down, get a different job, but then—you didn't, you kept it going, and I was like—oh, she wants to stay. But then like another year went by, and I was like—oh. She *doesn't* want to stay here, she wants to *leave.* Why isn't she leaving?

QZ: You wanted me to leave you alone here, to run everything / by yourself?

MATTHEW: It wasn't for me. You know that, you didn't stay for me. *(Pause)* I worked here because I *wanted* to, QZ, because I like it here, I feel *safe* here. But you— . . . I mean, you hate it here. *(Pause)* You hate it here, right?

(A silence between the two of them.

Bryan enters. He wears a makeshift eyepatch made from duct tape. He looks at QZ. Pause.)

Okay, I'll—. *(Pause)* I'll come back?

QZ: Thank you, Matty.

(Matthew exits, shutting the door. QZ and Bryan look at one another.)

BRYAN: You get a DUI?

QZ: No, thank God. I was mostly sober by the time it happened, cop felt bad for me.

(Pause.)

BRYAN: I'm—glad you're okay. I wish you would have let me pick you up.

(Pause. QZ looks at him.)

QZ: Bryan, what are—? What the fuck are we doing?

BRYAN: I don't know.

QZ: This place is trashed, we're not gonna make the next issue, my arm's in a sling, and what the fuck happened to your eye?

BRYAN: Matthew shot me.

QZ: Well good for him then. *(Pause)* When we were in high school, I never thought we would turn out to be such awful people. How did we turn out to be such awful people?

(Bryan moves closer to her, still maintaining his distance.)

BRYAN: QZ, I—. I really should tell you something.

(Pause.)

QZ: What?

(Bryan looks at QZ. Pause.)

BRYAN: I don't know how to tell you this, I— . . . Look, I should
have told you this the second I came back here, but I was
/ worried—

QZ: *Why the hell did you have to propose to me?* We were doing
fine—and then you fucking *propose?*

(Pause.)

BRYAN: Wait, you—? Did you—?

QZ: Jesus Christ, Bryan, of course I knew it was you.

(Pause.)

BRYAN: How long have you known?

QZ: Didn't take long to figure / out—

BRYAN: Shit, QZ, if you knew it was me then why didn't / you—!

QZ: Well why did you pretend you were someone else in the
first place?!

BRYAN: Because I knew you'd actually respond to Rick! You
never would have written me back!

QZ: YOU'RE RIGHT, I WOULDN'T HAVE. YOU'RE AN
ASSHOLE. RICK'S A GOOD GUY.

BRYAN: But why didn't—?! Why didn't you just *say* something?!

QZ: WHY DIDN'T *YOU* SAY SOMETHING?

BRYAN: BECAUSE THOSE LETTERS WERE THE ONLY
GOOD THING LEFT IN MY LIFE.

(Silence.)

QZ: Yeah, well. Me too. *(Pause)* Took me a few letters to realize it was you, actually.

BRYAN: What made you realize?

QZ: You used the word "beatific." You're such an asshole, who uses that word?

(Pause.)

BRYAN: When I didn't hear back from you after my last letter, I didn't know what to do—

QZ: That letter was beautiful, Bryan. I think it might be the most beautiful thing you've ever written. Reading it was— . . . It felt amazing, it felt *right*. Then I get to the end, and you sign—"Rick." You propose to me, and you sign—"Rick." *(Pause)* And when you first walked in here, and I saw you standing there I had this split second thought, like—*can we actually do this?* And I waited for you to say something, *anything*, but you just— . . . *(Pause)* Did you really expect to just show up here and I'd fall into your arms? You *left* me.

BRYAN: I know, I'm sorry—

QZ: Why did you do that?

BRYAN: That doesn't matter / now—

QZ: No. No more of this shit, you're going to tell me.

(Pause. Bryan looks at her.)

BRYAN: When Jim died and we found that note— . . . *(Pause)* Everything we were doing here, this whole paper, even what I felt for you, it all felt so— . . . I wasn't some trucker poet. We hadn't made something real or meaningful here. We started this place because of Jim. We thought we were saving him all those years, saving all those other guys, but in the end it all just—

QZ: You think I didn't want to save him too? I *loved* him,
I loved him since high school, just like you. We should
have made him quit trucking the second you got that
phone call from him. If I knew what he was capable of,
I would have set fire to his rig myself—

BRYAN: He didn't do that because he was still trucking, QZ,
it was bigger than that. *(Pause)* When I left, I thought
I'd just take the pickup and drive around for a few days,
maybe a week. Just to clear my head. After three or four
days, I was on this rural highway out in Wyoming in the
middle of the night, and I hadn't seen any other cars for
miles and miles, and these two little headlights show up in
the distance. And we get closer, and closer, and suddenly
it was like—all I had to do was one simple movement.
From there . . .

*(Bryan holds his hand out, miming a steering wheel at
twelve o'clock.)*

To there.

(Bryan moves his hand to ten o'clock.)

And that would be it. And the car gets right next to me,
and I swear to God it took *everything in me* not to do it.

(Silence.)

QZ: You know about a week before Jim died, Kelly and Dave
and those guys were over here, you remember that?

BRYAN: I think so?

QZ: Jim had just done that run up to Alaska, he was telling us
about tipping over on that mountain pass with all those
pigs in his truck? He felt so bad for them being out in the

cold, he packed two dozen of them into his cab with him so they wouldn't freeze to death?

(Bryan smiles.)

BRYAN: Yeah.

QZ: He was so—*happy*, being here with all of us, he was actually— . . . Later that night, he told me that when he was out trucking, he would think about this place as much as he could, because whenever he thought about us, he knew for certain that there were other people in the world. *(Pause)* We saved him as much as we could, Bryan. I don't know what happened to him out there, but when he was with us, when he was *here*—he wasn't a murderer. He was our best friend.

(Pause.)

BRYAN: So where does that leave us?

(Silence. Pause. QZ gets up, goes to the filing cabinet and takes out a large stack of letters. She puts them down in front of Bryan and sits next to him. Bryan looks at them for a moment, not saying anything. He exits momentarily, returns with a similar stack of letters. He brings them back to QZ and sets them next to hers. Silence.)

QZ: My *God*, we are so much better on paper, aren't we?

BRYAN: Yeah. We are.

(QZ and Bryan laugh a bit. Bryan reaches a hand across the desk toward QZ. They hold hands for a moment, looking at one another.)

So . . . ?

(Pause.)

QZ: What?
BRYAN: You never answered my question.

(Silence.)

QZ: Well, so. Ask me.

(Pause.)

BRYAN: I already did.
QZ: That was Rick. I want Bryan to propose to me.

(Pause.)

BRYAN: QZ. *(Pause)* Will you marry / me?
QZ: No.

(Pause. They slowly release one another. QZ looks at him.)

No.

(QZ takes a few breaths, then goes to the door, taking a key ring.)

I'm gonna take the pickup, they've got my car at a lot over in Missoula. All my stuff's still in it. Hopefully it's not all ruined.

(Pause.)

BRYAN: You coming back?

(Pause.)

QZ: I've lived in the same thirty-mile area my entire life, and when I was driving yesterday, when I just left? It felt amazing, like some big change was coming, something soon. New millennium, whatever. *(Pause)* Then—I ended up in a ditch, in the hospital, and then—back here. Where I always am. Back here, with you. New millennium, same old shit, I guess.

(Pause. QZ looks at the keys in her hand.)

BRYAN: Who knows? Maybe something will happen. Maybe we get to start over.

(Pause.)

QZ: I'm not coming back, Bryan.

(Silence. QZ goes to her stack of letters, taking it in her arms.)

I'm gonna tell Matty he can take the Honda, and he—... Just make sure he's gonna be okay, yeah?

(Pause.)

BRYAN: Yeah.

(She heads toward the door, then turns back to Bryan.)

QZ: I'll write you.

(QZ exits.)

Scene Seven

Several days later.

Matthew stands in the trailer with a couple of packed duffel bags.

Bryan enters from the back, wearing a proper eyepatch.

MATTHEW *(Referring to the eyepatch)*: Ahoy there! *(Awkward pause)* Is it—okay?

BRYAN: It's fine. Doctor said I'll be able to get rid of the patch in a couple days.

MATTHEW: It's kinda cool looking.

BRYAN: Yeah, I know.

(Pause.)

MATTHEW: I'm really sorry for shooting you in the eye?

BRYAN: It's fine.

MATTHEW: No but seriously.

BRYAN: I deserved it. It's fine. *(Pause)* Do you know where you're going to go?

MATTHEW: Haven't completely decided. I have a cousin in Eugene, she's a veterinarian. She said I can stay with her.

BRYAN: Sounds nice.

MATTHEW: Yeah, I don't—. I was thinking about maybe just doing some wandering, you know? Maybe just drive around, take some odd jobs. Maybe travel a bit before / I—

BRYAN: You really, really should go to Eugene.

(Pause.)

MATTHEW: Yeah, I guess—. I guess that's smart. *(Pause)* Are you sure about me taking the Honda? I mean the only other car is the Subaru, and I don't think that runs very well, I wouldn't take it too far.

BRYAN: It's fine.

MATTHEW: You gonna be able to do the drop-offs in that thing?

BRYAN: Well, I doubt we have much of a paper anymore. Gonna have to refund all the advertisers. Issue was due days ago and we don't have anything.

MATTHEW: Yeah we do.

BRYAN: What?

(Matthew takes an edition of the paper out of one of his duffels.)

What is this?

MATTHEW: It's nothing special, sorta sloppy. But I managed to pull it together. I just got rid of the content, made it all personals. *(Points at the paper)* See, it's a "special singles edition." I'd actually be surprised if it didn't sell better than our normal editions.

(Bryan looks through the paper.)

BRYAN: When the hell did you do this?

MATTHEW: I just threw it together, brought it to the printers that day. They did it pretty quick, they owed me. *(Pause)* There's still some drop-offs that need to be done. They're in the Subaru, should be pretty self-explanatory.

BRYAN *(Referring to the paper)*: My God there are a lot of personal ads here.

MATTHEW: Yeah, busy month. A lot more on the machine, too. *(Pause)* You sure you're gonna be okay out here all alone?

BRYAN: I'll be fine.

(Short pause.)

157

MATTHEW: You—gonna keep the paper going?

(Pause.)

BRYAN: Suppose I gotta survive somehow.
MATTHEW: You think you'll write anything?

(Pause.)

BRYAN: I think we've got enough to fill a paper every month. Don't need to confuse it with anything I'd write.

(Pause.)

MATTHEW: Look, I know it didn't work, I know that—. But this paper—it really did help me. You know that, right?
BRYAN: I know, it's / okay—
MATTHEW: Please, just—I've been trying to do this ever since you came back here, just—.

(Matthew takes out his wallet, takes out a folded-up newspaper clipping. He looks at it.)

(Reading) "You can find us in between Wallace and Mullan, off exit 419, about two miles south of the gas station. If you ask us what our agenda is, we'll tell you that we don't know. If you ask us why we started a newspaper for truckers, we'll tell you it's because we had to. Because after over fifteen years of driving the length of the country over and over, alone, spending / years—"
BRYAN: Matthew, / c'mon—
MATTHEW: Just—. Please. *(Continues reading)* ". . . spending years sleeping in parking lots that all blend together, eating at McDonald's and Wendy's that all look and smell the same, passing truck after truck on the interstate knowing each driver felt just as isolated as you, you start to feel like

you don't exist. So we had to do something. Something for the few of us who need it. Something to remind us, the few of us who live this way, that we still exist."

(Stops reading. Pause.)

I know you made this paper for truckers, but——. Growing up here, being—who I am . . . I sort of felt like I didn't exist either. But reading what you wrote every month—helped. A lot. *(Pause)* So just—thank you.

(Matthew puts the clipping on the desk in front of Bryan. He grabs his duffels.)

BRYAN: Listen, uh.

(Bryan grabs a pencil, searches for a piece of paper to write on. He grabs a newspaper from the ground, tears off a piece, starts writing.)

I went to high school with this girl—Allison Spector. You know the poetry club I started at Mullan High?
MATTHEW: Yeah.
BRYAN: Well, it was with her. More her idea than mine. Anyway, last I heard she was still in the—field, or whatever. She had a press out in Portland, just a small little thing.
MATTHEW: Are you serious?
BRYAN: Last time I did a run through Portland we met up, she was still publishing. I don't remember what it was called, but just look her up and tell her—I sent you. Like I said, I have no idea if she still does it anymore, that was years ago, but——.

(He hands the piece of paper to Matthew. Pause.)

Why don't you read me something?

MATTHEW: What do you mean?

BRYAN: Read me one of your poems or whatever. *(Pause)* C'mon, you made me listen to my own stuff, just read me something.

MATTHEW: No, I—I can't.

BRYAN: Yeah, you can, c'mon.

MATTHEW: But it's not—I've never even read this stuff out loud.

BRYAN: That's okay, just try it.

MATTHEW: No, I don't even know what I'd read to you, I / don't—

BRYAN: *Jesus* would you stop being such a little pussy and just *read me something?*

MATTHEW: OKAY okay. Geez.

(Matthew reaches into his duffel and takes out a notebook. He flips a few pages, landing on one.)

Okay, I can—. I guess I can read this one. *(Pause)* It's a tanka.

(Pause.)

BRYAN: What?

MATTHEW: It's like—it's this form of poetry, I think it's Japanese? It's five lines, the first and third lines have five syllables, and the rest / have—

BRYAN: Okay stop it, you're ruining it, stop. Just read it.

MATTHEW: Sorry. *(Reading:)*

> Stray cat on my porch
> gray striped eyes stare, then vanish;
> triggered memories
> a thought I don't recognize
> a smell I had forgotten.

(Pause) That's it. *(Pause, defeated)* It's a tanka.

(Silence. Matthew looks away.)

BRYAN: It's really good.
MATTHEW: Really?
BRYAN: Yeah. It's really, really good.

(Pause. Matthew smiles, puts the notebook back in his bag.)

MATTHEW: It's just a stupid poem, whatever. *(Pause)* Look, not to be annoying but—you're not going to kill yourself, right? I mean you're like—done with that idea, right?

(Pause.)

BRYAN: Yeah, pretty much.
MATTHEW: That's really good!
BRYAN: Yeah.
MATTHEW: You must feel so optimistic!

(Pause.)

BRYAN: I just—need to accept that my life isn't as noble or important or exciting as I thought it would be once. I just need to grow up.

(Pause.)

MATTHEW: I mean that's—sort of optimistic, I guess. 'Cause now there's nowhere to go but up.

(Matthew grabs his duffels and heads toward the door. He gives Bryan a wave as he exits. Bryan waves back. Bryan sits for a minute, silent.

He stands up, surveys the room, then looks down at all the papers on the ground. He begins to collect them, grabs a trash bag, and shoves them into the bag.

After he bags a few handfuls he moves to the answering machine and pushes play. The answering machine rewinds, then beeps and begins to play messages as Bryan collects the papers.)

MALE VOICE EIGHT: Tom, 541-235-2950, I'm in Eastern Oregon. Nice trucker, does seven thousand plus, CDL Class A with hazmat. Looking for nice woman for L-T-R, good hygiene, good looking in face. I enjoy the finer things in life, looking for a woman who does also.

(The answering machine beeps. Bryan realizes the bag is too small to collect all the papers. He exits outside momentarily, returns with a large outdoor trash barrel. The answering machine beeps.)

MALE VOICE NINE: Uh. Uhhhhhh—.

(The answering machine beeps. Bryan continues to clean up the papers, throwing them into the trash barrel.)

FEMALE VOICE TWO: Mandy, Idaho location, 208-348-9467. I would like to learn how to drive a truck but I do not have money to go to driving school. I have no family to help me. I'm single and forty and want to learn how to drive. No dogs, no cats. Very sincere. Please help.

(The answering machine beeps. As he's cleaning, Bryan finds Matthew's original edition of The Few. *He regards it for a moment, then throws it into the barrel.)*

FEMALE VOICE THREE: Montana, 406-343-2043, my name's Jessie. Full-figured woman with big breasts looking for man. Just got out of an L-T-R, looking to start a new one. I don't know how to swim. Send me a message and we will meet and see what happens. Please only men interested in large-breasted women.

(The answering machine beeps. Bryan has now collected all of the papers. He places the trash bag on the floor and continues to clean up various items—the broken printer, the empty whiskey bottle, etc. The answering machine beeps.)

FEMALE VOICE FOUR: Um, it's—. Ugh, fuck, forget it.

(The answering machine beeps. Bryan finds the BB gun, looks at it.)

FEMALE VOICE FIVE: Enjoy warm oil massages question mark. I can help exclamation point. Eastern Washington near I-90. 509-239-6792. Come to me I will rub you from head to toe and make you feel amazing. I will ease your tension and satisfy your needs.

(The answering machine beeps. Bryan moves to a desk and opens various drawers looking for a place to put the gun. He opens a drawer, but stops when he sees what's in it. He reaches inside and pulls out the jug of antifreeze. He sits down at the desk, holding the antifreeze.)

MALE VOICE TEN: Uh, Northern Utah, 'bout two hours outside Logan, 435-393-2274. Fifties, attractive looking for same. I like trucks, motorcycles, dogs, country music. I do car shows, Sturgis, flea markets.

(Bryan puts the antifreeze onto the desk in front of him. He looks at it for a moment, then leans forward, burying his head in his hands.)

Twice divorced, looking for a stable relationship. I smoke, no drugs, no alcohol. No kids. Looking forward to your reply.

(The answering machine beeps.)

FEMALE VOICE ONE: Hi, it's, uh. It's Cindy? I called before. It's Cindy. I left a real long personal, and then I asked you not to print it, but you did anyway, and—. *(Pause)* So I'm actually not calling with a personal ad, this is more of a—. *(Pause)* When I saw you printed my ad, at first I was so mortified, I had no idea what people would think, or— . . . I was ready to call you back and give you a piece of my mind, I'll tell you what. But—yesterday, I got a response from this person, this man. *(Pause)* We talked for almost five hours on the phone last night, past midnight, which for *me* is just—. I mean I don't really honestly remember the last time I talked to someone for that long. And he's really just—good. He's good. He's gentle, and he listens, and he— . . .

(Bryan lifts his head up, listening.)

So I—I'm calling to say thank you. I mean look, I don't know if this is gonna—*amount* to anything, or—. I've learned not to count on anything in my life. But even if we never talk again, even if it's just that one phone call last night, it really did—help. I felt like I was in a pretty bad way when I left that ad, and I didn't really know how it was all gonna end, but—. You really did something for me,

I told you not to print the ad, but you did anyway, and you didn't even charge me . . .

(Bryan looks at the clipping Matthew left on the desk, takes it in his hand, looking at it. Pause.)

Right now—at this moment? The future is looking better for me. Much better. It's like I can see the sun again. And I hope that everyone over in your office or whatever, I hope you're all—good. Thank you. Really, just—thank you.

(The answering machine beeps, then goes silent.
Bryan looks up, taking in a deep breath. He exhales.)

END OF PLAY

A Great Wilderness

Dedicated to the memory of Jerry Manning

PRODUCTION HISTORY

A Great Wilderness received its world premiere at Seattle Repertory Theatre (Jerry Manning, Artistic Director; Benjamin Moore, Managing Director) on January 17, 2014. The production was directed by Braden Abraham. The set design was by Scott Bradley, the costume design was by Erik Andor, the lighting design was by L.B. Morse, the original music and sound design were by Obadiah Eaves, and the dramaturgy was by John M. Baker; the production stage manager was Stina Lotti. The cast was:

WALT	Michael Winters
DANIEL	Jack Taylor
ABBY	Christine Estabrook
TIM	R. Hamilton Wright
EUNICE	Mari Nelson
JANET	Gretchen Krich
VOICEOVER ON THE TELEVISION	Evan Whitfield

The play opened at Williamstown Theatre Festival (Jenny Gersten, Artistic Director; Stephen Kaus, Producer) on July 9, 2014. The production was directed by Eric Ting. The set design was by Wilson Chin, the costume design was by Jessica Pabst, the lighting design was by Matthew Richards, and the sound design was by Brandon Wolcott; the production stage manager was Lindsey Turteltaub. The cast was:

WALT	Jeffrey DeMunn
DANIEL	Stephan Amenta
ABBY	Mia Dillon
TIM	Kevin Geer
EUNICE	Mia Barron
JANET	Tasha Lawrence

A Great Wilderness was commissioned by Seattle Repertory Theatre (Jerry Manning, Artistic Director), and was developed with the support of the O'Neill National Playwrights Conference (Wendy Goldberg, Artistic Director), the William Inge Theater Festival (Peter Ellenstein, Artistic Director), and the Playwrights' Center (Jeremy B. Cohen, Producing Artistic Director).

WALT	Male, mid-seventies
DANIEL	Male, sixteen
ABBY	Female, mid to late sixties
TIM	Male, mid to late sixties
EUNICE	Female, forties or early fifties
JANET	Female, late forties or early fifties
VOICEOVER ON THE TELEVISION	Male or female

Setting

The common room of a decaying camp on the outskirts of a wilderness area in Idaho. There are full boxes everywhere. Much of the space has been packed up. Only essential furniture remains, along with some camping gear, books including several numbered Bibles, a television, etc. A hallway leads to other bedrooms and a bathroom. A kitchen occupies a section of the stage.

NOTES

Dialogue written in *italics* is emphatic, deliberate; dialogue in ALL CAPS is impulsive, explosive.

A "/" indicates an overlap in dialogue. Whenever a "/" occurs, the following line of dialogue should begin.

Ellipses (. . .) indicate when a character is trailing off, dashes (—) indicate where a character is being cut off, either by another character or themselves.

The television frequently plays underneath the dialogue, and should be only slightly quieter than the actors. The effect should be that it's imposing, present—just short of irritating. The television dialogue is not constant, but there should always be a twee, cheaply produced soundtrack playing in the background whenever the DVD is playing.

Act One

Scene One

Late morning.

> *Daniel, sixteen, stands near the door holding a duffel bag. He looks around the room, obviously nervous.*

> *Walt stands on the opposite end of the room, looking at him, smiling warmly.*

> *A tense silence.*

WALT: Are you hungry? You've gotta be hungry.

(No response.)

I think I have—there's plenty of food, you can help yourself to whatever you like. And I'll be cooking us our meals, I'm actually pretty good at, uh. Your mom probably told you all this, she—.

(No response.)

Come in. Daniel. Please.

(Daniel pauses, then slowly moves inside, setting down his duffel.)

Was your ride okay?

DANIEL: It was fine.

WALT: The ride up the mountain can be bumpy, a lot better than twenty years ago though, I'll tell you that much. And it's pretty, uh, was it pretty?

DANIEL: I don't—. I was sitting in the middle, / I didn't really—

WALT: Oh, that's—

DANIEL: I feel sort of turned around, I don't really feel like I know where I am right / now—

WALT: That's really a shame. Bobby should have let you sit up front. Usually he lets my boys sit up front.

(Pause.)

DANIEL: The van was pretty full. Hunters or something.

WALT: Fishers, more likely. There's some very nice fly-fishing around here. Bobby's been shuttling my boys up here for years / now—

DANIEL: "Your" boys? That's what you call us?

(Pause.)

WALT: Sorry, I—. I won't call you that if you don't—. *(Short pause)* You're hungry. You've gotta be hungry.

(Pause.)

DANIEL: I'm okay.

(Daniel glances around the room a bit, his eyes landing on the book on the podium.)

WALT: Oh that's neat. Take a look, you'll like it.

(Walt goes to the book. Daniel approaches it cautiously.)

DANIEL: Is it a Bible?
WALT: No it's a dictionary, see—

(Walt grabs the magnifying glass.)

It's a compact edition of the complete Oxford English Dictionary, all twenty volumes in microprint. Here, look—

(Walt motions for Daniel to look through the magnifying glass.)

Over five hundred thousand words in here, you believe that?
DANIEL: Huh.
WALT: I've always loved dictionaries. Ugh, that makes me sound so boring, doesn't it? "I've always loved dictionaries."
DANIEL: Why?
WALT: I guess, I just—like knowing I have the help, if I need it. If I couldn't find the words. *(Pause)* I'm not explaining myself very well. I just like dictionaries.

(Awkward pause.)

Are you sure you're not hungry?

(Pause.)

DANIEL: Okay.

WALT: Sandwich?

DANIEL: Okay.

(Pause. Walt moves into the kitchen.)

WALT: You like anything in particular? I have turkey, roast beef—

DANIEL: Whatever's fine.

WALT: Well what would you like?

DANIEL: Whatever.

(Walt comes out of the kitchen.)

WALT: I know that this must be uncomfortable for you. And I'm sorry about—, there are usually many more people here, at times we've had nine or ten people staying in here at one time, some summers we had as many as thirty boys come through here. But I really want to make you comfortable, and safe, it's *important* to me that you feel safe. For the next few weeks, this is your home.

(Pause.)

DANIEL: I don't like roast beef.

WALT: So turkey?

DANIEL: Whatever.

WALT: I think there's baloney.

DANIEL: Turkey.

(Walt goes back into the kitchen, makes sandwiches. Daniel tentatively sits down.)

WALT: There are some really beautiful hiking trails we can do together, or if you just want to do them by yourself that's fine, I just ask that you don't go further than the ridge there if you're by yourself. There's a great lake you can get to, but it's a day's hike. I don't know if I could make it that far, I'm—. But once Tim and Abby come, maybe they'd like to take you.

DANIEL: Tim and Abby?

WALT: Yeah, they—. Didn't your mom explain this to you?

DANIEL: She didn't—. She didn't tell me a lot.

WALT: Oh. *(Pause)* Well, they—they're friends, Abby helped me start this place, her husband Tim has been a counselor here for many years. And they'll be taking over this place once I— . . . Your mom really didn't explain this to you?

DANIEL: No.

(Pause.)

WALT: You know there's candy in that jar in front of you if you want some—is there candy in there?

(Daniel opens a candy jar on the coffee table in front of him.)

DANIEL: Uh—yeah?

WALT: There's candy?

DANIEL: It's like—I think it's all Tic Tacs.

WALT: *Tic Tacs?* I'll get some candy. *Tic Tacs*, what is wrong with me?

DANIEL: So they're—your friends are coming here? To stay?

WALT: For a while, they'll help me pack up. And they'll be taking over this place next summer.

DANIEL: Are you moving?

(Walt finishes making a couple of sandwiches, brings them out to the main room, hands one to Daniel.)

WALT: I am. To an "assisted-living center" or some other euphemism, "Shady Gardens" or "Garden Grove" or some other stupid thing. A place for people so old they fill their candy jars with Tic Tacs. I'm moving right after you finish up here.

DANIEL: So I'm your last—patient or whatever?

WALT: "Patient"? Are you sick?

DANIEL: Am I?

(Pause.)

WALT: You look fine and healthy to me. *(Referring to the sandwich)* Try it.

(Daniel inspects the sandwich a bit.)

I didn't poison it, I promise.

DANIEL: What?

WALT: I'm kidding.

DANIEL: About *poisoning* me?

WALT: All right, sorry, I'm—. Sorry?

(Daniel pauses, then takes a bite of the sandwich.)

Okay?

(Pause. Daniel nods.)

The good thing about being the only one here, you can have any room you like.

(Daniel pulls out an iPhone.)

It can get a little cold at night, I'd rather you didn't use the space heater, I don't trust those things. I can give you a hot water bottle.

DANIEL: A what?

WALT: A hot water bottle, to sleep with, to keep you warm.

(Pause. Daniel looks at him.)

DANIEL: You want me to sleep with a bottle full of warm water?

WALT: No, it's—. It's not like—

DANIEL *(Referring to his iPhone)*: There's no signal here?

WALT: Here? Heck no. I've heard when you walk up the ridge you can sometimes get, uh, signal. And there's a phone here. It's a rotary phone, you know how to use a rotary phone?

DANIEL: I don't know what that is.

WALT: Oh.

(Awkward silence. Daniel stares forward.)

DANIEL *(Suddenly)*: You're not gonna like *shock* me or anything, right?

WALT: "Shock" you? No, / we're—

DANIEL: Because you really don't need to do that, I don't—. Mom just sort of shoved me into a van without telling me anything, like *anything*, like *I don't even know your name*, and I read on the internet that sometimes people use electricity or whatever, / but I don't need that.

WALT: No one's going / to—

DANIEL: And why am I the only one here?! I really wasn't expecting to be the only one and I'm already feeling really uncomfortable, I can't even call anyone and you're making *jokes* about *poisoning me*—

WALT: I'm Walt. My name is Walt. Call me Walt.

(Pause.)

We don't shock anyone. We don't hurt you, we don't scold
you, we don't try to beat you down. The only thing I've done,
the only thing I've been trying to do for thirty years, is to
raise you up. I know what you're feeling: you're feeling
tired, confused, angry. I used to think I had it worse when
I was a boy, but I'm convinced it's ten times harder nowadays, when all you have to do is open up a laptop and—.

(Pause.)

The first thing I want you to know, the first thing you need
to know—you are safe here.

(Pause.)

You are safe here.

(Pause.)

DANIEL: So what are—? What are you going to do to me?
WALT: I'm not going to do anything "to you." We're going to talk,
read scripture together, go on hikes, pray. I don't have any
set curriculum here, this is all about you. Getting back to
who you really are, the person you want to be.
DANIEL: A straight person.

(Pause.)

WALT: That's not really the best way to talk about it, it's not /
about—
DANIEL: What if I told you I wasn't sure I wanted to be straight?

(Pause.)

WALT: It's your life, Daniel. I'm not here to force you into anything. Like I said, this is about you. Finding the person you've always wanted to be. It's a kind of baptism. But you have to, uh, make a decision about what kind of baptism—, what you're being baptized into. Ugh, that was stupid, I'm sorry. Forget I said that. *(Pause)* What I think we should do now is—sit down and eat our sandwiches. I think that can be our start. *(Pause)* Yeah?

Scene Two

Several hours later.
Abby stands in the middle of the room, holding a suitcase and some bags from Walmart.

ABBY *(Calling out)*: Walt, you here?!

(Tim appears from the hallway, entering the main room.)

TIM: He's not in his bedroom.

(Abby goes to a window, looking out.)

He knows we're coming today, right?
ABBY: Well he did when I talked to him yesterday, he—. Oh, it's terrible in here, get the windows?

(Tim opens a couple of windows.)

Where's that air conditioner we got for him?
TIM: He never liked that thing. It's probably sitting in the shed rusting over.

181

(Abby moves down the hall.)

ABBY *(From off)*: Well we paid enough for it, I don't— . . .
(Short pause) He's already packed up.
TIM: What?

(Abby reenters.)

ABBY: I said he's already packed up. I thought he said he
wanted help packing.
TIM: Well it's not / completely—
ABBY: That road, I thought we were going to die. Those sheer
drops on the passenger side on the way up, I had forgotten
about those.
TIM: Better than it used to be.
ABBY: I'm still shaking. Where's that bottle of cognac?

*(Abby goes to the kitchen, starts putting away the supplies
in the Walmart bags.)*

TIM: We got it for Walt.
ABBY: Oh he won't mind, pour me a glass please?

(Pause. Tim opens his bag, takes out a bottle of cognac.)

TIM: Okay.
ABBY: Is it really that much trouble / to pour me a glass of—?
TIM: I'm doing it, honey, I'm pouring you a glass.

*(Tim pours two drinks, brings one to Abby. They drink. Abby
surveys the room, noticing a photo on the mantel. Pause.)*

What?
ABBY: No, I just—. *(Pause)* I haven't been here in a while.

TIM: It feel different?

ABBY: Not at all. Looks exactly like it did in the beginning, it—... *(Short pause)* I just hope Walt doesn't give me any grief. I have a feeling he's not too excited about going to the home.

TIM: You know, you really shouldn't call it "the home." Not in front of him at least.

ABBY: Oh who cares? It's a home, I'll call it a home if I want to.

TIM: I just—I don't think he'll like that, sounds like we're sending him off to an asylum.

(Abby goes back to the Walmart bags, unpacking them.)

ABBY: Well he's already given them the deposit, it's done. And the time has come. When he fell down last year, if Janet hadn't've stopped by that afternoon, I don't know what— *(Rooting through the bag)* You got boat twine? Why did you get boat twine?

TIM: I just don't want him to feel like we're up here to send him off / on some iceberg or something.

ABBY *(Still rooting through the bag)*: Well he knows we—... "Iceberg"? What the heck are you—? And *duct tape*? Tim, why on earth did you / buy this?

TIM: Oh I don't know, I just bought / some supplies—

ABBY: Are we helping him pack or taking him hostage?

(Pause. Tim sits down.)

TIM: I just—. *(Pause)* It's just sad to see this place go.

(Abby regards the room.)

ABBY: Sure.

(The door opens and Walt enters.)

WALT: Oh— / Hi—

TIM *(Getting up)*: Well there he is!

(Tim gets up and goes to Walt, embracing him.)

ABBY: Hello, Walter.

TIM: Where did you disappear off to?

WALT: Oh, I was just—. I was just out— . . .

(Walt disappears down the hall. Abby and Tim look at one another.)

ABBY: Walt?

WALT *(From off)*: Just, uh—. Sorry. *(Returning)* Sorry! Good to see you. Uh—Daniel isn't here, is he?

TIM: Daniel?

WALT: Yeah, uh—. The boy, was there a boy here?

TIM: No—

ABBY: Wait—you don't have a kid up here, do you?

(Pause.)

WALT: Well, I just—. I know it's sort of last minute, but / he really—

ABBY *(Exasperated)*: Walt, what were you / thinking?!

WALT: I'm sorry, I just—. His mother called me a few days ago, I / just thought—

ABBY: You're supposed to be moving into that place *next week*, they / have your—

WALT: They can wait an extra week or two, I'm still paying / for it—

TIM: You really think this is the best time for—?

WALT: Now listen, I'm sorry I didn't tell you, but—. But he's here, and he needs our help.

TIM: So—where is he?

WALT: Well see this is the, uh. I—don't really know.

ABBY: You don't know?

WALT: Well, he—he said something as he was leaving, he was at the door here, and he said something to me and I just, I can't remember what it was, but—. Ugh, I hate this, I hate it when I can't remember, I hear people saying things and the words travel in one ear / and out the—

ABBY: How long has he been gone?

WALT: Well, I don't know, what time is it?

TIM *(Checking his watch)*: It's—almost six?

WALT: Oh.

TIM: When did he leave?

WALT: I guess it was around, uh. I don't know, noon? *(Pause)* I guess I've been wandering around outside calling after him for about four hours now, I guess, I really lost track of time, uh. *(Pause)* Should we be concerned? *(Pause)* Maybe we should be concerned.

Scene Three

Later.

It's nearly dark outside. Walt is standing in the kitchen on the phone. Tim and Abby have opened a few boxes and are rooting around inside them.

WALT *(On the phone)*: —well, yeah, I'm not— *(Pause)* Wait, what? No, Janet, you're not—you're not understanding me, he's not *missing*, / he just went wandering outside or—

TIM: I'm not finding anything.

ABBY *(To Walt)*: You didn't label any of these, / I don't—

WALT *(To Abby)*: Try the—oh, I don't know. Open the— *(On the phone)* No. Janet, I don't want the—you know, I don't want people thinking / that we *lost* him for gosh sake—

ABBY: He lives in a *cabin* in the *woods* and he doesn't own a *flashlight?*

WALT *(On the phone)*: I understand that, I really do, but this isn't—it's only been a few hours, I don't know if it's time to, you know, call in the National / Guard or whathaveyou.

TIM: Do we have something in the car?

ABBY: No.

WALT *(On the phone)*: Can't you just— / I don't know, ride around yourself, look for him a bit? Listen, if he's not back in a few hours, I'll be the first one to, you know, call Search and Rescue.

TIM: What about the little—

ABBY: We haven't had that for years.

TIM: What about the flares?

ABBY: *Flares?*

TIM: I was just thinking / that I—

ABBY: It hasn't rained here in three weeks and you wanna walk around in the forest here with *flares*?

WALT *(On the phone)*: / Yes, exactly, that's what I'm—. Yes, thank you, yes.

TIM: I just thought he might, the kid might see them or something. Never mind.

ABBY: You're such a city boy.

TIM: You know I really don't like it when you call me that, Spokane isn't exactly / New York City—

ABBY: Oh I'm / just kidding, never mind.

WALT *(On the phone)*: Okay, great. Thank you, Janet, and—. Yes, I appreciate the, uh. Discretion. Thank you.

(Walt hangs up.)

She's gonna, uh. She'll take a ride around, some of the old logging trails, see if she spots him.

TIM: Should we call his parents?

WALT: I just don't want to blow this out of proportion, we've dealt with this before—

TIM: I'm sure it's fine, but maybe we / should—

WALT: Let's just—not alarm too many people right now, all right? If he doesn't show up, you know, in a few hours, then we'll get worried.

TIM: So if he's not back in a couple hours, we call Janet back.

WALT: Yeah, of course.

TIM: For sure if he's not back by / midnight—

WALT: *Yes I heard you yes. (Pause)* Maybe I shouldn't have done this, maybe I—. His mother was just so—*desperate*. She's already sent him to five or six different pastors—

TIM: Maybe you have a flashlight / out in the shed, or maybe—

WALT: Most of them sounded completely clueless, nowadays I'm not / even sure—

ABBY: Walt.

WALT: Hm?

ABBY: Flashlight.

WALT: Oh. *(Pause)* Oh you know I think there's one in that closet there.

ABBY: *Geez*, Walt.

(Walt goes to the closet, finds the flashlight.)

WALT: Here just give me a minute, let me figure out where I put my coat and I'll go with you—

ABBY: Walt, just let Tim go, stay here with me.

WALT: He doesn't even know who Tim is, for all you know you might scare him away—

TIM: He's not a frightened deer, he's cold and thirsty and he'll be glad to see / another person—

WALT: Now Tim just give me a second, I said I can go with you.

TIM: *Walt, you'd slow me down.*

(Pause. Walt looks away, hands Tim the flashlight.)

WALT: Okay.

TIM: I didn't mean for that to / sound—

WALT: No, you're right, I'm—. I'd slow you down. *(Pause)* I should be here if he comes back anyway.

TIM: Sure. *(Heading to the door)* Chances are he didn't go too far up the ridge, so I'll just head east a bit. He'll probably see my flashlight, come running.

WALT: Sure.

TIM: I won't go too far.

ABBY: Just watch where you're going, you're gonna / twist your ankle again if you don't watch where you're going—

TIM: I will. I said I will.

(Tim kisses Abby on the cheek and exits. A silence between Abby and Walt.)

ABBY: Walt, you really could have told us if you were planning on taking / on—

WALT: *Yes, I*—. I know. Abby, I've already said that I'm sorry, / I don't—

ABBY: All right, all right, I'll—. I'll stop, I'm stopping. *(Pause)* Look, I'm sure he's fine.

WALT: Sure.

ABBY: He's an Idaho kid, he'll be fine.

WALT: Mm-hm.

(Pause.)

ABBY: You didn't have to pack everything up by yourself, that's why we're here, you know.

WALT: I don't know, I just—wanted to get it all out of sight. Thought it'd make me feel better.

ABBY: Did it?

(Pause.)

WALT: No. No it, uh.

(Abby sits with Walt.)

ABBY: On the way up here I was thinking about all those trips
we did from town after we bought this place from the Boy
Scouts. That time you were bringing the chest freezer up
here, almost ran the pickup off the road.

WALT: I did not.

ABBY: You almost killed us both.

WALT: Oh that's such an exaggeration. And it wasn't the chest
freezer, it was the stove.

ABBY: It was the freezer. I remember because you bought it from
that Chinaman who ran the car dealership, you remember.

WALT: You know we're not supposed to say that now.

ABBY: What?

WALT: "Chinaman." It's racist or something.

ABBY: It's where he was from!

WALT: I know it, I didn't realize either, I used it a few years ago,
one of the boys told me I shouldn't use the word, that it's
insensitive.

ABBY: I don't even know what to say to that, it's where he's *from*.
People are such idiots nowadays.

(They share a little laugh.)

WALT: It's nice to see you both. I'm sorry you had to have this
drama the moment you got here.

ABBY: Any minute now Tim will walk in that door with him. We
can focus on getting you ready to go to the home.

WALT: I wish you wouldn't call it that, "the home."

ABBY: Oh, Tim got on me for saying that too. I just don't care. I'm gonna say "the home" and "Chinaman" if I dang well want to, they're my words. *(Pause)* Are you— . . . ? I mean, how are you—feeling about it?

(Pause.)

WALT: Had to happen sooner or later. I can hide up here in the mountains from everything but death.

ABBY: Geez, Walt.

WALT: I'm not trying to be dark, I just—. It's fine, it's God's will. There's a pool. *(Pause)* I'm just glad you two are taking over this place.

(Silence.)

ABBY: Walt, you know we—. You know Tim and I aren't getting any younger either, right?

WALT: Well, yeah. / What?

ABBY: It's just—. You have to realize, we have lives in Coeur d'Alene. I don't know if we can just pick everything up and move here for three months out of the year.

WALT: Wait, you—? What are you saying?

ABBY: Look, I didn't mean to bring this up immediately, but might as well just get it out there, no use keeping it from you.

WALT: You're not going to keep this place going?

ABBY: Okay, I never told you I would keep this place going, we never said that. It's not like we can just put our lives on hold for three months every year—

WALT: Well then I can hire people! If you / two don't—

ABBY: *Hire* people? Walt, where the heck would we get money to hire a staff? You only brought four kids up here last summer, and two of them you didn't even *charge* anything—

WALT: Okay, Abby—

ABBY: And your rest home isn't *free*, you know? Tim said that even some of the cheaper units can cost five thousand a month, and I know that you don't— . . . *Darn it*, I don't know why I have to be the one to do this, I don't know why I always have to be the adult.

(Walt gets up, wandering aimlessly. Silence. Abby softens, goes to him.)

Walt, you've done—good work. Great work. But you said yourself, this is God's will. You have to move on.

(Walt looks at her.)

WALT: And next year, when there's another boy, another ten boys, who are confused, and suffering, and alone, where are they gonna go? What's out there for them? How many more boys are gonna end up like— . . . ?

(Pause. Abby gets up, looking around for a moment. She finds her purse, roots around in it.)

I'm sorry.

ABBY: No, I'm—. Look I'm just thinking I could drive around a bit to see if I see / anything—

WALT: I said I'm sorry, I / didn't—

ABBY: There's no reason I shouldn't be out there looking for him as well, I'll just—.

(Abby heads toward the door.)

WALT: Abby, wait.

(Abby stops, not looking at Walt.)

191

Isaac died because he didn't have a place like this. I just want you to remember that.

(Abby looks at Walt. Silence.)

ABBY: I'll come right back if I find him.

(Pause. Abby exits.)

Scene Four

Later that night.
Tim, having just walked in the door, watches a DVD that has been left playing on the television. Walt is at a table, asleep.

VOICEOVER ON THE TELEVISION: —only one mile away, which was awarded a Medicare rating of eighty-three out of one hundred. Residents can choose from private condominiums, located only steps away from the golf course, or bedrooms in our Cottage House, a fourteen-unit assisted-living center for senior citizens with physical or mental difficulties.

(Tim approaches Walt, reaching a hand out toward his shoulder.)

Visit us at Shady Grove and you'll find our residents happy, alert, groomed, well-fed, and healthy. You'll find our staff caring, / friendly, jovial, and speaking with attention to speed and volume.

WALT *(Startled)*: OH—

TIM: Sorry! Sorry—

WALT: Tim, you really almost just killed me—

TIM: I'm sorry.

VOICEOVER ON THE TELEVISION: / Amenities include a hair salon, bank, gift shop, snack wagon, gym facilities, pool, and library. We also offer regular shuttles to many popular shopping destinations, as well as some of the best restaurants the Treasure Valley has to offer.

TIM: He hasn't come back yet?

WALT: No, you didn't see anything?

TIM: No, I—I went toward the lake, almost as far as the dead forest, I didn't see anything. You're sure he went that way? He didn't go back down the road?

WALT: I don't—I have no idea. He said something, then he was gone.

TIM: You *really* don't remember what he said?

WALT: Tim, if I knew what he said, don't you think I'd *tell you*?

TIM: All right, all right. Is Abby out looking for him?

WALT: Yeah, she's—. She's driving around a bit.

(Pause. Walt paces nervously, looks out a window. Tim looks at the television.)

VOICEOVER ON THE TELEVISION: Every day offers our residents new activities such as crafting, sing-along, reading, monthly communal birthday parties, / cocktail hour, church services, and art classes.

TIM: Is that—?

WALT: What?

TIM: On the TV. That's where you're going?

WALT: Oh, the—. Yeah.

VOICEOVER ON THE TELEVISION: Almost every hallway in Shady Grove prominently displays art by our residents, / like these seen here. Our art teachers are highly trained professionals who have years of experience with—

TIM: It looks nice.

WALT: Mm-hm.

TIM: Art classes, that's—

(Walt turns off the television. Short pause. Tim heads toward the door.)

I'm gonna head back out, I just wanted to make sure he didn't come back. I'm wondering if he took the trail up around the other side of the ridge, maybe / he—

WALT: Tim, Abby told me—. She told me that you're not taking over this place.

(Tim stops. Pause.)

TIM: Listen, I—. I want you to know that I really don't want to see this place close down, I tried to convince her that we could keep it running—

WALT: Mm-hm.

TIM: But you know Abby. She's been talking about you selling this place for at least five years now.

WALT: She has?

TIM: We argued about it the whole way here. I mean when was the last time she spent more than a few nights here? Six, seven years ago? Last summer she didn't want me coming up at all. *(Pause)* Listen, even if this place doesn't shut down—that doesn't mean we're giving up. I'm still counseling boys out of my office, I've got one I'm working with right now. And you can always come up to Coeur d'Alene to work with me—you could even do some counseling in Boise part-time, I could come down a few weeks out of the year to work with you, or— . . . *(Pause)* Point is—this isn't over.

(Pause.)

WALT: It's an interesting feeling.
TIM: What?
WALT: I don't know. Becoming a dinosaur.

(*Pause.*)

TIM: Wait—what do you mean?

(*Headlights shine through the window. The sound of an approaching car.*)

WALT: Is that Abby?

(*Tim opens the door, looking out.*)

TIM: No, it's—. I don't know.

(*Sound of a car door closing.*)

(*Calling out*) Hello?

(*After a moment, Eunice appears at the door. She looks at Tim for a second, then Walt, not saying anything.*)

Can we— . . . ?

(*Eunice pushes past Tim, goes inside.*)

Excuse me?

(*Eunice looks around, then heads down the hall.*)

Do you know who that is?
WALT: I have no— . . .

EUNICE *(From off)*: Danny?!

WALT: Oh.

(Eunice reenters.)

EUNICE: Where is he?

WALT: Well, we actually—

EUNICE: I got a text from him. I tried calling him back but he wouldn't answer, and the phone number you gave me for this place has been busy for hours. Where is he?

WALT: Oh that phone—

(Walt goes to the phone, looking at it.)

It's this stupid old rotary / phone—

EUNICE: *Where's Daniel?*

WALT: Okay, okay, just—. I'm Walt, we spoke on the phone. It's Eunice, right?

(Pause.)

EUNICE: Yes.

WALT: Eunice. Daniel went out for a walk this afternoon, he hasn't come back yet. But we'll find him, / I promise you—

EUNICE: Oh Lord please no—

TIM: It's really not as bad as it sounds—

EUNICE: Oh Lord, oh Lord / please no—

WALT: Sit down, please—

(Eunice sits down on the couch.)

TIM: Chances are he'll come back later tonight or— . . . He's probably not even lost, he might just be—I mean, you know how teenage boys can be, they can pull these kinds of things—

196

EUNICE: Not Daniel. Daniel doesn't do this.

TIM: You'd be surprised at what they're capable of, even the ones you / don't—

EUNICE: I'm sorry, who are you?

WALT: He works here, with me. And we've dealt with this kind of thing—

EUNICE: So what are you doing, have you called the police, the—I don't know—*ranger*, or—

WALT: There's a ranger here who's a good friend, has been for years, she's aware of it, she's on the lookout. If we don't hear from her in a few hours we'll make some more calls. Really, I know how stressful this must be but honestly— it's going to be okay.

TIM: What did the text say?

EUNICE: What?

TIM: You said he texted you?

EUNICE: Oh. Yeah.

TIM: What did it say?

EUNICE: It said "I'm gone."

(Pause.)

It just said "I'm gone."

Scene Five

Later that night, around midnight.

Janet, a park ranger, is standing in the cabin with an open notebook.

Walt, Tim, Abby, and Eunice sit in various places around the cabin.

JANET: I tell you, you could drive for *eight hours* and not see another living soul. *Hundreds* of miles. Or "kilometers" or whatever shit. I'm telling you, Australia—that's some *real* wilderness. Makes this all seem like a city park. My husband and I spent a couple weeks out there, and I can / tell you—

TIM: Janet—

JANET: I'm just saying! You shouldn't be too worried. If he was lost out in the outback, that's when you'd have to be worried. Plus they have these dingos.

ABBY: So what should we be doing? Is there anything that we / can—

JANET: I mean listen, you guys know how it goes, you've seen this before. Chances are he already ran into some hikers, this time of year it's damn near impossible not to run into anyone after this long. *(To Eunice)* Honey, you have *nothing* to worry about.

EUNICE: I'm sorry?

JANET: I'm saying, honey, you have nothing to worry about. This kind of situation happens once every couple years, not a single one has died on us yet.

EUNICE: Oh.

TIM: *Janet.*

ABBY: All right, there has to be something *we* can do?

JANET: Wouldn't hurt to do some driving around, honk the horn a bit. Maybe he found one of the old logging roads, could be following that. Lemme get you a map, we made new ones last year.

(Janet fishes around in one of her oversized pockets, pulls out a map.)

They're pretty nice now. Used satellites to make 'em, accurate as hell. If you guys wanna drive around, you never know. But honestly, my guess is by now he's run into some hikers, they're probably takin' him to the trail head right now. This reminds me of that one kid from ten years back or so? Remember that?

WALT: Uh.

JANET: The fat little shit from Twin Falls, got lost on one of Walt's nature hikes, wandered around for hours before he ran into that group on horseback or something—

ABBY: Okay, I can do some driving around—Tim, you can head toward the lake again?

TIM: Sure. Walt, you'll stick around here in case he comes back?

(Walt, lost in thought, doesn't respond.)

Walt.

WALT: Hm? Oh, yeah, I'll—. I'll stay here.

(Pause.)

TIM: Maybe you should get a little sleep?

WALT: I'm fine.

TIM: There's no use in sitting around / worrying—

WALT: *I said I'm fine, Tim, I—. (Pause)* If you find him, come right back, okay?

TIM: Sure.

(Tim and Abby leave.)

JANET: Okay! Now it's, uh—Eunice? Is that right?

EUNICE: Yes.

JANET: Pretty name.

EUNICE: Okay.

JANET: So it might help if I ask you a few questions, you feel up for that?

EUNICE: Yeah, of course.

JANET: Now just so I know, does your son have any wilderness training under his belt?

EUNICE: Wilderness training?

JANET: You know, was he a Boy Scout, did he go camping, you know—?

EUNICE: He was a Cub Scout. He quit when he was a—, what do you call it, Webelos?

JANET: Okay so he has some training then.

EUNICE: I don't think so. They mostly went bowling.

JANET: Fun! What about camping, would he have any skills along those lines?

EUNICE: He went camping a few times, I don't know. He hated it, I know that much.

JANET: Well anything you can tell us about / his—

EUNICE: Why does this matter, I don't—?

JANET: Well see the thing is, if we know he has some training, experience, we're gonna be better informed about where to look. If he even has some basic knowledge of wilderness survival, that might help us track him, whereas if he really doesn't know anything—

EUNICE: He doesn't know anything. You should treat this— situation like he doesn't know anything.

JANET: Okay! Now it doesn't get too cold at night this time of year, but just in case, was he wearing something warm when he left?

WALT: Yeah, he had—. I think it was—, was it like a—hooded sweatshirt?

JANET: So he had some layers on / then?

EUNICE: He doesn't own any hoodies.

WALT: I remember it was this, green? No, / it—

EUNICE: Shorts and a blue T-shirt, a tan jacket—if he was wearing it?

WALT: Yes, he—that sounds right. I think that sounds right. I'm sorry.

JANET: It's okay! Now did he say anything to you before he left, anything / about—?

WALT: No see that's just the thing, I can't remember what he—... I mean he did say something, I'm sure he said something to me, and I remember nodding or smiling, and then he left—

JANET: So you can't remember what he said? Maybe just really think about it.

WALT: I *am* really thinking about it. I really just—. I don't remember, I'm sorry.

JANET: Maybe if you think of it you could maybe give me a call, just if you think of it.

WALT: Yeah, I—. Yeah, of course.

(Eunice starts laughing softly to herself.)

JANET: You okay honey?

(Pause.)

EUNICE: This is so—... This is ridiculous. This is *so ridiculous.*

WALT: / Okay—

JANET: / Honey—

EUNICE: You people are—... I just can't stand your—*attitude* toward this. You come in here and you ask me if he was a *Boy Scout*, you can't even remember what he was wearing, or *what he said to you*—

JANET *(Surprisingly stern)*: Ma'am you're gonna have to take it down a notch right now. *(Pause)* Now there's a few things you need to understand here. I've known this man here for damn near eighteen years, and I can tell you that he cares for each of these boys like they were his own.

EUNICE: Fine, but that's not the whatever, *issue* right now, the issue is neither of you even seem *alarmed* about this—

JANET: You'd rather I freak out, go nuts, scream my head off?

EUNICE: No, I just—

JANET: I want you to know that I take this very seriously. Two summers ago, we had two hikers go missing. First eighteen hours, I wasn't too concerned. Vast majority of the time, people turn up within eighteen hours. But these guys, they didn't show up. So I dialed it up. I called up Search and Rescue, organized search parties on my own, got a friend of mine to take his helicopter up to do some rounds. Found them within four hours. They were thirsty and scared, but they were fine.

(Pause.)

My gut tells me your son is gonna be just fine, so right now I'm very calm about this whole thing. But believe me, if we get to the point where I need to dial it up, then believe me I'm gonna dial it up.

(Pause.)

EUNICE: Okay.

JANET: Okay! Now is there anything else you think might be relevant? I don't suppose he's ever been up here before, he wouldn't have any relationship to the area, would he?

(Pause.)

EUNICE: Well, he—. Yeah, he was up here once.

JANET: Oh yeah?

EUNICE: Yeah, his, uh—. His dad took him up here, couple years ago.

JANET: Close by here?

EUNICE: I mean, I don't know.

JANET: Could you maybe call up your husband and find out where it might have been roughly?

EUNICE: No, I couldn't.

(Pause.)

JANET: Okay then. Well I think I'm about done here. I just wanna make sure that someone stays here, at all times, there's a good chance that he's just gonna come straight back here to the cabin.

WALT: Sure.

(Janet puts away her notebook, heads to the door. Walt walks with her.)

Thanks, Janet.

JANET: Sure thing. When are you gonna be heading out by the way?

WALT: Uh, soon. Fairly soon, few weeks.

JANET: Well you gotta be sure and let Clint and I cook you dinner before you take off, okay?

WALT: Yeah, uh. Sure. *(Pause)* Thanks.

(Janet exits. Walt closes the door behind her. He turns to Eunice.)

Does his, uh. Is Daniel's father—does he know what's going on?

(Pause.)

EUNICE: He's fine.

WALT: You don't think he'd want to know?

EUNICE: To be honest Dennis probably wouldn't want to know. He wouldn't come up here, anyway.

(Eunice gets up, looks for her coat.)

Okay, I can't stand this, I'm going to go out there and look for him myself—

WALT: Now, really, that's not a / good idea—

EUNICE: I'm not just going to sit here and chat while my / son is out there *in complete darkness*—

WALT: Really Janet is much more qualified to be / handling these situations—

EUNICE: *Well I don't know what to do, I have no clue what to*— . . .

(Eunice stops, becoming upset. She looks away from Walt. Short pause.)

WALT: I understand the instinct, if I was ten years younger I'd be out there screaming his name myself. But there's no use in getting another person lost out in those woods. Honestly, the best thing we can do for him right now—is pray for him. Pray for him to *come back*.

(Walt goes to Eunice.)

Will you pray with me?

(Eunice looks at Walt. Pause.)

EUNICE: I don't— . . .

WALT: What?

EUNICE: I don't know, maybe I shouldn't have sent him here, maybe— . . . I mean, so he looked at a few videos on the internet, so what? You never glanced at a dirty magazine when you were a kid?

(Pause.)

WALT: Listen, I've dealt with this quite a lot, these things can get out of control pretty quickly. Nowadays, with the kids growing up with these computers, it's all too easy to find.

(Pause.)

EUNICE: So what did you— . . . You didn't *do* anything to him, did you?

WALT: What?

EUNICE: I mean I don't really know what goes on up here, I— I mean you didn't do anything weird, you didn't *shock* him, / or—?

WALT: *No*, I didn't—. Why does everyone think I *shock* people? We talked about this on the phone, I sent you all our literature—

EUNICE: Dennis always reads the literature, I didn't look. And I tried not to listen when we talked on the phone.

WALT: Why?

EUNICE: Dennis has sent him to so many pastors, weekend workshops, but this time—. Sending him up here, for weeks up in the woods, I—. I honestly didn't want to know what you— . . .

(Pause.)

WALT: It's just—talking, mostly. Talking, praying, reading scripture.

EUNICE: Well it's a nicer approach than Dennis had, I'll give you that.

(Pause. Walt looks at Eunice.)

WALT: Pray with me?

(After a moment, Eunice and Walt bow their heads.)

EUNICE: Dear Lord, I— . . . *(Pause)* Please keep Daniel safe out there, please—. Please find it in your wisdom to bring him back to— . . . *(Pause)* Please just let him find some stream to drink out of, let him find some berries or something to eat. Maybe a cozy little cave to sleep in? Maybe just make it nice for him out there, maybe— . . .

(Walt raises his head, looking at Eunice. Eunice pauses briefly, then continues.)

Maybe it's really nice for him out there, maybe he's happy. Maybe he's— . . .

(Eunice stops, opening her eyes. Pause. Walt attempts to continue the prayer.)

WALT: And Lord, we ask that you—

EUNICE: Do you think that someone like Daniel, do you think they can really—change? *(Pause)* I mean *you* changed, right?

(Walt looks at her, doesn't respond. Silence.)

I'm sorry, I just assumed that you—

WALT: Yes, I—. Many years ago I did—struggle with it.

EUNICE: And how did you—get rid of it?

WALT: If you don't mind, / I'd rather not—

EUNICE: Walt, I don't know if you can tell but I'm sort of at the end of my rope here, I— . . . *(Pause) I need someone to tell me that this can work.*

(Pause.)

WALT: You know for thirty years parents have been asking me that, they want some reassurance that it *will work*, and— . . .

206

(Pause.)

Just before I graduated high school, there was another boy in my class who I was—close with. We carried on for nearly a year before— . . .

(Pause.)

He had started going to this park, this place in Boise where men like him would go to find each other. Somehow his parents found out what was going on, and they sent him to some psychiatrist who would do those electroshock therapies you were so worried about.

(Pause.)

I was—terrified, I didn't know where to turn, so I sought out a church. A nice pastor named Clark took me under his wing. He made me realize—the problem was in *me*, there was something in *me* that wasn't right. And I needed to conquer it.

EUNICE: And it worked? You actually—changed?

(Pause.)

WALT: For me, it—. Yes, I— . . .

(Walt looks away, his eyes glazing over. Silence.)

EUNICE: What happened to him?
WALT: Pastor Clark? Oh, he died years ago—
EUNICE: No, the—. Your friend. The boy.

(Pause.)

WALT: I don't know.

(Pause.)

EUNICE: What was his name?

(Long silence. Walt stares forward.)

Are you okay?

(Pause.)

WALT: I don't remember. It doesn't matter, anyway.

(Walt bows his head, praying. Eunice watches him, not bowing her head.)

Dear Lord, we ask that you return Daniel to us. We ask that you keep him safe, and return him back to us. In Christ's name we pray. *(Short pause)* Amen.

(Eunice continues to watch him.)

Scene Six

Later that night.
Eunice watches the Shady Grove DVD. Most of the lights in the cabin are off.

VOICEOVER ON THE TELEVISION: It's about relating to people as people, not just patients. It's about making real connections with each of our residents. Our employees cherish life for the remarkable journey that it has been, and is still to come.

(Abby enters from outside.)

/ As one of Boise's oldest providers of senior care, we've had a lot of experience.

ABBY *(Calling out)*: Tim?!

EUNICE: He's not back yet.

ABBY: That stupid car is overheating again, he knows what to— . . .

(Abby sees Eunice watching the television. She stops.)

Are you— . . . ? You doing okay?

VOICEOVER ON THE TELEVISION: Assisted-living communities provide or coordinate oversight and—

(Abby turns off the television. An uncomfortable silence.)

ABBY: You know if you wanted to get some rest, I'd be happy to stay here in case—

EUNICE: No, I—. There's no way I could sleep. *(Pause)* So you and Tim, you're—counselors here, or whatever?

(Pause.)

ABBY: Tim more than me nowadays, but—yeah. *(Pause)* I was here at the beginning.

EUNICE: So Walt and you—the two of you founded this place?

ABBY: A long time ago, yes. *(Pause)* When we were married.

(Pause. Eunice looks at Abby.)

EUNICE: Oh. *(Pause)* I don't mean to— . . . In my church, divorce doesn't really exist.

ABBY: Well it didn't exist in ours either, it—. *(Pause)* It was a very difficult time.

(Pause.)

EUNICE: I just—. I hate myself for just sitting around. I should be out there shouting his name at the top of my lungs . . . But I'm not doing that. Why am I not doing that?

(Pause.)

ABBY: You're exhausted. You're exhausted and stressed. Every mother thinks she's terrible at it at some point.

(Pause. Abby joins Eunice.)

EUNICE: I grew up in this beautiful little town in northern Wyoming, about three hundred people? And we all knew each other, and we all went to the same church, and everything always just—*made sense*. Then I met Dennis at Bible college, he started his own church and it became one of the biggest in the state, and we had a baby, and it all—. God had given me a life that made sense. But Danny— . . .

(Pause.)

Ever since he was old enough to talk, he's always been so—*feminine*. All his friends were girls, he was never interested in sports, or—. So Dennis would take him on these camping trips, these camping trips that he thought would somehow *help*, or—. And when he caught Danny on the computer that day, Dennis just— . . . I'd never seen him like that. It just—didn't make sense. To either of us.

(Pause.)

And from then on, Dennis just—*refused* to interact with him. Mostly he'd just hide him away. When you're running a church you don't really want your feminine little secret running around and— . . .

(Pause.)

Maybe we should just let him be. Maybe he should just move out when he's eighteen, find some life within it. Maybe that's better for everyone.

(Pause. Abby goes to Eunice.)

ABBY: Our son Isaac—he was like that. I mean it wasn't obvious like that, we didn't get much of an idea of it before he—.

(Pause.)

I take that back, we had an idea of it. Walt and I both had an idea of it, we just didn't want to—say it out loud, I guess. And one night, Isaac had a boy over from his class, and I walk into their room in the morning, and they're—*on* one another.

(Pause.)

So we scolded him, we read scripture at him, sent him to church camps. And he tried and tried, but nothing seemed to work, nothing seemed to kick it out of him. We finally just said—there's nothing we can do. Just let him leave town, make a life. A life lived in sin, but—.

(Pause.)

211

Four months later, Isaac hanged himself in his apartment. His landlord found him. His landlord that he barely knew.

(Abby looks at Eunice. Pause.)

EUNICE: I—

ABBY: This is what you *have to understand*—this isn't just about temptation, or sexual immorality. We all sin, we all fall short of perfection and need forgiveness. But when you allow him to *accept* that part of himself, to embrace it, when you allow him to give up the fight—then you quietly *damn* him. This isn't about his life here on earth—better he spend *every moment* fighting that part of himself than surrender to death in this life *and* the next.

(Pause. Abby takes Eunice's hand, becoming upset. Eunice is frozen.)

So when you say to yourself that it might be better to let him go, try to make a life within it? You remember there is *no life within that.* Remember my son, Isaac.

(The front door opens. Tim enters.)

TIM: I didn't see anything, couldn't even— . . . *(Seeing Abby)* What?
ABBY: Nothing. The car is overheating again, / can you—?
TIM: What's wrong?

(Eunice goes to a window. She looks outside, lost in thought.)

ABBY: Nothing, I was just—. I'm fine.
TIM: What are you upset about?
ABBY: I said I'm fine, don't—. Just leave it alone.

(Walt enters from down the hall, just woken up.)

WALT: Did either / of you—?
ABBY: No.

(Walt looks at Abby.)

WALT: Is everything—?

(Janet enters from outside. Unseen by the rest of the group, Eunice starts to silently break down.)

ABBY: / It's fine.
JANET: Sorry to, uh. Sorry to barge in, but things have just gotten a little more complicated out there.
WALT: What does that mean?
JANET: I just got a call from a lookout about forty miles south of here. Some lightning just got a forest fire started—
WALT: Oh—
JANET: Don't know how big yet, but there haven't been many fires this season, so it could spread pretty quick. *(To Walt)* Listen I know you wanna keep this quiet, but I had to—... *(Seeing Eunice)* You okay there?

(Eunice collapses into herself. Abby goes to her.)

ABBY *(Going to Eunice)*: Okay, it's all right, just take a moment.
TIM: Is she / okay?
ABBY: She's fine. She just needs a moment.
JANET *(To Walt)*: What this means is the time has come to call in some other people here.
WALT: I just, I don't want to make this into a big scene—
JANET: I understand that, but—
TIM: We can't keep sitting on our hands here, / Walt—

WALT: I'm not sitting on my hands, / no one's—!

JANET: I already radio'd the sheriff, Search and Rescue is on the / way here, they've—

WALT: Search and Rescue?! It's only / been—

JANET: Walt, I'm sorry, it's outta my hands now. It's done.

TIM: So what can we do?

JANET: Search and Rescue's gonna start moving all over the area, but I was thinkin' I could make some calls and start organizing some search parties on my own, so / we can—

WALT *(Losing himself)*: No, we are not—... *I'm not having this turn into some sort of circus, I'm not—*...

(Walt trails off. Everyone falls silent. Walt looks away, sitting down. Silence.)

EUNICE *(A half prayer)*: He's drinking from streams. He's eating berries. He's sleeping in warm little caves. He's fishing, and making fires at night. *(Pause)* Right now he's— happy, he's looking up into the sky, right now. He's happy.

Act Two

Scene One

Midday, around noon.

Walt and Daniel sit on the couch, two plates with mostly eaten sandwiches on the coffee table in front of them. Daniel's duffel bag sits near him on the couch.

Walt is holding a purple heirloom tomato.

WALT: This is—? *(Pause)* What is it?

DANIEL: It's a tomato.

WALT: But it's purple.

DANIEL: It's an heirloom tomato.

WALT: "Heirloom"?

DANIEL: It's stupid. I'm just sort of into it. I know it's a weird thing to be into.

WALT: I'm into dictionaries and you're into tomatoes, we make a good team.

DANIEL: I just like them, they're not like regular tomatoes, they breed true.

WALT: And what does that mean?

DANIEL: It means like when you mate them with each other, they produce the same kind of tomato. Different than the hybridized tomatoes you buy at the store.

WALT: And you grow these in your backyard?

DANIEL: Mostly. Some in my room, too.

WALT: Are they—difficult to grow?

DANIEL: They're *really* difficult to grow. But I'm pretty good at it.

(Daniel reaches into his backpack, pulls out another tomato wrapped in a cloth.)

This one's a Green Zebra.

(Walt takes the tomato, looking at it.)

WALT: How on earth did you become interested in this?

DANIEL: I don't know, I just like gardening.

WALT: Hm.

(Pause.)

DANIEL: Is that okay?

WALT: What do you mean?

DANIEL: Is it okay that I like to garden?

WALT: Why the heck wouldn't it be okay?

DANIEL: I don't know, I—. Dad sent me to a couple pastors. They both said I shouldn't do it. That it's a woman thing or—, something. I don't know.

WALT: Oh. *(Pause)* People have probably told you some pretty—outlandish things about yourself.

DANIEL: This one guy I got sent to, in Colorado Springs, he said I was probably too close with my mother.

WALT: Are you?

DANIEL: I mean closer than I am to my dad, but not—. Not that close.

(Pause.)

WALT: A lot of things can happen, there are many things that can—contribute to this. It's usually pretty hard to figure out exactly where it came from.

DANIEL: Where do you think it comes from?

(Walt chuckles.)

WALT: You've only been here for less than an hour, Daniel, we don't have to get into the big questions so / quickly—

DANIEL: No, really. Where do you think it comes from?

(Pause.)

WALT: If I knew for certain it would make my job a lot easier. *(Pause)* Sin is inherent from Adam. We're all born with it. Maybe—there isn't a concrete reason. Maybe it's just something we have to overcome.

(Pause. Daniel takes out another tomato, hands it to Walt.)

DANIEL: This one's called Aunt Ruby's German Green.

WALT: Wow.

DANIEL: It's a stupid name but it's a great tomato. Tastes really good when you pick it early.

WALT: So why did you—? Why bring them all the way up here?

(Pause.)

DANIEL: I just—. I thought my dad might dig them up when I'm gone. I just had a feeling.

217

(Pause.)

WALT: Well, we'll keep them safe for you. I'll put them in the fridge.

DANIEL: That's bad for them actually. Just put them in a paper bag if you have one.

(Walt carefully takes the tomatoes, brings them to the kitchen, finds a paper bag, and puts them inside.)

WALT: There's a small garden outside. Might need some cleaning up but if you plant something now it might be ready by the time you leave. Something quick maybe.

DANIEL: That might be cool. You have seeds?

WALT: We can get some. We need to run into town before Tim and Abby get here, anyway. I think there's still a gardening center there. Or wait—did that close?

DANIEL: I can look it up. Do you have wifi, or—?

(Daniel takes out his iPhone.)

WALT: Oh, there's no internet at all up here.

(Pause.)

DANIEL: There's no—?

WALT: No, sorry, but the phone book / is—

DANIEL: Is it because of me?

WALT: Is what because of you?

DANIEL: Did you get rid of the internet because of me?

(Pause. Walt goes to Daniel.)

WALT: I've never had internet up here, I promise. *(Pause)* How many times had you—looked at things on the internet like that?

(Pause.)

DANIEL: I mean not a lot.

WALT: Every day?

DANIEL: No, not like—. It was just once. Seriously. They caught me doing it the very first time I did it.

(Pause.)

WALT: Was it photos, or—?

DANIEL: Do we have to talk about this? This is really embarrassing—

WALT: You have *nothing* to be embarrassed about. I want you to feel safe talking to me, about anything. I've been doing this for a while now, and I can't tell you how important it is to articulate what it is you're feeling. Once it's put into words, we can know what it is. Until then it's just this mass of confusion festering in your gut. If you put it into words—you can assess it. Control it.

(Pause.)

DANIEL: It was—. It was a video.

WALT: Of what?

(Pause.)

DANIEL: Like, two guys who were—. One guy like had the other guy—.

(Silence. Daniel looks away.)

WALT: Was it oral sex or anal sex? *(Pause)* Do you know what I'm talking about when I / say—?

DANIEL: *Yeah* I know what—. *(Pause)* Oral sex.

(Pause.)

WALT: How much of it did you watch?

DANIEL: Not a lot. Like a minute or so.

WALT: How did you feel? When you were watching it?

(Pause.)

DANIEL: Scared.

WALT: Good. *(Pause)* That's good.

(Walt sits down on the couch.)

We can head into town later today, there's a few things we need anyway. We could actually do some grilling tonight if you like, I know Tim and Abby would like that, they're coming all the way here from Coeur d'Alene, I'm sure they'll be hungry.

DANIEL: Do they—? Are they going to be—talking with me too?

WALT: Well I'm sure they'll say hello.

DANIEL: You know what I mean.

WALT: No, they won't be counseling you. They're just coming up for a few nights. You want another sandwich?

DANIEL: I'm fine, thanks. *(Pause)* So I'm like—the last one who's gonna come up here?

WALT: Well, last one while I'm still here. Tim and Abby will be taking it over next year. And I can still come up for part of the summer. And hopefully they'll pass it on eventually. Maybe even someone like you will be running it someday.

DANIEL: So why did you—? I mean what made you start it?

WALT: A lot of things, I suppose. I just know how hard it is, I know what it's like. My son Isaac dealt with it. That's the reason I wanted to start this in the first place.

DANIEL: Did he—? He was able to—change?

(Pause.)

WALT: He was—never really given the chance.

(Pause.)

Back then, we didn't really know how to deal with it. We did what so many people still do today—we treated it like a disease that needed to be cured. We lectured him, took him to Bible studies, threw scripture at him, and after a while he—had enough. He left the house, moved away. What we never did was *listen* to him, make him feel safe, and just—*listen*. All I ever wanted was for him to feel safe. Even when he left, I told him that all I ever wanted was for him to feel safe.

(Pause.)

So I suppose this place is our small effort to make sure that boys like Isaac have a place where they can feel safe.

(Pause.)

DANIEL: What happened to him?

(Pause. Walt looks at him.)

WALT: Four months after leaving home, he was gone. In a studio apartment, alone. Just like that—he was gone.

(Pause. Walt stands up.)

All right, I can let you get settled in before we make the run into town, like I said feel free to take whichever bedroom you like.

221

DANIEL: I think I might go for a walk?

WALT: Oh. That's—of course, that's fine. I can show you around if you like, there's a few / trails that—

DANIEL: I'd rather just—. If it's all right, I sorta just wanna be by myself. *(Pause)* I won't go far.

WALT: Oh. Well that's—fine.

(Daniel heads toward the door, opening it. The sound of a fire begins to fill the space, growing in volume. Walt grabs the dishes, heads to the kitchen, puts them in the sink. Daniel stops.)

DANIEL: Walt?

WALT: Yeah?

(Walt looks at Daniel. The sound of the fire grows and grows until it's almost deafening.

The lights snap to black, the fire continues for a few moments in darkness. Slowly, we begin to hear the sound of a phone ringing as the fire subsides.)

Scene Two

Just before dawn.

Walt has dragged a lamp next to the dictionary. He's squinting through the magnifying glass, trying to read. There is a small, dying fire in the fireplace.

The phone rings again. Walt ignores it for a while, then finally goes to the phone and answers it. Tim enters from outside, filthy and exhausted.

WALT: Hello?

(Walt hangs up the phone.)

TIM: Which one was that?

WALT: Oh, the—. I don't know, Spokane paper.

TIM: You're just hanging up on them now?

WALT: Well I tried talking to one of them from the—I don't know what paper it was, but she just asked me these leading questions. Still nothing?

TIM: Janet's got a couple search parties heading further north, Search and Rescue's bringing in helicopters from Montana.

(Short pause.)

WALT: It's really just awful, these journalists using this, *exploiting* this boy. They're probably having a great time with it. Anyway, if they want to blame me, then fine.

TIM: No one's blaming you. And I doubt Eunice and her husband would be, you know. Litigious about it. If they were, I could help you out.

(Walt makes his way back to the dictionary, picks up the magnifying glass, starts looking again.)

WALT: You want to become known as the lawyer who defends old men who kill boys?

TIM: Stop it, Walt, he's not—. What are you looking for?

WALT: Oh, I'm just—. I just couldn't think of the word, this—this reporter, she was being so . . . *devious*, you know. But not that word, that's not the right word. I wanted to tell her how she was being, but I couldn't find the word.

TIM: "Duplicitous"?

WALT: No, not that.

TIM: "Slimy"?

WALT: No, I—. "Slimy"? You think I couldn't recall the word "slimy"?

TIM: Well I don't know, I'm / just trying to—

WALT: I'll find it, it's—. Just let me find it.

(Tim looks at the fireplace.)

TIM: You starting a fire?
WALT: Oh, I couldn't—. I couldn't get it going.

(Tim goes to the fireplace.)

TIM: Walt you just stacked the wood, no wonder it's not catching.
WALT: I was distracted.
TIM: You have newspaper?
WALT *(Motioning to the kitchen)*: Yeah, you know where it is.

(Tim takes some newspaper out of a drawer in the kitchen, starts to make a fire.)

Quite a way to go out, huh? Very last boy I ever have up here, I lose him out in the forest?
TIM: We haven't lost him yet.
WALT: Spending all night out there, I don't—. I don't know.
TIM: There's plenty of streams out there, could find a thing or two to eat if he had to. Someone could survive a while out there.
WALT: I don't know, he was—. He was slight.

(Pause.)

TIM: You know who I heard from the other day?
WALT: Who?
TIM: That boy, Alan—something?
WALT: Alan?
TIM: Remember, the, uh—. Sixteen, seventeen years ago? He was from Indiana or something. He was the one who loved that Dungeons and Dragons game?

WALT: Oh—right.

TIM: He told me that you stayed up with him until two in the morning one night, letting him teach you how to play it.

WALT: It was so convoluted, I had no idea what he was saying to me.

TIM: He had heard something about you retiring, shutting down. Wanted to get in touch.

(Pause.)

He told me that he had been sent to three or four groups before that, I guess. All around the country. And he said that you were the only one who would just sit with him and *listen*, that you wouldn't just be spouting off about scripture or sin all the time. That you really just—listened to him. He said that after spending six weeks here, with you, he knew what it must have felt like to have a good father.

(Pause.)

And he has two boys of his own now, six and ten I think.

WALT: Well, there's one then, but— . . .

TIM: What?

WALT: Nothing.

(Tim lights the fire. He goes to Walt.)

TIM: No, what?

(Pause.)

WALT: Tim, we both know how many boys have come through here over the years. And we both know how many of them were actually able to—

TIM: It's not like we keep in touch with *all* of them, it's— . . . You had a positive impact on these boys' lives, we both did, even if they fell back into it later in life we gave them tools / to work on—

WALT: And how many of them fell back into it after getting married, having children? Not to mention the—. God help us, the *suicides*—

TIM: Now *stop*, we don't have complete control over this, sin is a powerful thing, it's—. *(Pause)* Walt, what is it that you're getting / at here?

WALT: I just want to be sure that we did *good*, that we didn't *hurt* them, or—.

(Silence. Tim stares at him.)

TIM: You know how I mentioned to you that I was counseling a boy right now, out of my office? Do you know how old this kid is? Take a guess.

WALT: What?

TIM: Seriously, guess.

WALT: Tim, I don't know / how—

TIM: Twelve. He's twelve years old. He's in the sixth grade, he's in *elementary school*. When you and Abby started doing this, how old were the youngest ones you had up here? Sixteen, *maybe* fifteen?

(Pause.)

Look, I know what people say about me, they don't understand how I can come up here every summer to work with you. Even within the church, I know people talk. They don't understand why I suddenly became so obsessed with this one issue. I tell them—it's not about this one issue, it's about the *culture*.

WALT: Tim, I understand, you know / that I—

TIM: No, Walt, actually I'm not sure if you do understand. You've been up here in the mountains for thirty years, you don't know what it's like down there anymore. When Abby and I got married, and she told me about this place— I admit, I didn't totally understand it. But eventually, I looked around and I realized—I'm in the middle of a culture that's shifting by the minute, that's replacing morality with—with *fashion*, that's redefining everything we think about God and— . . . When I first started coming up here fifteen years ago, there were four other programs in the state. When this place shuts down, I think I might be the only one left in the *entire Northwest*—

WALT: Tim, I'm not saying / that you—

TIM: And now you're telling me that all the time we've been *hurting* these boys? Walt, that boy isn't out there wandering in the forest because of something that you did here, he is out there because the *culture* has made him lost, made him *disgusting*, made him—

(The phone rings. And rings. Finally Walt goes to the phone, answering it. Walt listens for a minute then slams the receiver down. Silence.)

I'm sorry, I didn't mean to—. *(Pause)* Sorry, I didn't mean to climb up on the pulpit just now, but I—. I mean, if *you* don't have faith in this, then— . . .

(Tim trails off, becoming upset. Walt goes to him.)

WALT: We did good work.

TIM: Yes, we did.

WALT: You're still doing good work.

TIM: Yes, I am.

WALT: I just— . . . *(Pause)* We've spent a lot of time here together. I don't want to lose our friendship.

(Pause.)

TIM: Well of course not. Why would you— . . . ? *(Pause)* What do you mean?

(Walt looks at him for a moment, then goes back to the dictionary, picks up the magnifying glass, and starts searching through it again.)

WALT: You can go back to bed. If I hear anything I'll wake you.

(Tim watches him.)

Scene Three

Later that morning.

Abby is on the telephone. Eunice is watching the Shady Grove DVD holding a mug of coffee. She has not slept at all.

VOICEOVER ON THE TELEVISION: / — is to provide the highest possible care for our patients who need the assistance of rehabilitative and/or licensed nursing staff. Rehab or skilled care is about more than providing care twenty-four hours a day. It's about being there to listen. Our residents benefit from supportive services and custom healthcare options. Assisted-living communities provide or coordinate oversight and services to meet residents' individual needs.

ABBY: Gary, can you—? Sorry, this dang phone, it's so old, I can barely—

(Abby bangs the receiver against the counter.)

Gary? There we go, this is better, keep going.

(Pause, listens.)

No I'm handling everything, so it's not really—. Well of course he's—.

(Walt enters from outside, goes to Eunice.)

WALT: Heard anything?

EUNICE *(Still watching the TV)*: No.

WALT: You really have to watch that?

EUNICE: I'll keep it low.

ABBY *(On the phone)*: Sure. Yep, I'll be in touch then. Bye. *(Hangs up)* Well! Some good news finally.

WALT: What?

ABBY: I think I may have found a way to help you pay for this retirement home!

WALT: Abby, for Heaven's sake, I thought you had heard something about Daniel—

VOICEOVER ON THE TELEVISION: / Services are based on the residents' service plans, taking into account unforeseen needs as they arise. Typical services offered in assisted living include those found in housing with service communities, or expanded versions of those services, as well as assistance with daily activities such as bathing, grooming, dressing, and medication administration or management.

ABBY: I had done a little fishing around about the land and whatever, and I've found someone who sounds *very* interested, they want / to take a trip up here—

WALT: Abby, I don't want you making any deals, / I haven't agreed to sell this place—

ABBY: I haven't made a *deal*, this is just talk, I'm just trying to—

WALT: Who are they, anyway?

ABBY: Hm?

WALT: Who is it who wants the—, who's interested in it?

ABBY: Well it's a church!

WALT: Okay?

ABBY: I guess they're interested in starting some sort of camp type thing, / or—

WALT: What church / is it?

ABBY: And they have some time in the next couple weeks to take a trip up here—

WALT: Abby.

VOICEOVER ON THE TELEVISION: Some assisted-living communities / have designated areas and programming for individuals who require highly specialized care. This level of assisted living provides services tailored to every individual resident's needs. The care and services that are offered foster skills and interests within an environment that seeks to diminish fear and promote safety. We offer a full continuum of care for seniors and others in the greater Boise and Treasure Valley community. As the only Christian not-for-profit long-term-care community in the greater Boise area, we are known for our quality and excellence of service. Founded in 1964, we are also one of the area's oldest and most respected assisted-living communities. We have built our business on a reputation for providing consistent care and respect to residents on a wide spectrum of physical and mental health.

ABBY: It's the Life Fellowship people.

WALT: No.

ABBY: I just want you to keep an open mind about this.

EUNICE: Dennis *hates* the Life Fellowship people.

WALT: Well Dennis and I agree on something then. This watered-down doctrine, they have no idea what they even believe, they don't / even—

EUNICE: Oh he doesn't care about that, he bought four old vans from them last year and three of them broke down already.

ABBY: Look, Walt, we have our disagreements but you can't argue that a church taking over this place really isn't the / best—

WALT: What kind of "camp" are they talking about, what do you mean?

ABBY: Well I think they want sort of like a retreat, something like that.

WALT: A "retreat"?

ABBY: Oh, Walt, I don't know, they were just talking about something like—some place where the adults could meet / for—

WALT: So they want a place for a bunch of businessmen from Boise to come and get drunk—

ABBY: Well for gosh sake Walt, I thought you'd appreciate me putting in the effort, not like I'm getting paid for this.

(The phone rings.)

WALT: Look it's not that I'm not grateful, I just want to have a say in this.

ABBY: Well of course you have a—

(Abby answers the phone.)

VOICEOVER ON THE TELEVISION: / Shady Grove is particularly known for our art therapy program which works with patients suffering from Alzheimer's and related dementias. We offer courses in painting and sculpture, as well as workshops in drama, dance, poetry, and memoir. At Shady Grove, we believe that a healthy mind is an active mind, and that freedom of expression is key to allowing seniors to remain vital, present, and engaged with their surroundings. We strive to allow our seniors to pursue their lifelong hobbies and interests while continually introducing them to new activities. By exercising their minds and bodies on a daily basis, our seniors are made to feel productive and vital. This philosophy has been carefully developed over decades of providing care to seniors.

ABBY: Hello? *(Listens, then to Eunice)* Eunice.

EUNICE: Who is it?

ABBY: Dennis.

(Eunice gets up, takes the phone. She takes the receiver back to the couch with her, stretching the cord almost as far as it will go. She sits down, continues to watch the DVD.)

Okay listen Walt, I know this isn't your favorite church or whatever—

EUNICE *(On the phone)*: / Hello.

ABBY: —but they seem pretty interested and that Shady Grove place is by no means cheap, / and we—

WALT: Well maybe I'm not—.

ABBY: What?

EUNICE: / No, they haven't.

WALT: Nothing, this is just—. This is happening too fast.

EUNICE *(On the phone)*: / Yes, well, they're looking. I don't know, he had a coat? I don't know, Dennis. I wasn't here when he left.

ABBY: Wait, what were you going to say?

WALT: I've just been—. I've been thinking about it, and maybe I'm not sure I'm ready to leave yet.

ABBY: *What?*

EUNICE *(On the phone)*: / Well I just didn't want to bother you, you're so important, you hate to be bothered by little things like your son missing in the forest.

WALT: Look I just don't see why I have to act like I'm at death's door or something, I don't see why I—

EUNICE: / Okay.

ABBY: Walt, no one likes growing old, but you—. Tim said you couldn't even figure out how to make a fire last night—

WALT: *I wasn't*—! That's *not true*—

VOICEOVER ON THE TELEVISION: / Situated on a picturesque plot of three acres at the base of the Boise foothills, Shady Grove's atmosphere is one of tranquility, peace, and reflection. A babbling brook flows just behind Shady Grove's parking lot. A series of gentle, well-lit walking trails surround Shady Grove's perimeter, allowing residents the chance to get their daily exercise while admiring the beauty of God's creation.

EUNICE *(On the phone)*: / Yes, they've sent people for him, they called Search and Rescue. Well, yeah, you could actually come here, that would be something you could do.

ABBY: What if something happens to you up here, what if you fall down again, or—

WALT: *I'm not a cripple for Heaven's sake*—

ABBY: I didn't say that, but you can't really expect Tim and I to drive five hours down here / to—

WALT: Fine then, don't come! I'm an adult, I can handle this by myself!

EUNICE *(On the phone)*: / No, I know, you're important, stay home. I'm not being passive aggressive, I'm just stating a fact, you're so important. You're so, so important.

ABBY: Oh would you stop it with the histrionics?

WALT: I don't know why you two feel the need to come here and treat me like I'm a child or / something—

ABBY: Why we feel the need to—?! You asked us to come!

VOICEOVER ON THE TELEVISION: / Residents have easy access to a well-maintained eighteen-hole golf course, as well as tennis and squash courts, all found within five miles of Shady Grove. Daily shuttles provide easy access, and full-time residents can receive special discounted rates on yearly memberships. If you have any questions about

these memberships, please call our information line. One
of our employees will be happy to assist you.

WALT *(To Eunice)*: *Would you please turn off the TV?*

EUNICE *(To Walt)*: I'm good thanks. *(On the phone, rising in
intensity)* / Oh that sounds good, you pray for him. As
long as you pray for him I'm sure this'll all work out, that
sounds good. So you've done your best here, you've put
in so much effort, you've really taxed yourself, so I guess
we're done talking.

ABBY: You know Walt, I'm really not appreciating your tone
right now, I have to say.

WALT: Well I just don't care, I'm not selling this place, I'm
not moving into that stupid retirement home, I'm not just
handing over all this to a pack of idiots so they can come
up here and drink themselves stupid—

VOICEOVER ON THE TELEVISION: / When residents enter our
main complex, they are greeted with a welcoming lobby—

EUNICE *(On the phone)*: / Okay love you bye honey.

*(Eunice drops the phone on the ground, continues to watch
the DVD.)*

ABBY *(Severe)*: You could *die* up here Walt, you get worse every
month, you / don't—

WALT *(To Eunice)*: TURN OFF THE DAMN TELEVISION,
TURN IT OFF.

VOICEOVER ON THE TELEVISION: —as well as a restaurant-style
dining hall that always offers residents their choice of
entrée, side dish, and—

(Eunice turns off the television, looks at Walt. Silence.)

WALT: I'm sorry.

(Pause. Walt breathes.)

EUNICE: Yeah I'll give you two a minute.

(Eunice takes her coffee and exits down the hall. Pause.)

ABBY: I need you to be *reasonable* about this—
WALT: I *do not* get worse every month.
ABBY: Okay.
WALT: And *I know how to build a fire.*
ABBY: *Okay. (Pause)* All right I'm not bickering with you any-more. Lord, you'd think we were still married.

(Silence.)

WALT: I'm sorry.
ABBY: Hm.
WALT: *I'm sorry. (Pause)* Do you— . . . ? I'm starving, are you hungry?

(Pause.)

ABBY: Yeah, I could eat something.

(Walt goes into the kitchen, roots through the fridge a bit. Abby sits down.)

WALT: We don't have—. Well, we don't have much of anything actually.
ABBY: Sandwiches?
WALT: We don't have any more bread.
ABBY: Lunch meat?
WALT: Baloney.
ABBY: Ech. Bring it over.

(Walt takes a package of baloney out of the fridge, brings it to Abby.)

WALT: I'm sorry to be so—. It just feels wrong, talking business with all this going on.

ABBY: Look, I know you're not *relishing* this, giving this place up. But I really think you should just sell it while there's someone who's interested. It's just smart.

(Walt opens up the package of baloney, takes a piece out, starts eating it. Abby does the same.)

WALT: Life Fellowship, of all people.

ABBY: Walt.

(Pause. Walt looks at Abby.)

WALT: I'm not leaving.

(Pause.)

ABBY: So you're just gonna stay up here until you have an accident or something. Until you fall down again, but this time you can't reach the phone, and you just lie on the floor / and—

WALT: Yes. *(Pause)* Yes.

(The door opens and Tim appears, followed by Janet, more serious than before, holding a plastic bag.)

TIM: Hi—

WALT: Find anything?

JANET: Well, uh. Yeah, we did.

(Janet reaches into the bag, pulling out the jacket Daniel was wearing before.)

Was this—was he wearing something like this when he left?

(Walt looks.)

WALT: Yes. Yeah, I think that was it, but let me— *(Calling down the hall)* Eunice!

TIM: Wait, it might not be a good / idea—

WALT: No, just—she'll know best, she remembers what he was wearing when he left—

(Eunice appears in the hall. She sees the jacket.)

EUNICE: Is that—? Where did you find it?

JANET: You think this is his?

EUNICE: I think so, where did you find it?

JANET: A smokejumper found it, little over ten miles south of here. Close to where the fire's been heading. This is the right color, this is—?

(Eunice takes the jacket.)

EUNICE: Yeah, it—

(Eunice unfolds the jacket. One side is covered with a large blood stain. Silence.)

JANET: Is this—? You're sure it's his?

(Eunice doesn't answer, continues to look at the jacket.)

Okay. I guess we—. *(Pause)* Well, see—this sorta changes things.

Scene Four

A short time later.
   Walt looks out a window, Abby sits, Tim paces.

TIM: You know, I just don't—. I don't want us to jump to any
   conclusions here, we have no idea if he—. I mean, are we
   even sure it's his jacket?

ABBY: Tim.

TIM: I'm just saying. Even if it's his, we can't be sure that
   he's— . . . *(Pause, looking down the hall)* What's Janet
   saying to her in there?

ABBY: They're not plotting against us, you don't / need to—

TIM: I just don't want Janet getting her worked up, get her /
   thinking that—

WALT: I don't know why we're all just sitting around here, we
   could be doing something—

ABBY: Like what?

WALT: Well I don't know, we could be driving around ourselves,
   or—

ABBY: There are plenty of people out there looking for him who
   are much / more qualified—

TIM: But I mean it hasn't even been twenty-four hours yet,
   I could head toward where they found the jacket, I could
   take the car as / far as—

ABBY: All right, I'm sorry, but do you two really think— . . . ?

(Pause.)

WALT: What?

(Pause.)

ABBY: Look, I don't know anything about anything, but if he's lost that much blood, and been out there all night— . . . I'm not saying we should have a funeral, I'm just saying—

WALT: Saying that we should give up?

(Pause.)

ABBY: I'm saying we need to be *realistic* about this.

TIM: Sure, but is it really time to stop looking?

ABBY: Of course not, everyone is still out there looking for him, but I'm just saying that we—the three of us should— . . . *(Pause)* Look, I realize how this sounds, but I think we should start thinking about what to do, you know, what Walt should be saying to the media, just in case—

WALT: "The media."

(Short pause.)

ABBY: What?

WALT: "The media." There's a child out there, alone, and you're worried about—. It's all about appearances with you, isn't it? All about what people will think of us, it's never about the boy, it's never about Isaac, it's just about what people will think about *us*, it's / about—

ABBY: What did you just say?

(Pause.)

WALT: I just mean, you don't need to be constantly concerned with what people will think of us, people will think what-ever / they—

ABBY: You said "Isaac."

(Pause.)

WALT: No, I didn't.

ABBY: Yes you did, you said "Isaac."

TIM: Okay, / okay—

WALT: Well I didn't—. I meant "Daniel," I obviously meant "Daniel," I / just—

ABBY: No you didn't. No, you didn't.

(Pause. Abby looks away.)

You know, maybe— . . . *(Pause)* I think maybe it'd be a good idea for us to get out of here for a little / while—

TIM: Okay now, you've known each other too long to talk to each / other like—

ABBY: Tim, it's okay, I'm not—. I just think it'd be best for us to get a room in town for the / night.

WALT: Oh for heaven's / sake—

TIM: Now c'mon, let's just take a minute and catch / our breaths—

ABBY: Tim, could you get our bags?

WALT *(Harsh)*: *Abby, would you please not fall to pieces over this?*

(Silence. Abby stares at him.)

ABBY: After everything I've done here, everything I've done for you over the years, and now trying to help you *sell* it—

WALT: I never asked you to / sell this place—

ABBY: —and you bringing this kid up here at the last minute without even telling us, letting him wander outside *alone*, leaving us to deal with— . . . *(Pause)* You really think I did all of this for *appearances*, is that what you think?

WALT: *Well you did, didn't you?* You were so *ashamed* at mothering some kid who turned out that way, so concerned that people / thought—

TIM: *Okay guys, we—* . . .

(Silence.)

Look, maybe Abby's right, maybe we should get out of here for a while—

ABBY *(To Tim)*: Could you get our bags?

(Tim looks at her, then at Walt.)

Please.

(Pause. Tim exits down the hall.)

I supported you through all of this, taking over this place, starting this program. You think it was easy for me, going to all those churches, giving those talks about Isaac?

WALT: Oh let's be honest, Abby, you never minded the attention, / you didn't—

ABBY: *I loathed the attention. I loathed it.*

(Pause.)

I would get up there in front of all those parents and tell them about my son, about the *failure* of my life, my motherhood. For you, starting this place was—helpful, *healing* even, you got to come up here and go on hikes and light campfires and everyone thought you were so *noble* and so *good*—

WALT: You think I've been on some sort of vacation up here?! I've spent my entire *life* trying to save these boys, and now you're ready to give up on this place, just like you gave up on Isaac.

(Short pause.)

And that was *your* failure, not his. And it was my failure too, I let it happen. But I've dedicated my *life* to making up for that mistake, while you've just been running away from it. That's why you stopped coming up here, that's why you want to shut this place down. That's why our marriage ended, you know that.

(Pause.)

ABBY: Walter, our marriage ended because you never loved me.

(Silence.)

WALT: That's not true.
ABBY: I don't blame you.
WALT: That's not true.
ABBY: You're not capable of—.

(Abby stops herself. Silence. Tim reenters with the suitcases, looks at them. Pause.)

(To Walt) I'm going to tell the Life Fellowship people that they can go directly through you. They have your number.

(Pause.)

Just sell it, Walt. It's over. Allow it to be over.

(Abby exits, taking her suitcase. Tim goes to Walt. They look at one another for a brief moment.)

WALT: I'm sorry, / I don't—
TIM: It's fine, we—. We won't be far. Let's just— . . . Let's just let everyone cool down a bit.
WALT: Sure.

(Tim and Walt look at one another for a moment. Finally, Tim extends his arm for a handshake. Walt looks at him.)

TIM: We'll see you soon. Okay?

(*Walt looks at him for a moment longer, then shakes his hand. Tim takes his suitcase and exits. Walt watches him go.*
From outside we hear the sound of a car starting up, driving away.
Janet enters.)

JANET: Hey, Walt. So like I was just explaining to Eunice, all this means is that we're pulling out all the stops now.

WALT: Okay.

(*Eunice enters slowly from the hallway.*)

JANET: Sheriff's got more support coming up from Boise, they're gonna start focusing the search around where the jacket was found, if he dropped it there within / the last—

EUNICE (*To Janet*): Give us a minute. If that's okay?

(*Pause.*)

JANET: Okay then. I'll just be, uh—.

(*Janet goes outside. Walt goes to Eunice.*)

WALT: Eunice, I can't tell you how sorry I am, but I—. I *promise* we are not giving up, we *will* find / him—

EUNICE: Walt, *please*, you don't have to— . . . (*Pause*) Janet did this thing, she was like— . . . She was being so *positive* about everything, she—. But—realistically?—he's not coming back, is he?

WALT: We don't—. That's not certain / that he's—

EUNICE: Walt, *did you see his coat?* He has no idea how to survive out there in the woods, when his dad took him camping he could barely take ten steps without falling down or

243

cutting himself, you think after being out there *all night*, and losing that much blood—

WALT: It's been less than twenty-four hours, and we / have no idea—

EUNICE: Are you worried that I'm going to sue you? Because you don't need to worry about that, if that's what / you—

WALT: *No*, I'm not—. There's just no use in jumping to conclusions, assuming that / he's—

EUNICE: Well there is some use *for me*, there's some use for me in thinking that he's *dead*, that he's not going to come back, that he—. *(Pause)* Walt—say he comes back. Say he walks through that door, right now. Then what?

WALT: Look, there are—. Obviously he shouldn't continue on with me, but—

EUNICE: Okay, so we shove him into the next program, and the next one, and the next one . . . Eventually he marries someone he's not in love with, has *kids*? Lives the rest of his life beating himself down?

(Pause.)

Or—we let him leave. He tries to make a life within it. He turns his back on God, God turns his back on *him*, and he— . . .

WALT: *Or*, he works, and eventually finds real, meaningful change—

EUNICE: He lives with a man who can't stand to admit that he's his father. He *hates* himself. If that wasn't enough of a motivation to change, then excuse me but what would you or anyone else have to say that would be?

(Pause.)

What would be best for him—is if he never came out of that forest. If he curled up under some tree, and felt the sun on his face, and just—. And I say that as a mother who *loves* him. A mother who can't stand the thought of never seeing him again.

(Pause. Eunice goes to the door, opens it up. She lets Janet inside.)

(To Janet) You have my cell phone number, right?
JANET: Uh—sure?
EUNICE: You can call if you find anything.

(Pause.)

JANET: Wait, are you—? You're leaving?
EUNICE: Yeah.
JANET: Well are you gonna be in town, or—?

(Eunice grabs her purse, heads to the door. She stops, turns to Walt.)

EUNICE: He's better off out there. You know that.

(Eunice exits. Janet watches her go. The sound of a car door opening and shutting, an engine starting up, a car driving off.)

JANET: Well what the hell is she doing?
WALT: I think she's—going home.

(Pause. Janet watches her drive off.)

JANET: Well I know that she's upset, but geez. I mean I was pretty clear with her, we don't know anything for certain. We really don't.

WALT: Sure.

JANET: Was it something I said to her? I just hope I / didn't—

WALT: No, Janet, it's—. You're fine. *(Pause)* What do you think?

JANET: About the kid? *(Pause)* Well look, you just never know, I mean he could be out there wandering around still, maybe / he's—

WALT: Janet. What do you really think?

(Long pause. Janet thinks.)

JANET: I think—. *(Pause, direct)* I'd say at this point we're looking for a body. *(Pause)* I'm sorry, Walt.

(Walt sits down. Silence.)

Listen, Walt. I'm not trying to whatever, psychoanalyze you or whatever, but I don't want you thinking this is somehow your fault. Christ, he's not a five-year-old. It wasn't your fault he wandered off. What, were you supposed to keep him on a leash?

(Pause.)

You know, when I first moved out here, took this job—people told me about you. Some religious nut out in a cabin, brings in all these gay kids, converts them or whatever. I thought it was batshit crazy, to be honest.

WALT: You did?

JANET: Sure. I mean, I got nothing against gays. My cousin Shelly, she's been living with her partner for decades, happy as shit. Live and let live, that's what I say. So when I heard about you, I had this idea that you were hurting these kids, or—.

(Pause.)

I don't know about this conversion stuff, but one thing I do know? You weren't hurting these kids. You weren't forcing them to do or say anything. You took care of 'em.

(Silence. Janet looks at him.)

Right?

(Walt looks at her.)

Scene Five

The next morning, just before dawn.
    Walt, tired and unkempt, is bending down in front of the fireplace, trying to make a fire.
    The Shady Grove DVD plays in the background.

VOICEOVER ON THE TELEVISION: —a welcoming lobby, as well as a restaurant-style dining hall that always offers residents their choice of entrée, side dish, and dessert. All of Shady Grove's common areas are easily accessible from every apartment.

(The phone rings. Walt goes to it. He listens for a moment, then hangs up the phone with his finger, drops the receiver on the floor.)

All of our buildings are single-level, making moving easy for any resident, regardless of physical ability.

(Walt pokes at the fire a few times, unsuccessfully. He gets up, going to the kitchen, looking for some paper.)

247

The dementia-care program, "Understand Their Journey," is designed with a clear understanding of memory loss in order to provide the best resident-focused care. Our premise is simple: understand residents in their moment, rather than try to force them into our reality.

(Walt continues to search through the kitchen, unable to find any paper. He looks up, sees the dictionary in the room.)

By using this approach, we validate the resident's worldview and reality and allow them to live their lives in a way that feels familiar. Our caregivers focus on knowing a resident's wants, needs, and preferences based on their life story.

(Walt goes to the dictionary, looks at it briefly, and then tears several pages out of it. He continues to rip pages out, filling his hands. He goes to the fireplace, shoves the papers inside the fire.)

Understanding the resident's past experiences and preferences allows us to provide for their needs at every stage of their memory loss. We honor and validate our resident's reality, and support them to be purposeful and successful each day.

(Walt lights the pages, the fire starts immediately. He slowly begins to stand up, has a sharp pain in his hip and nearly falls over. He steadies himself, wincing.)

We also join the journey of families through support, education, and ongoing communication. We hold family orientations, supply a resource library, and offer family support groups. We also issue monthly publications we call *Moments*, highlighting a family member's treasured moments in life, and share those with the greater memory- care community.

(Walt heads back to the kitchen, looking for food. He sees the paper bag holding the heirloom tomatoes. He takes the bag and reaches inside, pulling out the purple one. He looks at it.)

Most importantly, we offer our residents suffering from dementia a caring, compassionate staff who undergo specialized dementia-care training.

(Walt starts to eat the heirloom tomato.)

Understanding how dementia affects the brain helps each caregiver better understand behaviors, communication barriers, and the overall needs of each patient.

(The door opens and Daniel appears. He is dirty, gaunt, and shining. The sound of the fire from before is heard, steadily increasing in volume. He looks at Walt. Walt continues to eat the heirloom tomato, not noticing Daniel.)

For residents needing care in speech rehabilitation, Shady Grove offers several services, most of which are typically covered by Medicare Part B.

(Walt senses someone looking at him, turns around, and sees Daniel. Walt drops the tomato. Walt and Daniel stare at one another, silent. The sound of the fire continues to grow, filling the space.)

Treatment plans include recovery of speech, language and memory skills, nonverbal communication, diet recommendations—

(The sound of the fire drowns out the television, the lights snap to black. The sound continues in the darkness for a few moments before lights rise on:)

Scene Six

A short time later, dawn.

Daniel sits on the couch. Janet, just woken up and not in her uniform, is bandaging a wound on his leg. A few mostly eaten heirloom tomatoes sit on the table in front of Daniel, along with the baloney.

Walt stands on the other side of the room, looking at Daniel.

JANET: You feeling faint at all, any dizziness?

(Daniel shakes his head.)

Numbness in your hands or feet, anything like that?

(Daniel shakes his head again.)

Walt—could you get him some more water?

(Walt looks at Daniel, saying nothing.)

Walt?
WALT: Oh, uh—. Yeah, I'll—.

(Walt goes to the kitchen, fills up a glass of water.)

JANET: You look okay to me, but I'm no doctor, so I think I should take you into town.

(Walt comes out of the kitchen, bringing the glass of water to Daniel.)

(To Walt) This cut doesn't look too deep, but we really should have someone look at it, just in case he needs stitches—
DANIEL: I have to—. I think I might have— . . .

(Pause. Daniel stares at Walt.)

WALT: Daniel—
DANIEL: I think I might have talked with God.

(Pause. Walt and Daniel stare at one another.)

JANET: O—kay then. *(Short pause)* I'll be right back, I just wanna radio some people, let them know you're okay.

(Janet heads toward the door. Walt looks at her.)

I'll be right outside. You—you keep him here, yeah? *(To Daniel)* I'll give your mom a call. She's sure gonna be glad to hear you're okay, yeah?

(Janet exits. Pause.)

DANIEL: I'm sorry for leaving like that—
WALT: It's okay—
DANIEL: But I think it was meant to happen this way. I've realized something, something so important, and I— . . .

(Pause.)

When I was out there, when I started wandering—I was thinking about middle school, my friend Josh who lived outside of town on this ranch? I would go over there during the summers, and we'd spend the nights in this Airstream outside his house, and I— . . .

(Silence.)

I loved him. It wasn't about sex, I just—loved him. And I was simple, so I didn't understand what that meant. So I told him how I felt.

(Pause.)

He told me to never tell anyone else, and that I shouldn't be around him anymore. He told me he would pray for me, that I could gain freedom from these feelings. I see him at school now. He doesn't look at me anymore.

(Pause. Walt goes to Daniel.)

WALT: Daniel—

DANIEL: I mean I think back to first grade, and even then—I remember having a crush on a boy in my class. In the *first grade*. It was such a part of me that I didn't even think about it, I just—.

(Pause.)

I thought I was going to die out there, I was *sure* that I was going to die out there, I was sure that God *meant* for me to die out there, that it would just be easier for everyone. But then I tripped on this rock and cut my leg, really deep— and I got my coat and I bandaged it up, and I thought for sure I was, like—. I thought if I wasn't dead already, I was going to die. And I got up, and I walked over this hill and looked down and there was just *fire*. Everywhere.

WALT: There was a forest fire, a storm south of here with some lightning, it had—

DANIEL: It was like God was showing me—the end. Of everything.

(Pause.)

Like everything was being wiped out. Everything was being killed, turned to ash. Reduced down to something so simple.

(Pause.)

I looked down, and my leg was healed. Stopped bleeding. I cut myself so deep, I was pretty sure I was looking at *bone*.

(Pause.)

It was like you said. It was like a baptism.

(Silence. Walt takes Daniel's glass.)

WALT: Here, Janet said / you should—
DANIEL: And I realized something when I was out there.

(Pause.)

Up until that moment—I thought Josh had abandoned me. I thought he was turning his back on me. But I realized— *I'm* the problem, there's something in *me* that isn't right. And if I work hard enough, I *can* change—right?

(Pause. Walt looks at Daniel.)

WALT: Daniel.
DANIEL: And I know it's still going to be work, but that work can start here, with you. I know that God has given me these feelings for a reason, like you said, it's about over-coming them.
WALT: Daniel—
DANIEL: And I'm ready to—, you know, I'm ready to spend the *rest of my life* working at it. It's like I finally / get it—
WALT: Daniel—
DANIEL: I finally get what everyone has been saying to me, what my dad has been saying to me, all these pastors, I finally / get—

WALT: What did you say to me?

(Pause.)

DANIEL: What?

WALT: When you left, right before you left. You were standing in that door, and you said something to me. What did you say to me?

(Pause.)

DANIEL: I said I felt safe with you. I told you I felt safe with you.

(Silence. Then, slowly, Walt starts to silently break down. His head falls into his hands.)

No, it's—. Walt, this is good! This is a really good thing. I feel really—*good* about the future.

(Walt looks at Daniel.)

And I'm sorry it had to happen like that, I'm sorry I had to scare you. I didn't mean to do that, I wish I could have—

WALT: No, it's not—. It's not that. *(Pause)* I just look at you, and you're so young. I think about myself, when I was your age.

(Pause.)

I could have been anything.

(Black.)

END OF PLAY

Rest

Rest received its world premiere at South Coast Repertory (Marc Masterson, Artistic Director; Paula Tomei, Managing Director) on April 4, 2014. The production was directed by Martin Benson. The set design was by John Iacovelli, the costume design was by Angela Balogh Calin, the lighting design was by Donna Ruzika, the original music and sound design were by Michael Roth, and the dramaturgy was by John M. Baker; the production stage manager was Sue Karutz. The cast was:

ETTA	Lynn Milgrim
KEN	Wyatt Fenner
GERALD	Richard Doyle
JEREMY	Rob Nagle
GINNY	Libby West
FAYE	Sue Cremin
TOM	Hal Landon Jr.

The play received its Midwest premiere at Victory Gardens Theater (Chay Yew, Artistic Director; Christopher Mannelli, Managing Director) on September 19, 2014. The production was directed by Joanie Schultz. The set design was by Chelsea Warren, the costume design was by Janice Pytel, the lighting design was by Lee Keenan, and the sound design was by Thomas Dixon; the production stage manager was Tina M. Jach. The cast was:

ETTA	Mary Ann Thebus
KEN	Matt Farabee
GERALD	William J. Norris
JEREMY	Steve Key
GINNY	McKenzie Chinn
FAYE	Amanda Drinkall
TOM	Ernest Perry Jr.

Rest was commissioned by South Coast Repertory (Marc Masterson, Artistic Director) and developed with the support of the Ojai Playwrights Conference (Robert Egan, Artistic Director), the Dorset Theatre Festival (Dina Janis, Artistic Director) and the Clubbed Thumb Writers' Group (Maria Striar, Artistic Director).

Characters

The residents:

ETTA	Female, early to mid-eighties
TOM	Male, eighties
GERALD	Male, ninety-one

The staff:

FAYE	Female, late thirties
GINNY	Female, late thirties
JEREMY	Male, forties
KEN	Male, twenty

Setting

The entrance area and common room of a small, white, dry-walled rest home in northern Idaho in January. One side of the stage is dominated by large, automatic sliding glass doors that make just a bit too much noise whenever they open. Through the doors there is a foyer, and another set of unseen sliding glass doors offstage. Near the glass doors is a small reception desk with a dusty old computer on top, a telephone, a jar filled with hard candy, etc. A large window is on one side of the stage. Above the reception desk is a large dry-erase calendar on which very few events or activities are written. An empty wheelchair or two might be appropriate. To the other side of the stage is a small common area with a couch, a recliner or two, some folding chairs, a coffee table, and a television.

The entire place has been mostly packed up, and labeled boxes are littered across the space. The feel of the stage should be institutional, sterile, and contained.

Notes

Dialogue written in *italics* is emphatic, deliberate; dialogue in ALL CAPS is impulsive, explosive.

A "/" indicates an overlap in dialogue. Whenever a "/" appears, the following line of dialogue should begin.

Ellipses (. . .) indicate when a character is trailing off, dashes (—) indicate where a character is being cut off, either by another character or themselves.

Act One

Scene One

Afternoon, nearing dusk.
    Etta sits on a chair. Ken sits near her.

ETTA: The end of our adulthood, I suppose. We sort of unexpectedly (and expectedly I guess) slid back into infancy. Gerald in diapers, struggling to put names to faces, words to objects, meaning to—. *(Short pause)* You really want me to talk about this?

KEN: Really. Please.

ETTA: I'm like a stereotype, telling you all this. Like some old woman stereotype, droning on about her life.

KEN: No, really, I—. Please.

(Pause. Etta looks at him.)

ETTA: It's not a bad place to spend three days. Not a particularly good one either, but. The ambience is par for the course, maybe subpar now that it's been dismantled a bit. The food is awful, but I'm hoping you can help us on that front. You're a good cook?

KEN: I guess?

ETTA: You have experience?

KEN: I mean, kinda? I worked at a Taco Bell in high school.

ETTA: Well that's not nothing, I guess. *(Pause)* It's really worth it, working here for just a few days like this?

KEN: I could use the extra money. Even if it's just three days. And I mean I think it'll be good for me, I think— . . . *(Pause)* Grace, the woman I'm replacing, she just—left?

ETTA: Think she just found something else, like everyone did. It was amazing how fast everyone left, the moment they said we were being shut down there was this exodus.

(Ginny enters carrying a box. She goes to a corner with several packed boxes, places it with them, organizes a bit.)

There used to be seventy or so residents here, after a few weeks it was down to just my husband Gerald and I, plus Tom. Only staff left are Faye and Ginny—

(Ginny half waves at Ken, then exits.)

—plus the one who hired you. Last soldiers left standing.

KEN: So—where will you go?

(Pause.)

ETTA: We have a place set up at the Good Samaritan Village.

KEN: Oh right, the one over by the—. I bet it's nice there.

ETTA: Very well may be. But for Gerald it'll be a new place he doesn't recognize, a larger place, a more disorienting and certainly more frightening—. Well. *(Pause)* To be honest I'm not sure why it had to shut down, I think whatever corporation owned this place decided they could make more money selling it than they could—. They said it was about resident complaints, but that's just ridiculous. We had a couple of loudmouths from Montana in here (these people from Montana you'd think they'd be heartier) and they thought they were being treated poorly, something about—

(Gerald enters, looks at Etta. Ken looks at Gerald.)

Hi, Gerald.

KEN *(To Gerald, loud)*: Hi—I'm Ken? I'm going to be working in the kitchen for the next few days?

ETTA: He's not deaf, dear. *(To Gerald)* Do you need something, Gerald?

(Gerald looks at her, searching.)

GERALD: No, I—.

   . . .

   . . .

   Uh.

(Pause.)

ETTA: This is Ken. Say hello to Ken.

(Gerald nods at Ken.)

He's replacing Grace for the next few days. You remember Grace? *(Pause)* Grace, the cook. *Grace.*

GERALD: I'm not hungry, I—.

(Gerald goes to a shelf with a small stereo on top, presses play. From the stereo we hear Arvo Pärt's "Für Alina," loud and tinny. Gerald listens. Etta turns to Ken.)

KEN *(Awkwardly)*: I'm—sorry.

ETTA: What for?

KEN: Sorry it just—. Sorry.

(Pause.)

ETTA: He has some good days. Well, *had*. Good days are behind us at this point. *(To Gerald)* Gerald.

GERALD: Hm?

ETTA: The music is so loud, please.

(Gerald turns down the music.)

He's nine years older than me, we were married when I was twenty-five, he was thirty-four. People would remark on the age difference, and we'd say "well when we're in our seventies or eighties it won't seem like much difference at all." Suppose we were wrong about that one.

GERALD: I don't—.

. . .

. . .

I don't remember what I came in here for.

. . .

I don't remember.

ETTA: I know, Gerald.

(Gerald looks at Ken and Etta for a moment, then leaves the room, leaving the music on. Etta goes to the stereo and turns off the music.)

KEN: It's really—beautiful.

ETTA: I'm sorry?

KEN: I mean—. You've been together so long.

ETTA: Oh.

KEN: You must love each other so much.

ETTA: He doesn't remember who I am anymore, dear.

(Pause. Etta goes back to Ken, sits down.)

KEN *(Stricken)*: Oh, wow . . . I'm *so, so sorry—*

ETTA: Oh, no, it's fine—

KEN: That's just *so sad.*

ETTA: Okay.

KEN: *It's so, so—*

ETTA: All right you're going to have to stop that right now.

KEN: Sorry, I—. I don't know, not being able to recognize the person you *love—*

ETTA: I mean he was never too forthcoming with love anyway, I think he thought it was tacky, or—. Not that he didn't love me, he just didn't—. We had a shorthand for it. He never liked to say "I love you" before bed, he was embarrassed by it frankly, so we started just saying "see you in the future."

KEN: The—future?

ETTA: Yes, when we both wake up, the next day. "See you in the future." The future sounded much more optimistic back then, I suppose.

(Faye enters with a box and earbuds in her ears. She puts the box with the others, organizes a bit.)

You couldn't tell now, but he was a—brilliant man. PhD in musicology, professor emeritus at the university. He always thought he was the smartest person in the room, most of the time he was right. He loved to put people in their place, he loved to make his points. Honestly he was never happier than when he was saying something about something.

(Faye exits.)

Someone your age, you should be working somewhere else. Somewhere a little less depressing maybe.

KEN: Well it's—. I just think it—could be good for me.

ETTA: Oh?

KEN: When I saw this job posting at first I wasn't even going to apply even though I could *really* use this money, but when I thought about it, I thought that maybe it could be a good opportunity for me to— . . . *(Pause)* I think I just need to realize that, you know, dying isn't—bad. It's a good thing, it's kind of—beautiful.

(Pause.)

ETTA: You think when I die, you think that's going to be "beautiful"?

KEN: Have you accepted Jesus into your heart?

ETTA: Oh honey. *(Pause)* Three days you'll be here, right? You can make it three days.

KEN: Sorry, that came out weird, I'm not trying to be— *(Pause)* My pastor thought it was time for me to get out, to find work, interact with people more—and when I told him about this job, he thought it might be—*good* for me.

ETTA: "Good" for you?

KEN: Yeah. I sorta have a hard time with, like—death?

(Short pause.)

ETTA: You really shouldn't have taken this job.

KEN: No it'll be good, I mean—. I'm reborn now, I'm finding peace, and maturity, and—I just need to realize that this a place full of people who are about to be reunited with God, that it's really a—*positive* thing. Right?

(Gerald reenters, upset.)

GERALD: *Every time that I—.*
   . . .
Every time I go in there, you know.
   . . .
   . . .
Every damn time I go in there, the—. The people without faces at the end of the bed.
   . . .
People without faces.
   . . .
You know that?

(Etta goes to him, keeping her distance.)

ETTA: Yes, Gerald.
GERALD: People without faces, at the end of the bed.
   . . .
   . . .
I said that there are people without faces.
At the end of the bed.
   . . .
Looking at me without any eyes.

(Gerald stops, looks at Etta. He slowly calms down. Silence.)

I know you.

(Pause.)

ETTA: Yes.

(They look at each other for a moment.
Jeremy enters holding a few forms and an ID. He hands
Ken the ID. Gerald makes his way out of the room.)

JEREMY *(To Ken)*: All right, here's your license back, I think
we're good to go. Grace left us enough in the freezer to get
us through the night, so. See you in the morning.
KEN: Great, thanks.

(Jeremy exits. Ken looks at Etta.)

It was really nice talking to you.
ETTA: You too, dear.

(Ken goes to the sliding glass doors. They open. He looks
outside, hesitates. He turns back to Etta.)

Just a few days with us, honey. You'll be fine.

Scene Two

Late morning, the next day.
Tom is sitting on a recliner closer to the television, which is
on at a low level. It plays an emergency broadcast from a local
station warning of a winter storm.
Ginny stands, watching the television. Faye is at a window,
nervously looking outside.
A tense silence.

FAYE: Do we know—, like, *when* he left? Did she say anything?
GINNY: No.

(The sliding glass doors open abruptly. Faye and Ginny look at the doors expectantly. The doors remain open for a moment, then close. Short pause. Ginny turns back to the window.)

FAYE: It's getting really bad out there.

GINNY: I'm sure someone's found him.

FAYE: If someone found him, wouldn't we have heard by now?

GINNY: When he did this last August, it took almost all day for him to walk into that Kmart and—

FAYE: Yeah in *August*, it's like twenty degrees outside, if he's out there it's not going to take long before he— . . . *(Short pause)* Okay, I'm sick of just standing around, maybe we should circle the building again?

GINNY: The police will be here any second, they're gonna be able to—

(Etta enters, tense and worried. Faye stops herself. Etta glances at Faye, then sits, half watching the television. Silence. Faye goes to Etta.)

FAYE: I'm sure this is all going to work out.

ETTA: Hm.

FAYE: He's done this before. Someone always finds him.

ETTA: Yes.

(Ken enters with a tray of snacks for Tom. The sliding doors open again. Everyone stops, looks at them. Silence. The doors close. Ken looks at Faye. She forces a smile back at him. Ken gives Tom the snacks, then exits.)

GINNY: You know I'm sure by this point he's found some house, or—. You know that trailer park is only about half a mile from here.

FAYE: That's true, and if someone saw him walking by they would / have—

ETTA: Yes thank you.

FAYE: And when the police get here, they'll be able to drive around and see if they—

ETTA: Thank you, yes. We don't need to talk about it, thank you.

(Etta stops, struggling.)

FAYE: Oh, hon.

(Faye gets up, goes to Etta.)

ETTA: I'm sorry.

FAYE: You have nothing to be sorry about—

ETTA: I'm fine—

GINNY: Oh, hon.

ETTA: *Please* don't patronize me, I don't like it.

(Jeremy enters. Etta begins to gather herself.)

JEREMY *(To Faye)*: Have they called? *(Sees Etta)* Oh, honey—

ETTA: *Everyone stop.*

(Awkward silence. Tom finally looks away from the television, at Etta.)

TOM: Gerald wander outside again, Etta?

(Pause.)

ETTA: Yes, Tom.

TOM: Can't find him?

ETTA: No, Tom.

TOM: Very sorry to hear that.

ETTA: Yes thank you.

(Silence. Tom goes back to watching the television.)

JEREMY *(To Faye)*: Nothing?

FAYE: No.

JEREMY: But why don't—? Aren't there like, *emergency vehicles* or—?

ETTA: Everyone please stop talking about it, it's really just not helping, I—.

(Etta stands up, starts to exit, and then turns back.)

Look I realize that you're all being nice about this, but I have to say that the way you all express sympathy and concern, it's very annoying. I'm sorry if that's rude of me to say (I'm not really sorry actually) but it's the truth, it's really very annoying.

(Etta exits. Ken enters, goes to Tom.)

JEREMY: Shouldn't we be—doing *something*? I just feel like we should go out there, maybe one of us should do some driving around, or—. Ginny, did you bring the SUV?

GINNY: / Matt took it, I have the wagon.

KEN *(To Tom)*: You want anything else, Mr. M.?

TOM: Coffee?

KEN *(To Ginny and Faye)*: Can he have coffee?

GINNY: He really shouldn't—. Oh fuck it, give him coffee.

FAYE: Ginny.

GINNY: Oh he can't hear me.

(Ken exits.)

What about the sons, should we call them?

FAYE: Yeah, I guess we should / probably—

JEREMY: *No,* we're not—. There's no reason to get family involved right / now—

FAYE: Jeremy, he's *missing* for Christ's sake—

JEREMY: He is not—! Now we don't know that, he / could be—

FAYE: Of course we "know" that, he's not here and we don't / know where—

GINNY: Okay, okay—

(The sliding doors open again. They all look at them. Pause.)

JEREMY: *Jesus,* it's still doing that?!

(The sliding doors close. Jeremy grabs a folding chair, sets it under the doors, and starts fiddling with them.)

You know I'm actually *glad* we got shut down, seriously. It's not worth having a heart attack before I'm fifty. The stupid plastic surgeons that bought this place, let them deal with this stupid door. See if they can—

(Jeremy gets shocked by the door.)

FUCK.

GINNY: Okay, I think we're done playing with the door. C'mon.

(Ginny goes to Jeremy, helps him off the chair.)

JEREMY: It shocked me!

GINNY: I know, honey.

JEREMY: It really shocked me. It really just did that.

(The phone rings. Faye goes to answer it.)

FAYE *(On the phone)*: / Pine Manor Assisted Living.

JEREMY: I'm sorry.

GINNY: It's fine.

FAYE *(On the phone)*: / Yeah, we spoke earlier, I think.

JEREMY: Do you think I should call Eileen? She's gonna chew me out so bad, I know she's / gonna—

GINNY: Nothing's happened to him yet, calm down.

JEREMY: I just don't—. I mean could we get in trouble for this? Could we go to *jail* or something for this?

FAYE: / I understand that, but I'm just wondering what *we* should be doing, like if there's something we could do in the meantime, or— . . .

GINNY: Dear *God* Jeremy, we are / not going to—

JEREMY: Well it's not like crazy, right? We do have some responsibility here, if it looks like we were just *hanging out* while a resident with severe dementia just wanders into the—

(The sliding doors open again. Jeremy and Ginny look. A pause. Jeremy buries his face in his hands.)

FAYE *(On the phone)*: Okay, thank you.

(The doors close. Faye hangs up.)

GINNY *(To Faye)*: Anything?

FAYE: Branch Road is completely snowed in on the north side. So they couldn't even look.

JEREMY: They *closed the road?*

FAYE: Guess they had to. They're gonna try swinging around and taking the highway, see if they can come from the other side.

JEREMY: Oh, God.

(Ken returns with coffee and gives it to Tom.)

KEN: What's wrong?

FAYE: Branch is snowed in on the north side.

KEN: Woah.

JEREMY: Okay, I can't stand just sitting around here, I'm going to go drive over toward the highway, see if I find him.

(Jeremy stands up, grabbing his coat from behind the reception desk. Ken exits.)

GINNY: I don't know if that's a great idea, Jeremy, why don't you just circle the building a few more times, check the parking lot—?

JEREMY: I've already done that, *someone* has to be out there looking for him—

FAYE: Jeremy, stop, does your Corolla even have four-wheel drive?

JEREMY: Well I'll walk then!

FAYE: *Walk?* This is the worst blizzard we've had in years, you're not even wearing a hat—

GINNY: Look you're not in New Mexico anymore, this isn't exactly—

JEREMY: Stop it, stop treating me like I'm a kid or something just because I'm from New Mexico! I've been here for two years, I've seen snow, I know what I'm getting into, just—. *(Pause)* I *am* your boss, you know?!

(Jeremy moves to the sliding doors. They don't open. He waves his hand in front of the sensor. Nothing happens.

Jeremy seethes. He turns around and heads toward the back.)

I'll go out the *fucking stupid* back door.

(Jeremy exits. Silence, apart from the television. Faye and Ginny look at one another.)

FAYE: He's gonna get himself hurt out there.

GINNY: Oh let him get hurt then.

FAYE: No, really, maybe—. Maybe I should go with him.

(Faye grabs her coat.)

GINNY: Faye, / don't—

FAYE: Look maybe he's right, maybe we should look for Gerald if the police can't get through—

GINNY: You can't see two feet in front of your face out there, you think you / can find—

FAYE: Well I'm sick of just sitting here not knowing if he's out there freezing to death or something—

GINNY: I guarantee you someone has already found him and / they are—

FAYE: No, you don't know that, Ginny, just let me—

(Ginny goes to Faye.)

GINNY: Faye, you're *pregnant*, you can't just—

FAYE: *Ginny.*

(Faye motions to Tom, who continues to watch television.)

GINNY: Oh he can't hear me, calm down.

(Faye relents, puts her coat back.)

FAYE: I just can't stand thinking about him wandering out there. I know he's done this before, but with this storm, and all that farmland east of us—

275

GINNY: Even if he walked down the farm access road, which I doubt, there are cars coming down that thing every twenty minutes at least. Someone would have seen him. What's more likely is that he went walking toward town and someone found him after ten minutes. *(Pause)* And even if—I mean I don't think he is, but even if—the man's over ninety for God's sake, and he's just getting worse— these past few months he's wandered outside at least five or six times, this was bound to—. *(Pause)* Never mind. He's fine. I'm sure he's fine.

(Faye takes a breath. Silence.)

Why are you still so weird about me telling people?
FAYE: Oh my God.
GINNY: I just don't / know why—
FAYE: Okay, look, maybe we should be / focusing on—
GINNY: *Faye.*

(Faye relents.)

FAYE: I just don't—. I don't see why we have to make some big *announcement.*
GINNY: No one's saying we have to make a big announcement. I just don't know why it has to be this big secret—
FAYE: Well maybe it's personal, maybe / it's—
GINNY: You're not *embarrassed*, are you? Matt and I aren't embarrassed, so / you—
FAYE: *No*, it's not that, Ginny, I—. *(Pause)* It's just been— tough lately.

(Pause.)

GINNY: Yeah, hon, I know. I know it. But it's been a *year* now—

FAYE: I know, Ginny, but I just / feel like—

GINNY: You can make the decision to move on with the rest of your life, you know?

FAYE: I just— . . . Look I mean I only started working here to be around him more, and now that he's gone I feel like I— . . .

GINNY: I know, I was here too, I know what— . . . But you don't have to *wallow* in this, just—. There are good things in your life right now, just focus on the good things. Okay?

(Pause. Faye looks at her.)

What?

(The phone rings. Faye looks away from Ginny.)

FAYE: Okay.

(Ginny looks at Faye for a moment longer. The phone rings again. Ginny answers it.)

GINNY *(On the phone)*: Pine Manor, this is Ginny.

(Jeremy reenters, red-faced, cradling his right hand.)

FAYE: What?

GINNY *(On the phone)*: Yes, hi, have you— . . . ?

FAYE: Jeremy, what?

JEREMY: Nothing, I—. *(Pause)* The back door is frozen shut and I got upset and hit it and I really hurt my hand I don't know if I broke it—

GINNY: / Well how long is this supposed to last?

FAYE: Okay, come here. Lemme look at it.

JEREMY: I just like hate myself sometimes.

(Faye looks at Jeremy's hand.)

277

FAYE: No, you're—. I don't think it's broken, it doesn't look broken.

JEREMY: Seriously I hate myself so much sometimes, / I really—

FAYE: Okay take a breath. Sit down, you're okay.

(Jeremy sits down. Ken reenters, goes to Tom.)

GINNY *(On the phone)*: / Wait—so what does that mean, what are you saying?

KEN *(To Tom)*: You all done, Mr. M.?

TOM: More coffee, please?

KEN: Oh I don't know, Mr. M., I don't know if we / should—

TOM: It doesn't do anything to me.

KEN: Um—Ginny? Is it okay if—?

(Ginny waves Ken away.)

GINNY *(On the phone)*: / Are you—? You're sure?

KEN: Uh. Okay, I'll—.

(Ken exits. Jeremy and Faye watch Ginny.)

GINNY *(On the phone)*: Yeah, I understand that, but—

JEREMY: What is it?

GINNY *(On the phone)*: Well, no, probably not. *(Pause)* Okay. Okay, yeah.

(Ginny hangs up. She looks at everyone.)

JEREMY: They find him?

GINNY: No, they uh. They didn't and—the highway's closed.

(Pause.)

JEREMY: Wait, the *highway*?

GINNY: Fifty miles of it, anyway. They can't get out here.

JEREMY: What about the farm access road?

GINNY: It's all closed, Jeremy. Everything.

(Pause.)

JEREMY: But so what are they gonna do, are they gonna—?

GINNY: They can't, Jeremy. They just can't. Not until this passes, anyway. *(Pause)* They said to wait here, keep an eye out for him and—"hope for the best."

(Pause. Ken reenters with coffee, hands it to Tom.)

JEREMY: They said—? They said "hope for the best," they really said that?

(Silence. The sliding doors open again, linger for a moment, then close.)

Scene Three

Early evening.
   Etta sits near the television, which is on at a low level. She barely pays attention to it, lost in thought.
   Faye enters, carrying a box full of medical supplies.
   Etta looks at her, smiles vaguely.

FAYE: Can I get you / anything?

ETTA: Oh, no, I—. People aren't still outside, are they?

FAYE: Jeremy and Ginny are circling the parking lot one last time before it gets too dark.

ETTA: They really shouldn't be out there in this weather, they— ... *(Referring to the medical supplies)* What's that?

279

FAYE: Oh, it's—. Honestly it's just a lot of junk. I felt so help-less, I had to do something. We're supposed to sort it, see what's worth selling to the hospital.

(Faye goes toward Etta. Etta peers into the box.)

ETTA: Oh Lord, that's a catheter, isn't it?

FAYE: Yes, it is.

ETTA: And it's in there with a jar of *tongue depressors*?

FAYE: Yeah, Jeremy isn't very—organized.

ETTA: I feel sorry for him.

FAYE: Why?

ETTA: I mean he doesn't know what he's doing. Some parent corporation hires that idiot to run this place, you can't blame him.

FAYE: Mrs. Erickson—

ETTA: Well I don't mean it like—. I'm not trying to *insult* the poor idiot, I'm just saying.

(Faye laughs a little. Etta smiles.)

I'm being so *rude* today, aren't I? I'm being so rude.

(Pause.)

FAYE: Can I—? Would you like me to sit with you?

(Pause.)

ETTA: Now I hope you know I'm not looking for some pity party, I hope you know that.

FAYE: I'm not giving you one. Promise.

(Pause. Faye sits down, looks at the television.)

They saying anything new?

ETTA: No, not really. They're saying five feet, maybe six up toward Deary.

(Faye takes a thermometer out of the box, looks at it.)

Snow outside our room was almost up to the window when I was in there. Oh Faye, is that a rectal thermometer? I hope you're going to wash your hands.

FAYE: I'm sure it's been washed.

(Etta looks at her. Pause. Faye considers, then puts down the thermometer.)

Yeah, maybe I—.

(Faye goes to the front desk, takes a bottle of Purell and squirts some into her hand. Etta turns the television off. Faye looks at Etta for a moment.)

Look, Mrs. Erickson, I'm just so sorry that—

ETTA: Oh here we go.

FAYE: What?

ETTA: I believe I told you *specifically* that I wasn't / interested in—

FAYE *(Unintentionally high-pitched)*: I know honey, but I'm just sorry that—

ETTA: I swear, no one under fifty nowadays knows how to express sympathy in a way that's not completely condescending.

FAYE: Well you didn't even let me say anything.

(Pause.)

ETTA: All right, have a crack at it.

(Pause. Faye looks at her.)

FAYE *(Direct, simple)*: I'm very sorry that you're going through this. I still have faith we'll find him, but nevertheless this must be difficult. And if there's any way I can help, please let me know.

(Pause.)

ETTA: That was better.
FAYE: You see?
ETTA: Your voice didn't go up into that sickly sweet register, it was much better.
FAYE: Thank you.

(Pause.)

ETTA: It's so odd not having him around, my days for so many years have been full of my desperate attempts to *orient* him. Every five seconds, "that's a picture of our son Benny, dear," "this is Tommy, he's here to change our sheets," "this is our room, there are two beds because we *both* sleep here." Maybe it's what kept me from senility, constantly reminding myself where I was, what I was— . . . *(Pause)* You've been here what, six years?
FAYE: Seven. Well, I guess almost eight.
ETTA: Do you think Gerald—, that he's gotten worse, this past year or so? *(Pause)* In your opinion. I'm just curious.

(Pause.)

FAYE: Yeah, I mean—. I think so, yes. When I first got here he seemed to recognize me, but recently he—. And he seemed to be listening to his music more back then.
ETTA: Well he never really stopped that.
FAYE: Really?

ETTA: The only part of his brain that refused to shut off. Even after every other part of his mind seemed to fall away, he never lost the music, I could always cling to that one last part of him. Not surprising, I suppose. It takes a pretty strong will to grow up in rural Wyoming and decide to become a musicologist specializing in postmodern sacred choral works.

FAYE: I guess I never knew much about him, I knew he was a music teacher at the university and / that he—

ETTA: Music *professor*. In his better days he would have really gone after you for calling him a music teacher, music *professor*. University of Idaho gave him tenure faster than you could believe. Taught as long as he could. The university was good to him, I'll say that much. But after a while—. He'd miss a class now and then, students would complain, the dean tolerated it. But about twelve years ago, he walked into a lecture hall, turned on a recording of the Latvian Radio Choir performing Arvo Pärt's *Berliner Messe* (his favorite, he listened to it constantly), and sat listening to it silently for about ten minutes before touching himself inappropriately in front of fifty or so horrified freshmen.

FAYE: Oh.

ETTA: Yes, *oh*, I think we all breathed a collective *oh* when that happened. The signs were there before that, of course, but we dismissed them, *I* dismissed them. *(Pause)* If he knew what he had turned into, he would—. He'd be so humiliated.

(Pause.)

FAYE: Have you talked to Dave and Benny yet?

(Pause.)

ETTA: Well, they—. *(Pause)* Look to be honest I haven't called them yet, but I don't want to hear anything about it.

FAYE: You haven't—?

ETTA: I said I don't want to hear anything about it.

FAYE: I didn't say anything, I just—. I thought maybe you'd want to let them know—

ETTA: Oh I just don't see any reason in getting them all worked up, they're so sensitive, especially when it comes to their father. They'd have Gerald hooked up to an iron lung before they were ready to say good-bye to him, I'm telling you. If I tell Dave he's missing he's liable to snowshoe in here from Minneapolis, it's not—. There's just nothing they can do, there's nothing any of us can do, we can't— . . .

(Etta struggles.)

Excuse me.

FAYE: Oh honey—

(Etta glares at her. Silence. Etta takes a deep breath. Faye doesn't know what to say.)

ETTA: All right, enough.

FAYE: What?

(Etta goes upstage to a box, rummages around a bit, pulls out a bottle of port.)

ETTA: This has been collecting dust on our bureau since the millennium (it's not even good or anything) and I don't feel like taking it with me.

(Etta grabs two paper cups from reception, goes to Faye.)

FAYE: Oh, you go ahead, I'm fine.

ETTA: Oh just a little.

FAYE: I think it would put me to / sleep, I—

ETTA: A little bit won't hurt the baby, you'll be fine.

(Pause.)

FAYE: I'm sorry?

ETTA: I said a little bit won't hurt it. People are so sensitive about that nowadays, when I was pregnant I drank and smoked the / whole—

FAYE: How did—? How did you know about—?

(Pause.)

ETTA: Oh you're—? I'm sorry I'd assumed you'd be telling people by now.

FAYE: Did Ginny tell you?

ETTA: Faye, I was a receptionist at a doctor's office for thirty-four years, I know what—. I mean you haven't even had coffee.

(Etta pours a normal glass for herself, a small glass for Faye.)

Look a lot of women nowadays are having babies without getting married, it's nothing you have to worry about. Not with me, anyway. I hope I didn't embarrass you, I didn't mean to embarrass you.

(Pause.)

FAYE: No, it's—fine. *(Pause)* It's not, um. Well it's not really—mine?

(Pause.)

ETTA: I'm sorry?

FAYE: I'm having it for Ginny.

ETTA: "For Ginny"?

FAYE: I mean not like—wow, you'd think I'd have figured out how to explain this by now. A few years ago, Ginny had pelvic cancer, and because of the radiation she can't—. Anyway, this year she and Matt have been talking about a kid, finding a surrogate, so I— . . .

(Pause.)

ETTA: Offered.

FAYE: Yeah, I—. I offered.

ETTA: Huh. *(Pause)* Did you do the—? The in vitro / fertilization—?

FAYE: No, it's—. It's mine, biologically. *(Pause)* But I mean it's not *mine*, it's Ginny's.

ETTA: Well of course it's yours dear.

(Silence. Faye and Etta drink.)

FAYE: I mean she's my best friend, she's been my best friend since high school and I knew what she was going through, and— . . . And they're giving me some money, which believe me is going to be helpful, especially since I'm losing my job, and— . . . But it's not just that. After this last year, I just wanted to do something—forward-looking, something— . . . *(Silence)* It's just been a—weird year for me. Losing Dad and everything.

ETTA: Yes, I'd imagine.

FAYE: I mean the entire reason I became a CNA and started working here was so I could take care of him after his diagnosis, and now— . . . *(Short pause)* Sorry, I don't / need to—

ETTA: No, Faye, it's fine, you—. *(Pause)* Up until now I just assumed you didn't want to talk about it. When he passed, there was such a—tremendous silence surrounding it.

FAYE: Yeah, there was. Still is.

(Pause.)

ETTA: When his cancer had gotten worse, those last few months, / did you—?

FAYE: You know I actually don't—. I'm not sure if I can talk about it, I don't know if I—?

ETTA: I'm sorry—

FAYE: No, it's—. *(Awkward pause)* Sorry, this is all to say— I guess I thought having a baby would be doing something *good*, something life-affirming. Something—about the future.

(Pause.)

ETTA: I see. *(Pause)* Does it feel that way?

(Pause. Faye looks at her.
  Ginny enters wearing a coat and holding a flashlight, sees Faye with the port. Pause.)

GINNY: What are you—?

(Pause.)

FAYE: Oh, it's just—

GINNY: You're drinking?

FAYE: We were just—. We were just having a little drink. I just had barely a sip.

ETTA: I pushed it on her, I take full responsibility.

(Silence.)

FAYE: Ginny, I really wasn't—
GINNY: Maybe that's not a good idea.

(Silence. Faye puts the cup down. Ginny puts the flashlight down, takes off her coat and hangs it up.)

FAYE: Did you find anything?
GINNY: No, we—. Back door's still frozen shut. It's impossible to see anything out there, anyway. *(Pause)* Ken said dinner's gonna be a little late. Another forty-five minutes or so.

(Pause.)

FAYE: Okay.

(Ginny exits. Pause. Etta picks up the bottle of port.)

ETTA: I'm sorry, I shouldn't have pushed this on you, it was—. *(Pause)* I'll put it away.

(Etta starts making her way out of the room.)

FAYE: I think I—. I've made a mistake—
ETTA: It was just a little sip of port wine, it's not—
FAYE: I don't mean that, I mean—. *(Pause)* I don't think I should have done this, I don't know what to— . . .

(Faye trails off. Silence.)

ETTA: This baby? You're talking about the baby?
FAYE: I'm sorry, I don't know / why I'm—
ETTA: You're worried about giving it up? You're worried you'll want to keep it?

FAYE: No, it's not that at all, I'm just worried that I—. I'm worried that I shouldn't be having a baby *at all*, like—how much shit is going to happen to them, how much will they suffer, all because I needed money and Ginny wants to feel needed, and—. *(Pause)* God, I sound so awful. I hear what I'm saying, it sounds so awful.

(Silence.)

ETTA: We do place an inherent value on life, don't we? Life, in and of itself, is always good, no matter what. So we're told.

(Pause. Faye looks at Etta.)

FAYE: I mean, do you think that Gerald—?

(Faye stops herself, looks away.)

ETTA: What?
FAYE: No, forget it.
ETTA: Ask me.

(Pause.)

FAYE: I really don't want this to sound—. I don't want to offend you, but—
ETTA: You're wondering if Gerald might be better off if he . . . ? *(Pause)* I don't know. I don't know what to think. To be honest I've never felt more helpless and lost in my entire life. *(Pause)* You're making a life. Creating something new. Take comfort in it. Try to take comfort in it.

(Tom enters. He heads straight to the television and turns it on.)

FAYE: I'm gonna see if Ken needs help with anything.

(Faye exits. Etta looks at the television, goes and sits with Tom. The broadcast continues to talk about the storm. Silence as they watch the television.)

ETTA: No end in sight to this, huh?
TOM: They all end eventually.
ETTA: Hm.

(Silence. They watch.)

TOM: Etta. *(No response)* Etta—
ETTA: Yes, Tom, I know. *(Pause)* I know.

Scene Four

A short time later.

    Ken is at the window, nervously staring outside. Jeremy enters with a clipboard.

JEREMY: Hey / I was—
KEN *(Startled)*: AH—
JEREMY: GEEZ—
KEN: Sorry, / sorry—
JEREMY: Calm down, it's me, it's / just me—
KEN: I'm sorry, I just—. *(Pause)* Sorry.

    (Pause.)

JEREMY: You worried about the storm?
KEN: No it's not that, I actually like it, I was—. I was trying to calm myself down by watching the snow. *(Pause)* I'm sort of an anxious person?

JEREMY: Yeah, I—. I see that. *(Pause)* So listen, I know you're still cooking but when you're done I was thinking you could inventory what's left of the kitchen supplies?

KEN: Yeah, I can do it. Sorry.

(Pause.)

JEREMY: You worried about Gerald, is that what's going on?

KEN: Yeah, I guess, but not in the right way? *(Pause)* I was in the kitchen, and the vents were on and they're kinda loud, and I realized that someone could be like right behind me and I wouldn't know it, and I kept thinking that I'd turn around and someone would be—. I just wanted to come out here where it was quieter, where someone couldn't sneak up on me.

JEREMY: Guess that didn't work.

KEN: No, it—. *(Pause)* Look this is gonna make me sound terrible, but I have this fear that I'm gonna turn around and Gerald will be standing there, or worse his *body* will be— . . .

(Pause.)

JEREMY: That's like a really weird fear.

KEN: Yeah I— . . . I don't know I'm sort of weird with this kind of stuff. I took this job because my pastor thought it would be good for me, and— . . . *(Pause)* What made you start working here?

JEREMY: What do you—mean?

KEN: I mean did you want to have a closer relationship to the elderly, or did end-of-life care appeal to—?

JEREMY: I got divorced.

KEN: Oh.

JEREMY: Yeah, I just needed a—. I don't know, I needed to get outta there. *(Pause)* We were only together for like eight months, but it was a *lifetime*. Those eight months were like a *lifetime*.

(Pause.)

KEN: How did you guys meet?
JEREMY: Match Dot Com.
KEN: That's really beautiful.

(Pause.)

JEREMY: And now I'm in Idaho, and I don't have a job, and I have no idea what the fuck I'm going to do.

(Pause.)

KEN: I mean listen, I think we all have our own paths. I think God has a plan for you, maybe you just don't know what it is yet.

(Pause.)

JEREMY: If God has a plan for me, then he like *really* hasn't thought it through very much. *(Pause)* Wait, so—why did your pastor want you to work here?
KEN: Oh, I just—. I sort of get overwhelmed easily, especially when it comes to death and dying, and . . . My pastor just thought that maybe, working here, I'd gain a—positive relationship with death.
JEREMY: I mean, I don't think most people have a super positive relationship with death.
KEN: Yeah, but I, like— . . . *(Pause)* My stepdad OD'd on our kitchen floor when I was ten. I found him. He had been

dead for hours. Growing up my mom wasn't super—stable, and this last year things have gotten worse for her, so finally I just had to leave and— . . . *(Short pause) Anyway*, things have been a lot better lately! I got out of there, moved here, and this church in town has been good for me, Pastor Jake is really— . . . And I just think that God's plan can sort of be surprising. Sometimes he puts us on paths that we don't really expect.

(Silence.)

JEREMY: Yeah so like if we have some spatulas, then you can write "spatulas" in the first column there and in the second column you can—

(A kitchen timer in Ken's pocket goes off. He pulls it out, looks at it.)

KEN: Meatloaf's done.
JEREMY: Oh.
KEN: I'll get started on the inventory after dinner.
JEREMY: Cool.

(Ken takes the clipboard from Jeremy. He starts to exit toward the kitchen.)

Ken?
KEN: Yeah?
JEREMY: You, like—have a place to stay and everything, right?
KEN: There's a couch in the church basement.
JEREMY: Oh. *(Short pause)* Is it—okay?
KEN: I mean it's better than my car.

(Ken smiles at Jeremy. Pause.)

JEREMY: And you really think that there's still a plan for you?
KEN: I mean—sure. God led me here for some reason—right?

(Ginny enters with an old card table.)

GINNY: Jeremy the dining room is *freezing*—
JEREMY: Well yeah, I turned the heat off last night—
GINNY: Where did you expect us to eat for the next two days?!
JEREMY: They told me to cut corners, you think I should heat a
  two-thousand-square-foot dining room for / three people?!
GINNY: Okay just get the folding chairs, please?
JEREMY: *God. Fine.*

*(Jeremy exits. Ken goes to Ginny. They try to stand the card
table up unsuccessfully.)*

KEN: This leg is broken I think—
GINNY: No, there's a trick to it, I just don't remember what—.

(Faye enters with a packed box.)

(To Faye) You remember how to do this?

(Faye puts the box down, goes to Ginny.)

FAYE: It's the one leg, you have to like pop it out or it won't—

*(Faye messes with one leg of the card table. They manage
to stand it up. Ken heads toward the kitchen.)*

KEN: Meatloaf's done, so we're ready I think.
GINNY: Okay.

*(Ken exits.
   Silence. Ginny and Faye stand together awkwardly.)*

FAYE: Listen, Ginny, I'm sorry about earlier?

GINNY: Oh, no—

FAYE: Really, I / owe you—

GINNY: Honey I've thought about it and I was totally over-reacting. I mean it was just a little sip of wine, / how could it—

FAYE: Well that still doesn't / make it—

GINNY: It's not a big deal. But listen, can we— . . . ? *(Pause)* Are we—okay?

(Pause. Tom enters.)

TOM: Dinner?

GINNY: On its way, Mr. M.

(Tom sits on the recliner. Ginny turns back to Faye.)

FAYE: Ginny—

GINNY: I know this is a lot for you to take on, but I just—, something's up and / I don't—

FAYE: I'm fine.

TOM: I would like my dinner now.

GINNY *(To Tom, loud)*: It's coming Tom, can't make it come any faster. *(To Faye)* Faye, I'm sick of feeling like I've lost my best friend or something and not knowing / why—

FAYE: I don't / know if I—

GINNY: If it's me, if I said something or did something then / you can—

FAYE: *No*, it's not you, it's— . . .

(Silence. Faye considers. She looks at Ginny.)

You're still happy about this baby, right?

(Pause. Ginny looks at her.)

GINNY: What?

FAYE: I mean, when we decided to do this, it felt so—*beautiful*, I felt like I was doing something so special for you and Matt, like I was helping you create this life, it felt so—. . . *(Pause)* But when we did the ultrasound last week, and we actually *saw* the baby for the first time, you asked me how I felt and I told you I felt so happy, but— . . . I didn't feel that way. I'm not sure what I felt, but I— . . . I mean I *am* happy, but— . . . *(Pause)* I'm not explaining myself very well.

(Silence. Ginny looks away, goes back to the table.)

What? *(No response)* You asked me what was wrong.

GINNY: And you told me.

(Pause.)

FAYE: All right, Ginny, you're not allowed to *force* me to tell you what I'm feeling and then get mad at me / for—

GINNY: Well I didn't think that you were gonna tell me you don't want to have this baby all of the sudden.

FAYE: Okay, I didn't say that—

GINNY: I thought you were gonna say you were worried it would be hard to give the baby up, or you're tired or morning sickness, or—. *Normal pregnancy things.*

FAYE: Look it's not like I'm not going to go through with it, I'm just telling you—

GINNY: "Not going to go through with it"? What does that mean, why did you just say that?

FAYE: I *said* it's *not* like I'm *not* going to go through / with it—

GINNY: But you've thought about it.

FAYE: No! Of course not!

GINNY: If you think that *that* is an option here—

FAYE: Oh my God, Ginny—

TOM: I am very hungry right now, I would like / my—

GINNY: SHUT UP, Tom.

FAYE: *Stop. Ginny. Stop.*

> (*Silence. Ginny breathes, trying to calm herself down. Faye goes to Tom.*)

Mr. M., it's on its way, I promise. Okay?

> (*Tom nods at her. Faye goes back to Ginny.*)

Nothing's happening with the baby. It's gonna be healthy, I'm gonna have it, you guys are gonna raise it, just like we've talked about. Okay?

> (*Pause.*)

You asked me what I was feeling, and I told you. This isn't about some big crisis, this isn't about—.This is just about something I'm feeling. That's all.

> (*Pause.*)

GINNY: So what you're feeling—is that you wish you hadn't done this.

> (*Pause. Faye doesn't respond.*
>   *Jeremy enters with folding chairs.*)

JEREMY: No place settings?

GINNY: I'll get some.

> (*Ginny brushes past Jeremy, exits.*)

JEREMY: What?
FAYE: Nothing.
JEREMY: Did I say something?
FAYE: No, Jeremy.

(*Pause.*)

JEREMY: Were you talking about me?
FAYE: *No*, oh my God.

(*Ken reenters with a large pan of meatloaf and heads toward the table. Ginny follows after him with place settings.*)

KEN: I got this recipe from a lady at my church, if it's half as good as she makes it then you guys are gonna love it.

(*Faye goes to Ginny.*)

FAYE: Ginny—

(*Ginny ignores Faye.*)

GINNY (*Calling out*): Etta. Dinner.

(*Ginny exits. Faye watches her leave.
Ken starts to carve up the meatloaf.*)

KEN: Mr. M., you wanna stay there or you wanna come eat with us at the table?
TOM: I'm fine here.
JEREMY (*To Faye*): Any calls?
FAYE: No, sorry.

(*Ken brings Tom a plate of meatloaf.*)

KEN: How's the storm looking?

TOM: Bad. Bad, bad, bad.

KEN: I have potatoes too, I'll get them.

(Ken exits, Etta enters.)

ETTA: What is it?

TOM: Meatloaf.

ETTA: Ech. Are there potatoes?

FAYE: Ken's getting some.

(Ginny reenters with a pitcher of water.)

Here I can get that—

(Ginny ignores Faye, brushes past her, puts the pitcher of water on the table. Throughout the following, no one pays any attention to anything Tom says.)

I can get / the cups—

GINNY: I'm fine.

(Ginny exits down the hall again.)

JEREMY: What's wrong?

FAYE: Nothing, it's fine—

JEREMY: Seriously is this about the stupid dining hall? If I leave the heat on in the entire building / then the—

FAYE *(A little too severe)*: *Oh for Christ's sake, Jeremy*—

JEREMY: / *Sorry*, sorry—

ETTA: You know what? Why don't we finish that bottle of port, why don't we have that with dinner.

(Etta gets up, heading toward the bottle of port.)

299

TOM: I'd like some.

ETTA: It's not very good, but—

(Ken almost runs into Etta as he returns with the potatoes.)

/ Eh eh eh—

KEN: Sorry, sorry—

(Etta exits. Ken heads to the table with the potatoes. Ginny reenters with cups, sits at the table.)

We didn't have a lot of butter, I hope they taste okay.

FAYE: / I'm sure they're fine.

GINNY *(To Jeremy)*: You talked at all with the police / about—?

JEREMY: Not for a couple hours.

GINNY: Should we call them or something?

JEREMY: I mean they'd call if they heard anything.

GINNY: God I feel so *powerless*, I can't stand it.

(Etta reenters with the bottle of port. She starts pouring people drinks.)

TOM: / This meatloaf has no salt.

KEN: Oh you know what—we need a serving spoon?

JEREMY: You know where they are?

KEN: Yeah I think so hold on—

(Ken exits.)

FAYE *(Whispering, to Ginny)*: Look I'm sorry—

GINNY *(Ignoring Faye)*: Etta, I'll have some.

ETTA: I'm sure everyone's in the mood / for a little.

FAYE: I'm fine, thank you—

JEREMY: Go ahead, have some.

FAYE: No, thanks, I can't.

TOM: / This meatloaf has no salt in it.

JEREMY: You "can't"?

FAYE: I mean I'm fine.

JEREMY: If you're in recovery or something maybe we shouldn't—

FAYE: / No, I'm not—

GINNY: She just doesn't want the wine, Jeremy, leave it alone.

(Ken reenters with a serving spoon, puts it in the potatoes.)

KEN: / Okay! Are we all good?

TOM: It's because she's pregnant.

FAYE: I think so, Etta you want some water?

ETTA: No, thank you, I'm fine.

(Everyone is seated, about to eat.)

KEN: Maybe we should say a prayer. *(Pause)* I mean for Gerald. Maybe it would be nice to say a prayer for Gerald?

(Pause. Everyone looks at Etta.)

ETTA: Yes, I—. I suppose that would be nice, I think that's very appropriate.

(Ken looks at Jeremy. Pause.)

JEREMY: What?

KEN: Would you like to—?

JEREMY: Me? Oh—I mean I'm not—. I'm probably not the one to do this, I'm really not religious. I've never like—prayed before.

GINNY: You've never *prayed*? Everybody's *prayed*.

JEREMY: My parents thought organized religion was evil, I mean they took me to chanting circles a couple times but they never really, like—

ETTA: Yes I would like Jeremy to do it.

(Pause. Everyone awkwardly lowers their heads.)

JEREMY: Um. So . . . I would—*we* would just like to ask you to return Gerald to us. Please give him back to us, please find it—in your wisdom?—to deliver him. To us. *(Pause)* Please keep him safe, and—nourish him?—with food, and with—drink. *(Pause)* And please God, help us. *(Pause)* Please help us. Please God help me.

(People open their eyes, looking at Jeremy, who continues.)

(Losing it a little) Please God help me. Please just—. *Please help me. (Pause, regaining himself)* And thank you for the—. For the food. *(Pause)* Amen.

(Everyone starts to eat.)

KEN *(To Jeremy)*: Did that feel good?
JEREMY: It was—fine.
KEN: You know God is always there if you need help, he's / the—
FAYE *(Referring to the meatloaf)*: Oh Ken there's no salt in this.
KEN: What?
FAYE: I think you forgot the salt.
KEN: Really?

(Ken tastes the meatloaf.)

JEREMY: Yeah it's like dog food, it tastes like dog food.
KEN: I'm so sorry—
ETTA: It has a nice flavor, it just needs some salt—
KEN: I'll go get it, I'm so sorry—

(Ken exits to the kitchen.)

ETTA: It's still better than Grace's cooking, I'll say that.
FAYE: Oh she wasn't that bad. She made those shrimp thingies?
ETTA: I know you liked her, but I / swear—
GINNY: So I have some good news for everyone.

(Pause.)

JEREMY: Oh yeah?
GINNY: I know it's a strange time to bring it up, but I guess we could all use some good news right about now, right?
FAYE: Ginny, what / are you doing?
GINNY: So for a while now, Matt and I have been talking more and more about becoming parents, but it's complicated because I'm actually not able to have a baby of my own. But this past year we both realized that we really want a kid, so we decided to find a surrogate.
FAYE: / Ginny—
GINNY: And it's Faye. Faye's going to have our baby.

(Pause.)

JEREMY: Oh wow—
GINNY: And she's in her second trimester, so we're going to start telling people. *(To Faye)* Yeah?

(Pause.)

FAYE: Yeah.
JEREMY: Well that's—. I mean, congrats! That's really great.
GINNY: Thanks. I know, weird timing, but. Just thought it would be nice to share some good news.

(Faye looks at Ginny. Pause. Ken reenters.)

303

KEN: Sorry guys, I only found one shaker and it's empty? Do we have any more. *(No response)* Guys?

FAYE: Yeah, I can show you.

(Faye exits with Ken. Awkward pause at the table.)

ETTA: Well. Congratulations.

GINNY: Thank you.

ETTA: Second trimester, well. Is it a boy or a girl?

(Pause.)

GINNY: We, uh. We don't know.

ETTA: You want to be surprised?

GINNY: I guess so, I mean Matt and I— . . . *(Pause)* I guess we just didn't really talk about it.

(Pause.)

ETTA: Boys are easier. Which do you want?

(Pause.)

GINNY: I don't know.

ETTA: Boys are easier. Hope for a boy.

(Pause. The sliding doors open, linger for a moment, then close. Another pause.)

JEREMY: Are you giving Faye money for it?

(Pause.)

GINNY: We're—. Yes, she gets a—fee, that's how it's usually done.

JEREMY: Oh. That's—.

(Pause. Jeremy drums his fingers on the card table. Silence.)

How much you paying her?

(Etta and Ginny don't look at him. Another silence.)

Geez I can't like say *anything.*

(Faye and Ken reenter with salt. Ken holds a bottle of sauce.)

KEN: I also found some barbeque sauce if anyone wants to—

(Ken stops, looking out the window.)

GINNY: What? *(Pause)* Ken?

(Ken moves to the window, looking out.)

What?

KEN: I just—. *(Pause)* I thought I saw something. Like a—person. I thought I saw a person out there.

FAYE: Are you sure?

KEN: Well no, but I—. I really think I just saw someone out there—

(Jeremy and Ginny go to the window, looking.)

(Pointing) Right there, see? *(Pause)* I swear I saw someone standing there, I saw—I thought I saw someone standing and then fall down.

JEREMY: Where?

KEN: At the end of the field, like—like past the farm access road, near the base of the mountain.

(Ken goes behind the reception desk, taking his coat.)

I'm gonna go see, I just want to make sure it's not him.

305

(Tom looks at Etta.)

ETTA: Now Ken, I really—. I really don't think he's out there—

KEN: Well I'm probably wrong but I just want to check—

GINNY: That's gotta be half a mile away, you gonna be okay walking in this? The police said we shouldn't be / outside in this—

KEN: I'll be careful, I just want to make sure that it isn't—

(Ken goes to the sliding doors and stands in front of them. They don't open.)

TOM: / Etta?

KEN: How do I? How do I make it open?

(Ken tries to pull the door open.)

Is it locked or something?

JEREMY: Oh, I don't know, Trent always took care of this stuff, I don't know / how to work it—

KEN: Look if that's him he needs us *now*, he might be freezing to death—

JEREMY: Well I don't know!

(Ken kicks the door.)

TOM: *Etta.*

KEN: What about the back door?

GINNY: That's been frozen shut for hours—

KEN: Should I just / break it open or something?

GINNY: All right, there's a crowbar in in the utility closet—

JEREMY: / You guys can't pry open the door, you'll break it!

KEN: Where?

GINNY: The closet toward the back of the / hallway—

ETTA: NO, PLEASE JUST— . . .

(Pause. Everyone stops. Etta is shaking, visibly upset.)

He's *not out there*, I promise you, he's— . . .

(Pause.)

FAYE: Etta, what? *(Pause)* What is it?

(Silence. Finally, Tom stands up, facing everyone.)

TOM: You can all calm down. *(Pause)* Gerald's in his bedroom. *(Pause)* He's in his bedroom.

(Black.)

Act Two

___

Scene One

A short time later.

    Jeremy, Ken, Faye, Ginny, and Tom all stand or sit near Etta, who sits nervously in a chair.

    The storm has gotten worse. The wind outside howls every so often. Snow is now up to the base of the windows.

    A long, tense silence.

FAYE: So you— . . . Last night, you just—decided?

(Silence. Jeremy buries his face in his hands.)

JEREMY: Oh my God. Oh, my God.

(Pause.)

ETTA: You all have to understand for the last twelve years—
twelve years—his mind has just—evaporated. Daily rou-
tines, memories, faces, eventually whole sections of his
life, friends and family and—. And now, with the prospect
of moving him into a new facility, a new confusing land-
scape, more unfamiliar faces—

GINNY: If you were worried about moving, you could have
talked to us / about—

ETTA: There's nothing you could have done, this is what I'm
saying, there's nothing anyone could have done.

JEREMY: / Oh my God.

GINNY: We could have worked this out, we could have *talked
about this*—

ETTA: And what would you have told me? "Hang in there," "we
all love Gerald," "stick by the people you love," you'd just
throw these—*slogans* at me like I was looking for a morale
booster or / something—

FAYE: *Okay*, guys, just—. . .

*(Another silence. The sliding doors open, linger for a moment,
then close.)*

GINNY: Did Tom—did he *help* you do this, / or—?

ETTA: *No*, of course not, I—. I just didn't know what to do after
it was over, I needed to talk with someone, figure out what
to do—and we decided that we would at least just wait
until morning, that I would tell you all that he had died
in his sleep, but in the middle of the night I realized that
they might be able to tell, that if they did an autopsy or
something they might realize that / I—

FAYE: But why didn't you just *tell* us? You let us spend all day
thinking that he had wandered off / outside—

ETTA: Now this is the thing, I *never* told you that he wandered
off, you just saw me in the morning and when I told you

I didn't know where he was, you— . . . I mean he had done this so many times before, wandered outside, you all just assumed he'd done it again and I— . . . Look, I know that I should have told you right then but I just had this moment of *panic*, I didn't know what to do, how to tell you what I had done—

GINNY: But why last night? He's been like this for years, what happened last night?

(Pause.)

ETTA: I'm not proud of keeping this from you all as long as I did, but before I could figure out how to handle this you were all convinced he had gone outside, and I know I should have said something hours ago, but / I just—

KEN: How did you do it?

(Pause. Etta looks away.)

TOM: Lock on the medication locker has been broken for weeks, you all know that. *(Pause)* He just—drifted off. It was very peaceful.

(Silence. Everyone breathes.)

GINNY: Jeremy how long have I been telling you about that stupid medication / locker—

JEREMY: So this is *my* fault?! *You're* responsible for medication on the night / shifts—

GINNY: Well I'm not responsible for the / fucking *locks* on the—

FAYE: / Okay, guys—

JEREMY: *And* you're the one who searched the patient wing this morning, you didn't think to check his *bedroom*?

GINNY: Why the hell would I check his bedroom?! Etta said he was gone, you think I'm / gonna barge into their bedroom and—

FAYE: *Okay guys enough, just—* . . . Just stop.

(Pause. Tom moves to the card table. He sits down, serves himself a slice of meatloaf, and pours some salt on it.)

Etta, you realize— . . . You know this is, this is something you could get in serious trouble for—

ETTA: Why do you think I waited this long to say anything? Of course I / know that—

JEREMY: Okay, okay, everybody just—. *(Pause)* I need to think. *(Pause) Fuck.*

GINNY: Etta, have you— . . . Have you told Dave and Benny?

ETTA: What?

GINNY: Dave and Benny. Did you tell them that you—did this?

ETTA: Of course I didn't, they'd never forgive me, they'd never . . .

(Pause. Ginny looks at everyone.)

GINNY: So—we're the only ones who know about this.

(Pause.)

JEREMY: Wait, *yeah*—

FAYE: What do you mean?

GINNY: I'm just saying there's a way to handle this, maybe, without making a big / deal about—

JEREMY: *Yeah, we can*—we can tell them that we finally found Gerald in an empty room, that he hadn't gone outside after all, and we / just—

ETTA: I'm sorry, I can't—. Excuse me. *(Pause)* I'm so sorry everyone.

312

(Etta, overcome, makes her way to her room. Faye looks at Ginny and Jeremy.)

FAYE: Nice, guys.

GINNY: We didn't / mean to—

JEREMY: Look, sorry, I just mean—I doubt they're gonna do some extensive autopsy or anything, I mean it's not like we have a fancy coroner, Clive is just some—guy, I think he's an accountant or something, he's not / like—

FAYE: This is crazy, we can't just pretend / that he—

JEREMY: Okay fine, we call the police and tell them—what? That one of our residents decided to *murder* her husband?

FAYE: No, because that's not what happened—

GINNY: With everything that's happened here, I just don't see why we can't make this—simple. I know it's weird, but would it really change anything?

JEREMY: *Exactly*, Gerald's—gone, he's gone, and nothing we say or don't say is going to change that, and I for one don't want to get involved in some messy legal whatever, and I certainly don't want to see Etta get in trouble for God's sake. I mean really, what's the difference?

KEN: But we can't—, I mean we— . . .

(Pause. Faye, Jeremy, and Ginny look at Ken.)

Look I know I'm new here, I know that I don't have the experience or whatever, but—. I don't know if I can just *pretend* that I don't know what really happened.

(Pause.)

JEREMY: Ken, Gerald was ninety years old—

TOM: Ninety-one.

JEREMY: Ninety-one years old, his own wife says that there was barely any of him left, this isn't some cold-blooded—

313

KEN: I know, but it's not— . . . I mean he was alive, he looked at me, we *met* each / other and he—

(The sliding doors open.)

GINNY: Ken, we've all been dealing with Gerald for a very long time, / he really wasn't—
KEN: *I know*, but he's not— . . .

(The sliding doors close.)

All I'm saying is that, it—*he* mattered, *his death* matters, and / we can't just pretend that—
GINNY: / Of course it does—
JEREMY: / Oh for Christ's sake—
KEN: *I just*—. I just don't know if I can lie about it.

(Ken looks at Faye. Pause.)

FAYE: I don't— . . . *(Pause)* God, I don't know. I don't know what to do.
JEREMY: / *Seriously?*
GINNY: Guys—Gerald started going downhill *twelve years ago*, and Etta's right, it would have been awful for him to move into Good Sam's this / late in the game—
JEREMY: / Exactly—
FAYE: But is that reason enough to just—get *rid* of him?
JEREMY: / She wasn't "getting rid" of—
KEN: I mean look, I know I don't know anything about this, and I know that he's been like this for a while, but I can't just act like what she did last night / was okay—
GINNY: But it's done! It's already done, we can't change that, what happened last night doesn't matter, / what we're talking about is—
FAYE: / Doesn't "matter"?

JEREMY: / Okay—

GINNY: I don't mean that, I just mean—

(The sliding doors open.)

JEREMY: Okay, I am not debating this with some *kid* that I hired
to be our cook for three days—

FAYE: Okay, / okay—

(The sliding doors close.)

JEREMY: No, I'm serious, I am the boss here, and I say that we
are going to tell the police that we found Gerald / in the—

KEN: Look you can't *make* me say something that's not true—

JEREMY: / Well then just don't say anything, how about—?!

FAYE: / Jeremy, you're not helping—

GINNY: Ken, we're not asking you to lie—

TOM: OKAY.

(Everyone falls silent. They look at Tom. Pause.)

Okay. *(Pause)* Five or six years ago, for some reason
you all got the idea that I was deaf. I went along with it
because, frankly, not being expected to engage with you
people suited me just fine. But, unfortunately, my hearing
is as good as it's ever been, and I've been listening to all
of you go on and on, and I know you'd like to think that
I don't have an opinion but I do. And here it is: shut up.
(Pause) Shut your mouths. *(Pause)* You're all so obsessed
with this idiotic *debate*, with the moral whatevers of your
own tiny little universes, but you know what actually matters? There's a broken woman who just lost her husband,
and she needs your help. Therefore: stop making this
about yourselves. Shut up.

(Tom makes his way out of the room, taking his plate of meatloaf with him.

The doors open, linger for a moment, then close. Pause.)

GINNY: All right, let's—. Let's at least deal with this body that we have down the hall?

(Pause.)

JEREMY: Okay.

GINNY: Nineteen is cleared out, right?

JEREMY: Yeah.

GINNY: Okay, we can put him in there, I'll crack the windows so the room is cold, we don't want him to start—. *(Pause)* You can go get him?

JEREMY: Yeah, we'll—. Ken, help me get him, okay?

KEN: Oh, I—. *(Pause)* I don't really do so well around dead bodies? I don't / know if—

FAYE: Okay, Jeremy, I can help you, just—

KEN: No, no, I—. *(Pause)* I'll do it.

FAYE: You sure?

KEN: Yeah. *(Pause)* Sorry.

(Everyone starts to make their way out of the room. Ken stops.)

Look, I'm sorry for—like, lecturing you guys or whatever. I just wanna make sure that—. I want to make sure we feel okay about this. *(Pause)* I'm going to pray about it, okay? *(Pause)* Do me a favor, just—pray about it.

Scene Two

Later that night.

Tom drinks coffee and watches the television, which plays a late-night program at a very low level.

Etta enters holding a notepad. She looks at Tom.

TOM: You doing okay?

ETTA: Yeah, I just—. I can't sleep, I tried for hours. I've been up trying to be productive, I thought I'd start on his obituary. I've barely written anything, I don't know what—. *(Pause)* You can't sleep either?

TOM: I worked a night shift for forty-two years. I sleep when my body needs sleep.

(Etta sits down.)

ETTA: What were they all saying about me?

TOM: People say what people say, Etta. Doesn't matter.

ETTA: Do they think I'm crazy?

TOM: I don't know.

ETTA: Do they think I'm a murderer?

(The television suddenly turns to static.)

TOM: Damn.

(Tom grabs the remote, changes the channel a few times. It's all static.)

Well that's that, isn't it?

(Tom turns off the television.)

317

When I first got here, I used to do these jigsaw puzzles, you remember that? There was this television here but I was determined to do something more constructive, something less passive. So I'd do these damn jigsaw puzzles all the time, filled most of my room with them. Spent years doing it. Eventually I look around my room and realize I've spent years reconstructing photographs and paintings that a company had disassembled for me. Never felt more like a rat in a cage in my entire life. *(Pause)* Turning on the television seemed strangely like a more productive activity.

(Tom gets up, takes his coffee cup to a trash can, and empties it into the can.)

TOM: Gerald was a music teacher, that's right?
ETTA: Professor.
TOM: Professor, sure. Music professor. I was a night watchman at a grain tower complex outside Bovill for most my life. Never understood why it even needed a watchman, as if someone is going to come and steal two tons of lentils or whathaveyou in the middle of the night.

(Tom goes to a water cooler, fills his coffee cup with water.)

Point is, my life has been fairly mechanical and simple, and I'm not complaining, I've had a full life. Two beautiful daughters, many wonderful years with Dorothy before the leukemia. But for Gerald, a music professor, I suppose that was more the life of the mind. So when you lose the mind, I suppose there's not much life left? *(Pause)* Anyway, I'm no philosopher.

(Faye enters and starts cleaning up the table. Etta looks at Faye. Pause.)

ETTA: I can't imagine what you must be thinking of me right now.

FAYE: Etta, we—. Look we were all surprised, but it's not like we all don't—understand where this is coming from. I think the important thing for us is just to make sure that you're going to be okay.

ETTA: What did you—? What did you end up doing with him?

FAYE: Ken and Jeremy took him to an empty room.

(Pause.)

ETTA: What room?

(Pause.)

FAYE: Do you really want to—?

ETTA: I won't go stare at him or anything, I just—. I would like to know what room he's in.

(Pause.)

FAYE: Nineteen, I think.

ETTA: Marcy's old room?

FAYE: Yeah.

ETTA: Marcy's old room. All right.

(Silence.)

TOM: Television's out now, phones might follow soon. Last I heard the snow'll let up in the morning, so.

(Tom makes his way down the hall.)

Goodnight, then.

(Tom exits. Silence.)

FAYE *(Referring to Etta's notebook)*: What's that?

ETTA: Oh, I figured I should write his obituary, start to write it anyway. I've barely written anything.

FAYE: You want some help?

ETTA: Well, I—

FAYE: Seriously, I can't sleep either, I don't mind.

(Short pause.)

ETTA: Okay.

(Etta sits down, hands Faye the notepad. Faye sits as well.)

FAYE *(Reading)*: "Dr. Gerald Alan Erickson, ninety-one. Born May twenty-sixth, 1922. Professor and father." *(Pause)* That's all you have?

ETTA: I just don't know what I'm supposed to, you know. I don't know how to do this, I just don't care about these things—

FAYE: Well it's okay, why don't—? Just start chronologically, where was he born?

ETTA: Oh he wouldn't want to bother with that, he hated where he came from. A farm outside some tiny little town in Wyoming, he never talked about it.

FAYE: Okay, you—. Maybe—his parents' names?

ETTA: He never got along so well with them, he'd want that out.

(Pause.)

FAYE: Okay, then—you could list where he got his degrees?

ETTA: Well that's sort of dry, isn't it?

FAYE: It was important to him though, right?

ETTA: Absolutely not, he believed college was a big scam. Used to say that going to a library was a better education than any university could give you.

320

FAYE: He taught at a university and he felt that way?

ETTA: Gerald was a—unique animal, we'll say that. He didn't want to have some normal job, he wanted to spend his days doing the only thing that was important to him, so he found a way to do it. Doesn't mean he had faith in it. He was a terrible teacher, everyone said it. Brilliant man, terrible teacher.

FAYE: Okay, there's—. I mean it's sort of standard, but you could say something like, "devoted father to two / boys—"

ETTA: Eh.

(Pause.)

FAYE: What?

ETTA: I mean, "devoted"? I don't—. I mean I suppose you could put that in.

(Pause.)

FAYE: He wasn't—?

ETTA: I mean he was fine, he was a fine father, he paid the bills, he showed them affection when they needed it, but "devoted"? He was a normal father.

FAYE: So brilliant man, terrible teacher, normal father. That's what we have so far.

ETTA: Well see this is my point, this is why I'm having trouble! He's not—an easy man to encapsulate, I'll say that much. Two paragraphs to sum him up sort of contradict his entire personality, he was the antithesis of brevity.

(Pause.)

FAYE: You can always tell people where they could send flowers or cards. Do you know what your unit number at Good Sam's is going to be? You could include that?

ETTA: Oh, well, I don't——. I'm not so sure about that now.

(Pause.)

FAYE: What do you mean?

ETTA: I mean they had us all set up for this two-person unit, so I'm not even sure if they'll have a place for me—

FAYE: I'm sure they'll be able to accommodate you—

ETTA: And to be honest I'm not even sure I want to go over there, you know that terrible Trisha woman who worked here a few years ago? I heard she got hired over there, and I / don't—

FAYE: Well so what—? What are you going to do?

ETTA: Well, for the last fifty-odd years of my life I haven't had much of a say in where I was going to live, or how I was going to——. *(Pause)* There's this little town in Iowa, this little town called Tiffin where I was born, that was full of these Mennonites. We lived in this little one-story house that was near the only grocery store in town, and there was nothing but sprawling farmland in every direction, and the winters were so bitter and the summers were so wonderful. *(Pause)* I haven't been there since 1978, you believe that? Gerald didn't much care for family history, he never really understood why I had this urge to go back. Maybe there's some little house like the one I grew up in, someplace close I can rent. Buy a little car, garden during the spring and summer.

(Pause.)

FAYE: You—. You're going to move to Iowa?

ETTA: I mean it sounds ridiculous, I know it sounds ridiculous, but—. I mean I don't know what else is keeping me here.

(Pause. Faye puts down the notebook, stands up, paces a bit.)

What?

(Pause.)

FAYE: You're moving to Iowa?

ETTA: Well it was just a *thought*, I don't know, I—

FAYE: You think you're going to be able to live by yourself, you won't need anyone around to—

ETTA: Well Faye honestly you and I both know that the reason I'm living in this place doesn't have anything to do with *me*, it was all about—.

(Silence. Faye looks away.)

All right now, I know you're thinking something, just come out and / say it—

FAYE: So you're free now.

(Pause.)

ETTA: I'm "free"?

FAYE: That's sort of how it sounds, sounds like you've freed yourself from something, shook off the dead weight, or—. *(Pause)* I don't mean that, I didn't mean it like that. But it does almost seem like you're—*happy* about this.

(Pause. Etta stands up.)

ETTA: I'm going to my room.

FAYE: No, wait—

ETTA: I don't know what it is you're / trying to do—

FAYE: Look I just—. If you're going to have us all—*cover* for you like this, I need to know that—. I need to know that you did this for Gerald, that you were helping him, that you weren't just—

ETTA: You're a girl. You're a silly girl. *(Pause)* You have no idea what that man was / going through—

FAYE: You've said that before, and I hear you. We all hear you, I can imagine how hard it was for him, and for you—

ETTA: No, actually, you *couldn't* imagine it, you couldn't *begin* to imagine it, I / promise you—

FAYE: Okay, you know what? You don't have a monopoly on grief! And you certainly don't seem too broken up about losing him, so I don't / know why—

ETTA: Do you think last night was *easy* for me?! You of all people should understand this, the way your father suffered those last few years, the / way he—

FAYE: He *did* suffer, but you know what I did?! I *fought* with him, we both fought as hard as we could, because *that's what you do.*

(Pause. Etta looks at Faye.)

ETTA: I see, now we're getting to it. That's what this is all about?

FAYE: Okay, never mind, it doesn't even / matter now—

ETTA: What I did last night—you think I made that decision *lightly?*

FAYE: No, what I'm saying is maybe that decision was wrong, maybe it was *vulgar.* I fought with my dad as hard as I could because those last few years were *worth it*, they / were—

ETTA *(Losing herself a bit)*: Were they? I saw what happened to him later on, throwing up every night, his leg amputated. Did your father think it was worth all that suffering, or was that just you?

(Pause. Faye looks at her. Etta breathes, calming down.)

I'm sorry.

(Faye begins to head out of the room.)

FAYE: All right, I think we're done with the fucking heart-to-
   heart—
ETTA: *Stop.*

(Faye stops, not looking at Etta.)

Faye, you— . . . *(Pause)* Obviously there's no way I can
make you understand what happened last night, but you
must realize—you have no idea what this has been like for
Gerald, *or* for me. You're at the beginning of your entire
life, you're having a baby, you / don't—
FAYE: *It's not even my baby. (Pause)* And trust me I'm not so
   happy about having my whole life in front of me because
   right now it's looking pretty *long and lonely*, and I— . . .
   (Pause) Shit.

(Silence.)

ETTA: Keep going.

(Pause. Faye looks at her.)

FAYE: I mean at least when he was still here, I had some reason to wake up in the morning, but when he died I looked
   around and realized—I never even *wanted* to be a CNA,
   I never wanted a job like this, now I'm just *constantly* sur-
   rounded by people who are sick and dying, and— . . .

325

(Pause. Faye becomes more and more upset.)

ETTA: And?

FAYE: And I have no idea what to do now, and I'm so terrified that I'm just having this baby to try to make myself feel better, for *completely* selfish reasons, and I don't think that's fair to Ginny, *or* this kid, and— . . .

(Pause.)

ETTA: And?

FAYE: *And, I*— . . . I am *so fucking terrified* of the rest of my life. I think about the rest of my life, and I'm *terrified.*

(Silence. Faye's entire body is tense.)

ETTA: Okay. *(Pause)* Breathe, Faye.

(Faye takes in a breath, relaxing. Etta goes to her.)

Better?

(Pause.)

FAYE: I—

(Suddenly the power goes out and the stage goes completely dark. A loud beeping is heard.)

ETTA: What's—?

FAYE: Uh—okay, just stay there—

ETTA: What's that noise, why is it doing that?

FAYE: I don't know, just—just stay there until I can find a flashlight—

(Faye tries to get to the front desk, but she trips and nearly falls to the floor.)

Shit—

ETTA: What is it?

FAYE: It's fine, I just—. I rolled my ankle—

(Etta tries to get to Faye.)

ETTA: Well here, let me—

FAYE: *No*, Mrs. Erickson, please stay there—

(Ken enters quickly.)

KEN: Guys what's going on?! What do we do?!

FAYE: We just lost power, calm down, it's / not a big—

KEN *(Growing more frantic)*: Is it going to come back on? When is it gonna come back on?

(Jeremy enters.)

JEREMY: What the hell is / that beeping?!

FAYE: I don't know, I—. Jeremy, can you help me, I think I sprained my ankle or something—

KEN: Are you okay?!

JEREMY: Here, just a second—

(Jeremy makes his way to the front desk and finds a flashlight. Tom and Ginny enter, Ginny using the flashlight on her cell phone.)

GINNY: Everyone okay?

JEREMY: Yeah, just—

(Ginny sees Faye.)

327

GINNY: What?

FAYE: Nothing, I just hurt my / ankle it's not—

JEREMY: Why isn't the emergency generator on? God is *everything* broken here?!

(Ginny goes to Faye, helping her.)

KEN: Guys I'm really uncomfortable, this is really difficult for me—

(Tom makes his way to the source of the beeping, unplugs a small box from an outlet. The beeping stops.)

ETTA: Oh, thank God.

TOM: We have candles?

JEREMY: Yeah, in the kitchen closet. Ken, can you go get those?

GINNY *(To Faye)*: / Can you put any weight on it?

KEN: Uh, I don't—. I don't know if I can—

FAYE *(To Ginny)*: / I think so, I think it's fine—

JEREMY: *Jesus Christ*, fine I'll get them!

(Jeremy exits to the kitchen. Tom helps Etta to a seat. They both sit down.)

GINNY *(To Faye)*: Here, let's get it elevated—

(Ginny helps Faye to a seat, brings another chair to elevate her ankle. Ken grows more and more frantic.)

KEN: Guys, I don't—. This is bad, this is really bad.

FAYE: Ken, don't worry about it, we have candles and / plenty of water—

GINNY: Don't we have that old portable generator in the basement?

ETTA: Oh we won't need that, this likely won't last more than the night—

KEN: GUYS I JUST—. *(Pause)* Sorry but I—. I can't really handle the dark.

GINNY: You don't need to be scared, just stay in here with us—

KEN: NO I MEAN I CAN'T—. I don't know if I can be here, seriously, I really hate the dark, and especially in a place like this, and there's a body down the hall—

(Jeremy reenters with candles and some lighters. He lights one, puts it toward the center of the room.)

JEREMY: Where's that portable generator? Don't we have a portable generator?

GINNY: In the basement I think.

FAYE: We don't have gas though, do we?

JEREMY: We can check, there might be some down there. Ken, c'mon.

KEN: What?!

JEREMY: Come with me to the basement, we'll see if the portable generator is down there—

ETTA: Now honestly I think / we can survive one night without power, don't you think?

KEN: No, I can't, I really don't think I can go down there right now, I don't think I can—

JEREMY: / Okay I got the stupid candles, and I am *not* carrying up that generator all by myself—

FAYE *(To Etta)*: What about heat? We might need to plug / in some space heaters, or—

ETTA *(To Faye)*: We have blankets, we'll be okay with—

KEN *(Exploding)*: NO I CAN'T DO THIS, I CAN'T BE HERE RIGHT NOW, I CAN'T—. *(Short pause)* GUYS I'M SORRY I DIDN'T TELL YOU THIS BEFORE BUT I HAVE THESE EMOTIONAL PROBLEMS—

(Ken starts to hyperventilate. He goes down to the floor, putting his head in between his knees. Ginny goes to the floor, putting a hand on Ken.)

GINNY: Okay, shh—

(Ken flinches, Ginny takes her hand away.)

FAYE *(To Ken)*: What's gonna make you feel better? Can you tell me what'll help?

(Faye goes to Ken.)

KEN: I DON'T KNOW THAT'S THE PROBLEM—
FAYE: Okay, okay you—. Just—breathe with me, okay? Just breathe—

(Faye breathes slowly in and out; it's not helping Ken.)

Ken, can you just calm down a little and breathe?

(Ken continues to hyperventilate. Ginny goes to him.)

GINNY: We could say a prayer? You like that, right? Would that help?

(Pause.)

KEN: I DON'T KNOW MAYBE—?
FAYE: Okay yeah, that's good. Let's try praying. Okay?

(Pause. Ginny thinks.)

GINNY: Dear Lord. We ask you now, that you could—. That you could come into our hearts, and comfort us. That you could—bring us peace.

FAYE: We ask that you—deliver us from this, that you turn the power back on, and make this storm go away.

(Ken's breathing starts to become a little more normal.)

And we ask that you—. *(Pause)* We ask for your help. All of us, we ask for your help. We're—sort of small, insignificant people with small and insignificant lives and we're asking you for some help with that because we don't really know what to do here. We don't really know what to— . . .

(Pause. Ginny and Faye look at one another. Ken's breathing calms slightly.)

GINNY: And we ask that you'll give us—confidence, that you'll give us confidence that we will all—know what's right. That you'll help us to do right.

(Pause.)

FAYE: That you'll help us to do right. That you'll help us to do the right thing with Gerald—and with everything else.

*(Ken's breathing is now almost normal. He rocks back and forth a little.
    Silence.)*

KEN: . . . please help us . . . *(Pause)* . . . Lord, please help us . . .

(Silence. Ken's breathing finally becomes normal.)

ETTA: Amen.

Scene Three

Much later, in the middle of the night.

The wind has become slightly calmer. The lights remain off. Faye sits on the couch with her leg elevated.

Tom lies asleep on a recliner, Etta near him, asleep on a couch. Jeremy is asleep on the floor under some blankets, facing upstage. Ken is also asleep somewhere on the floor. Ginny is asleep in a chair.

Faye, unable to sleep, slowly reaches for a lighter. She lights a single candle, looks at it.

Silence.

GINNY (*Softly*): You can't sleep?

(*Pause.*)

FAYE: Nah.

(*Throughout the scene, Ginny and Faye speak in very hushed voices: a near whisper. Silences and pauses are long and still.*)

GINNY: How's the—?
FAYE: It's—fine. I'm not sure if I even sprained it. It's not that bad.

(*Pause.*)

GINNY: You took some Tylenol?
FAYE: Yeah.

(*Ken mumbles in his sleep a bit, turning over. Ginny moves onto the couch with Faye, sitting a few feet away from her. Silence.*)

GINNY: I caught Matt masturbating a couple days ago.

(Pause.)

FAYE: Oh.

GINNY: To porn, on his laptop. *(Pause)* By the end of the conversation I was the one apologizing, I have no idea how we got there.

(Silence.)

FAYE: I'm sorry—

GINNY: It's okay.

FAYE: It wasn't fair of me to unload that on you, I / didn't—

GINNY: Faye, I got mad at you because I'm not sure I'm completely confident about this baby either. I got mad because I was hoping that between the two of us you'd be the more optimistic one. *(Pause)* Matt spent almost eight thousand dollars redoing the basement so he can have a room where he can play his video games. He knows that I'm about to lose my job, he knows we have a baby coming soon, and he just dropped *eight thousand dollars* redoing the basement. I think it's mostly so he has a place where he can masturbate. He put a lock on the door a couple days ago. *(Pause)* He's probably masturbating right now. *(Pause)* Right this second.

(Etta snores a little, shifting a bit. Silence.)

He'll be a good dad though, yeah? *(Pause)* I mean a kid would like him.

(Silence.)

FAYE: I actually think he's going to be a really good dad.

333

(Pause.)

GINNY: Really?

FAYE: Yeah. Really. He's fun, and he's caring, and—. *(Pause)* And I mean having a kid could be good for him.

GINNY: Force him to grow up you mean.

FAYE: I didn't mean that—

GINNY: You did but that's fine, maybe you're right. *(Pause)* God, what an awful little hope to cling to.

(Silence. Faye looks out the window.)

FAYE: It stopped snowing.

GINNY: It did?

(Faye and Ginny both look out the window.)

FAYE: That's good.

GINNY: Yeah.

FAYE: Maybe it's slowing down.

(Silence.)

GINNY: You know when we were juniors in high school, I went with Dean and those guys to John's Alley. Did I ever tell you that?

FAYE: You went to John's Alley in *high school?*

GINNY: You know Dean, he knew everyone there, they didn't—. *(Pause)* Anyway I got very drunk very quickly, and before I knew it Dean was trying to take me back to his car, and I didn't—. *(Pause)* Your dad was driving by. He pulled over, grabbed me, dragged me into his pickup. I was so mad at him, I couldn't even—. At one point he stopped the pickup, and he looked at me and he said, "*You are a smart and decent person."* And he took me home. Never even told my folks. *(Pause)* I never thanked him for that.

(Ginny shivers a bit, pulling a blanket around herself.
Faye moves over to Ginny, putting a blanket around the two of them. They sit in silence for a moment.)

FAYE: Matt's a good guy.
GINNY: Yeah?
FAYE: And he's going to be a good father. And you're going to be a good mother.

(Pause.)

GINNY: I hope so.
FAYE: You are. *(Pause)* And this is a good thing. *(Pause)* This is only a good thing.

(Silence. Then suddenly:)

JEREMY: Guys I'm really scared about the future.

(Pause. Jeremy hasn't moved. Still facing upstage:)

I don't have a job and I don't know why I'm in Idaho.

(Silence.)

FAYE: You'll be okay, Jeremy.
JEREMY: I don't know.
GINNY: It's gonna be okay.
JEREMY: I don't know. I'm really scared. *(Pause)* I'm really scared.

(Pause.)

FAYE: Jeremy, c'mere.

(Jeremy gets up, going to Ginny and Faye. He sits in between the two of them. Faye and Ginny spread a blanket over all three of them. Silence.)

JEREMY: Do you guys think I'd be good at architecture? I've always thought I'd be good at architecture. *(Pause)* Maybe I should do architecture. *(Pause)* Or like work at Macy's.

(Pause.)

GINNY: My friend Diana works there.
JEREMY: Really?
GINNY: Yeah. She's a manager. I could call her if you want.
JEREMY: I actually think I have a really good eye for fashion. *(Pause)* Could you tell her that?
GINNY: Yeah, sure.
JEREMY: Okay. *(Pause)* Okay well—that's something. *(Pause)* That's something. That makes me feel a little better.

(The sliding doors open suddenly. Everyone wakes up with a jolt. They all look. The doors linger for a moment, then close.)

Scene Four

The following morning. Sunlight streams through the window. Power has been restored. Tom sits on the recliner watching the television.

Etta sits with Faye, holding the notebook from before.

ETTA: I mean I thought about it, and I'm sure it doesn't really exist anymore. Not the way I remember it, I mean. I imagine it's all been built up now, Walmarts and Applebees and everything else, I doubt my house is even still there.

FAYE: So you're—not going to go?

(Pause.)

ETTA: You know I'm just not sure, I think maybe packing everything up and just going out there is foolish and naive, but I think maybe it's worth a visit at least. *(Pause)* Do you think it's worth a visit?

FAYE: I think you should visit. *(Pause)* Iowa's close to Minneapolis, you know. You could be closer to Dave.

ETTA: Oh he'd love that, wouldn't he.

(Ken enters with food.)

KEN: Eggs!

FAYE: Sounds good.

KEN: I used salt!

(Ken brings a plate to Tom, exits.)

ETTA: All right. I should make some phone calls, I have to call this funeral director and let him quote me some very unreasonable prices for caskets.

FAYE: Did you ever—? Did you think more about the obituary?

ETTA: Yes. Yes, I did, I gave it some thought.

FAYE: Do you want any help with it, or—?

ETTA: No, I believe I have it, I think I'm happy with it.

FAYE: That's good. *(Pause)* Can I read it?

(Pause. Etta looks at her, relents. She hands Faye her notebook.)

(Reading) "Dr. Gerald Alan Erickson, ninety-one—"

ETTA: Oh we're reading it out loud, is that really what we're doing? *(Pause)* Fine then.

(Pause.)

FAYE *(Reading)*: "Dr. Gerald Alan Erickson, ninety-one. Born May twenty-sixth, 1922. Professor Emeritus of Arts and Sciences at the University of Idaho. Devoted father to— *(Stops reading, smiles at Etta)* "Devoted" father?
ETTA: Oh shut up, give it to me.

(Etta grabs the notebook away from Faye.)

(Reading, somewhat quickly) "Devoted father to two boys, David and Benjamin Erickson of Minneapolis and Cleveland, respectively. Dr. Erickson received his bachelor of arts from the University of Wyoming, and a PhD in musicology from Cornell University."

(Ginny enters, unseen by Etta. Tom and Ginny start to listen to Etta.)

"Specializing in postmodern sacred choral work, and most recently interested in the work of composer Arvo Pärt, Dr. Erickson had the opportunity three times in his life to meet the composer, which he considered to be some of the greatest moments of his life."

(Pause.)

"Introverted and deeply personal, Dr. Erickson remained a mystery to most people who had only short interactions with him. To some, his manner could even seem off-putting or cold. But to those closest to him, to those who knew him best, he was a deeply heartfelt man whose towering intellect was matched only by his capacity for love."

(Etta pauses, collecting herself. She takes a few breaths, then reads.)

(Simply) "Dr. Erickson is survived by his wife, Etta."

(Pause. Etta puts the notebook down.)

That's it. *(Pause)* It's okay?

(Ken enters.)

KEN: More eggs! And toast!

(Ken bring the eggs to Faye, the toast to Etta. Jeremy enters.)

JEREMY: Just got off the phone, they're on the way.
FAYE: What did you tell them?
JEREMY: All that worrying, I barely had to say anything, I just said we were mistaken, that he hadn't gone outside, that he had wandered into a room and just—. They didn't ask much.
GINNY: So they've opened up the highway?
JEREMY: Just to emergency vehicles, but they said later today they're planning on opening it up for everybody.
GINNY: Oh thank God.

(Etta heads down the hall.)

KEN: Mrs. Erickson, you don't want to eat?
ETTA: I'll be hungry in a minute, I have to call this funeral director.

FAYE: Etta, you know—. You know they're going to be here any minute, to get Gerald. *(Pause)* If you don't want to be around we understand, we just—

ETTA: Frankly I'm not certain I want to be here when they wheel him out of here. *(Pause, then to everyone:)* I don't know how to properly say thank you for something like this, but just—. Thank you.

(Etta exits down the hall. Ginny sits down with Faye, who picks at her eggs.)

KEN *(To Ginny)*: You want something to eat?

GINNY: Oh no, I think I'm okay.

KEN: Jeremy?

JEREMY: Um, sure. I guess.

KEN: Cool.

(Ken turns, starts to head toward the kitchen.)

JEREMY: Uh, Ken—?

(Ken stops, turns to Jeremy. Jeremy goes to him.)

So are you—? I mean, I didn't tell them anything, you know. I didn't tell them what actually happened.

KEN: I know.

JEREMY: Are you—okay with that?

(Pause.)

KEN: I think—. *(Pause)* I think God has a specific way of working, and sometimes I just don't have a say in it. That's what I think.

(Pause.)

JEREMY: Okay, I guess——. I guess I get that. *(Pause)* Hey, and you know, you— . . . I mean, I know you have a place to stay at the church or whatever, but like——. I mean if you ever need a place to stay, I have a futon.

KEN: Oh, wow, thank you.

JEREMY: It's super uncomfortable.

KEN: Oh.

(Awkward pause. Ken nods at him, continues toward the back.)

JEREMY: Oh, and— . . .

(Ken stops, looks at Jeremy.)

I just want you to know, I'm not like—*anti*-religion or anything.

KEN: Oh, sure.

JEREMY: I mean I'm not like——. I've just never been to——. *(Pause)* The church you go to, it's here in town?

KEN: Yeah.

JEREMY: Oh. *(Pause)* So like, what's it called?

KEN: It's called Mountain Fellowship? They're on Hillcrest, near the subdivision?

JEREMY: Oh that new church? The one that went up this year?

KEN: Yeah.

JEREMY: That's cool. I like that building.

(Pause.)

KEN: Oh.

(Silence.)

You know, you—. *(Pause)* I mean you could come sometime?

JEREMY: Oh.

KEN: I mean we're not like—. We really believe that people should come because they *want* to, we're not like knocking on doors and evangelizing all the time like some churches. But like, if you *wanted* to?

JEREMY: Yeah, maybe, I—. Maybe. *(Pause)* But listen I think evolution is totally like a *fact* and that gay people are awesome and so I wouldn't / want to—

KEN: No that's fine, it's—we're not like that. Really.

(Pause.)

JEREMY: Oh. *(Pause)* Cool.

KEN: Cool.

(Ken smiles at him.)

TOM: Coffee please?

KEN: It's brewing Mr. M., I promise. I'll be right back.

(Ken exits toward the kitchen. Jeremy joins Tom in front of the television.)

JEREMY *(To Tom)*: What's on?

TOM: Divorce court show. Show where they're in a court and people are getting divorced.

JEREMY: Nice!

(Jeremy and Tom watch the television. Silence.)

GINNY *(To Faye)*: How're you doing?

(Pause.)

FAYE: Okay. *(Pause)* Not sure. *(Pause)* You?

(Pause. Ken reenters with coffee for Tom, gives it to him.)

GINNY: Not sure either. *(Pause)* We'll see what happens, I guess.

(Ginny and Faye look at one another. Ken goes to the table, starts to clean up the dishes. Then something down the hall catches Faye's eye. She stands up.)

What?

(Faye exits down the hall.
  Ginny looks down the hall, sees something, then slowly stands as well. Ken looks down the hall, stops.
  Etta and Faye emerge, wheeling a hospital bed. Gerald is on the bed, motionless, covered in sheets.
  Jeremy sees the bed and stands up as well. Tom sees it, turns off the television, stands.
  Etta and Faye wheel the bed to the center of the stage, then stop.
  Silence.)

ETTA: I thought I, uh. *(Pause)* I decided I wanted to do it. I wanted to bring him out myself. *(Pause)* I hope that's all right.

(Pause.)

FAYE: It's fine.

(Pause.)

343

ETTA: The, uh. *(Pause)* It's not settled yet, but the service will most likely be this coming Saturday. Short's Funeral Chapel. Late morning. *(Pause)* If—any of you would like to come.

(Silence. Then outside, the sound of an approaching car, a car engine shutting off. Everyone looks toward the doors.
Etta goes to the bed, looking at Gerald.
Silence.
The sound of a car door closing.
Silence.
Then, for the first time, we hear the sound of the outer glass doors sliding open.
A slight pause.
The inner doors slide open. Just as they finish opening, the stage goes dark, except for a small pool of light surrounding Gerald and Etta.
In the background, we hear the opening of Arvo Pärt's "Für Alina."
Etta pulls the sheets down from over Gerald's head. He opens his eyes.)

You're listening to it again tonight? *(Pause)* You haven't listened to this one in years and now you're listening to it all the time. You used to tell me it was overrated, that objectively speaking it was one of Pärt's least interesting compositions. You remember?

(Etta starts tucking Gerald into bed.)

GERALD: The music, it—.
. . .
. . .
I'm not hearing it.

344

ETTA: We can't turn it up louder, it's past seven, we're not /
supposed—
GERALD: No it's there, I'm listening to it, I'm—.

. . .

. . .

I'm not hearing it.

(Pause.)

ETTA: There's a storm coming, that's what they're saying. Big
one. So I don't want you out wandering around, I want you
to stay in bed. Gerald?

(Gerald looks at her.)

Did you hear what I said?
GERALD: I—
ETTA: There's a big storm coming. So you must *stay here*. Under-
stand?
GERALD: The music, it—.

. . .

. . .

There are silences in the music.

(Pause.)

ETTA: Yes, the music has / some—
GERALD: The people without faces, the ones at the end of the
bed, the—.
They look at me through the silences in the music.

. . .

Through the whole-note rests,
each rest—
the people without faces

345

staring at me,
staring at—

. . .

. . .

. . .

I can't hear the music.

(Etta stares at him.)

ETTA: Gerald, you—. *(Pause)* You know what this is, it's Arvo
Pärt, you know this.
GERALD: I can't hear the music.

*(Etta takes his head gently in her hands, making him look
at her.)*

ETTA: *You know this. (Pause)* It's Arvo Pärt, it's "Für Alina" by
Arvo Pärt, you used to / say that—
GERALD: I can't hear it.

. . .

. . .

I can't.

*(Etta stares at him for a moment in silence, then searches
around in the sheets.)*

ETTA: All right, I think—. I think you should go to sleep, I think
we're done with the music for tonight.

*(Etta finds the remote to the stereo in the sheets, and turns
off the music.)*

You'll go to sleep and you'll feel better in the morning.
You'll feel better after a good night's rest, I promise that
you'll—

GERALD: Am I at home?

   . . .

   . . .

Am I home?

(Etta stares at him, saying nothing. He stares back at her. Finally, he gives up, looking away. He leans back in bed, staring up. Silence.)

I'm cold.

(Silence. Etta slowly lifts up the sheets and crawls into bed with him. She wraps her arms around Gerald.)

ETTA: You'll feel better in the morning, just—.

(Pause.)

Close your eyes.

(Gerald finally closes his eyes. Silence.)

See you in the future.

(Pause.)

GERALD: I don't— . . .

   . . .

I don't know what you mean.

   . . .

   . . .

   . . .

I don't know what you mean.

(Pause.)

ETTA: See you in the future.

(Etta continues to hold him.)

END OF PLAY

A Permanent Image

Production History

A Permanent Image was commissioned by Boise Contemporary Theater (Matthew Cameron Clark, Founding Artistic Director; Helene Peterson, Managing Director), where it received its world premiere on November 22, 2011. It was directed by Kip Fagan. The set design was by Etta Lilienthal, the costume design was by Jessica Pabst, the lighting design was by Raquel Davis, the sound design was by Jay Spriggs, the video design was by Andy Lawless, and the dramaturgy was by John M. Baker; the production stage manager was Kristy J. Martin. The cast was:

CAROL	Lynne McCollough
BO	Matthew Cameron Clark
ALLY	Danielle Slavick
MARTIN	Arthur Glen Hughes

SETTING

The interior of a small, ranch-style house in Viola, a small town of about seven hundred people in northern Idaho. There are some withered plants, some shelves with pictures and trinkets on them, a well-worn couch, a TV with a wood frame, a dining table, and some sad-looking Christmas decorations including a fake tree. Everything in the space—aside from the Christmas decorations and the screen of the television—has been crudely painted white: every piece of furniture, framed picture, shelf, trinket, book, magazine, the floor, the walls. The effect should be that the Christmas decorations are the only bit of color on an otherwise completely white set.

Dialogue written in *italics* is emphatic, deliberate; dialogue in ALL CAPS is impulsive, explosive.

A "/" indicates an overlap in dialogue. Whenever a "/" occurs, the following line of dialogue should begin.

Ellipses (. . .) indicate when a character is trailing off, dashes (—) indicate where a character is being cut off, either by another character or themselves.

Act One

———

Home Video

The TV flickers to life and we see a shot of Martin sitting on the living room couch. The living room appears as it did before it was painted white.

MARTIN: I'm not really sure how to do this. Carol wants me to do this.
CAROL *(Offscreen)*: We *both* want you to / do this.
MARTIN: We both—we both want this, we both do.

(Pause.)

Now you may think we're gonna apologize, or whatever. We're not gonna do that, that's pointless. Waste of tape.

(Pause.)

I guess the universe is expanding? I don't understand it completely, but it's something about how we all started out from this little thing, the big bang or whatever, and now everything in the universe is just splaying out in all these directions, and some people actually think it's getting faster—it's actually been proven, it's all / getting—

CAROL *(Offscreen)*: Martin: would you just get / to the—

MARTIN: You gonna let me talk or not?

CAROL *(Offscreen)*: I'm letting you talk! Just get to the point!

MARTIN: Anyway—a lot of people think that eventually it's all just gonna go in reverse, come crashing down. All of us, everything in the universe shoved back into this tight little ball. Eventually.

(Pause.)

I actually find that comforting. You need to know that I— that *we*—find it comforting.

(The TV turns off and the lights rise on:)

Scene One

Bo sits on the couch, center stage, looking around the space. Carol is busying herself with minutiae: arranging things, coming in and out of the kitchen, bringing Bo snacks. A small stereo plays "Angels We Have Heard On High" in the background.

CAROL: —and she was a real pill about it, believe me. But I told her, if you're going to let that stupid dog roam around the whole town all day long, then I'm going to shoot it if I see it in my garden. It's just BB's anyway, not like it would—. And I wouldn't aim for its head. Just give it a little shock, that's it. It's not cruel. Do you want a beer? *(No response)* Bo?

(Pause.)

BO: Yeah okay.

(Carol exits to the kitchen, continuing to talk.)

CAROL: So she brings me the vet bill for something like three hundred dollars, she said she had them x-ray the stupid dog and everything, and after all that there's just a few BB's inside of him, not in his organs or anything—

(Carol enters with two Budweisers, hands one to Bo, opens one for herself.)

—just right underneath the skin. So he's fine, and she wants three hundred dollars from me or something. She's such a dunce.

BO: You're having one?

CAROL: Yeah, I'm having one. What the hell is that supposed to mean?

BO: No, it's just.

CAROL: It's just a beer for God's sake, doesn't mean anything.

BO: I just didn't know you were drinking.

CAROL: I'm not drinking, it's *beer*.

BO: Mom.

CAROL: One beer, for God's sake.

BO: Mom.

CAROL: What?

(Silence. Bo stares at her.)

BO: *Mom.*

CAROL: *WHAT I said?!*
BO: *Why the hell is everything painted white?!*

(*Carol looks at him for a few moments. She's about to say something, then stops herself. She stands up, exits to the kitchen.*)

CAROL (*From the kitchen*): I bought these stupid snack trays at Costco. They're sort of stupid, I have a lot of them.

(*Carol reenters with a small snack tray of meat, cheese, and crackers. She sits on the couch with Bo.*)

I bought them because I thought we might have people over after the funeral but I don't think I want to do that so let's just eat them.
BO: I'm not—I'm not hungry.
CAROL: Well there's a lot of them. You look thin anyway.
BO: Mom.
CAROL: God would you stop saying that?
BO: Did you—when did you do all this?
CAROL: Oh I don't know. Couple days ago.
BO: Right after Dad died?
CAROL: Oh I don't know.
BO: You *don't know*?
CAROL: *GAH* would you stop it? You're really at me today.
BO: Have you been drinking?
CAROL: Again with the drinking!
BO: How much have you been drinking these past few days?
CAROL: Oh dear Lord. Yesterday I had three beers. Day before, I don't remember, I think I had a glass of wine. Again with the drinking!
BO: That's all? Seriously?
CAROL: Bo please stop.
BO: Well what—?! What do you expect me to do?!

CAROL: What?!

BO: THE HOUSE!

CAROL: IT'S MY HOME I CAN DO WHATEVER I WANT. I just needed a change, okay? And I didn't have the money to buy all new things so I just thought this was a good idea, and I still think it's a good idea and I would appreciate some support with this.

BO: Oh my God.

CAROL: Oh stop it. Have some food. *(Pawing at the snack tray)* What is this, salami? Ech. Have it.

(Bo stands up, looking around.)

BO: But I mean—the pictures? My God, is this a magazine? You painted over a magazine?

CAROL: I was out in the shed and there was all this white paint, I thought why not? Anyway, I'm bored by this conversation.

BO: Mom, do I need to call someone? Do I need to call the hospital or something?

CAROL: Bo, I haven't gone crazy. I know it seems that way but I really haven't. *(Pause)* Were your flights okay?

(Pause.)

BO: They were fine.

CAROL: I called you three days ago, I don't know why you had to wait until today to travel. Christmas Eve of all days, the airports must've been awful.

BO: I couldn't get out until today. It wasn't that bad.

CAROL: Did you go home first?

BO: No, I told you, I just flew straight here.

CAROL: You spend too much time traveling. It's not healthy, you should spend more time at home. Though New York isn't much better.

BO: You've never even been there.

CAROL: Of course I've never been there, I don't want to get *raped*.

BO: Oh my God.

CAROL: I don't know why you're spending your life to go to such god-awful places.

BO: It's my job.

CAROL: Why can't you take pictures of normal things?

BO: No one wants pictures of normal things.

CAROL: That's ridiculous. What, am I going to put a framed picture of some corpse or whatever on my mantel? Take pictures of sunsets, cats, babies with spaghetti on their heads or whatever, I'll put that on a mantel.

BO: Uh-huh.

CAROL: Anyway, Ally's coming tonight. Laura and Max are coming later for some reason, God knows why. When was the last time you saw her?

BO: I don't know. Few years.

CAROL: Funeral's tomorrow at five, at two we're doing the body watching thing.

BO: You mean the viewing?

CAROL: Whatever. I'm having him cremated.

BO: Dad always said he didn't want to be cremated.

CAROL: Oh he didn't know what he was saying. Did you bring clothes for the funeral?

BO: Yeah, I—

CAROL: We can go to the Dress for Less if you need to.

BO: No, I don't—. Okay, did you do this because you're— grieving? Are you trying to like, forget about Dad, or—

CAROL: You know just because you went to college doesn't mean you're a psychiatrist.

BO: It doesn't take a psychiatrist to know that this is fucking crazy!

CAROL: DON'T USE THAT WORD.

BO: It's just I'm not sure how to deal with this, Mom! This is obviously some cry for attention, or / some kind of—

CAROL: Oh thank you. Thank you, Doctor Freud.

BO: I don't know what to do with this!

CAROL: You don't have to do anything!

BO: Obviously I do!

CAROL: FINE THEN LOCK ME UP!

BO: Oh here we go.

CAROL: CALL THE AUTHORITIES! PADDY WAGON! CRAZY / WOMAN!

BO: Mom—

CAROL: MAN DIES AND HIS WIFE GOES INSANITY, THERE'S YOUR HEADLINE!

BO: WHAT ARE YOU TALKING ABOUT?!

CAROL: WHY ARE WE FIGHTING ALREADY?!

BO: WE'RE NOT FIGHTING!

CAROL: I JUST PAINTED EVERYTHING WHITE! I'M NOT CRAZY!

BO: FINE THEN!

CAROL: OKAY?

BO: OKAY!

CAROL: HAVE THE STUPID SNACK TRAY!

(Lights snap to black, then rise on:)

Scene Two

That night.

Bo is sitting next to a box marked "April–May 1992." His suitcase is open on the floor.

There is a small projector set up. Bo plays an old Super 8 film, projecting it onto the wall. The shot is blurry and distorted, but it's clear that it's a shot of a small child sleeping in a bed. Nothing is moving in the picture. Bo moves to the projector, stops the film.

He takes the film out of the projector, puts it back in the box, starts rooting through it a bit.

Ally appears in the doorway, wearing jeans and a parka, and holding a duffel bag. Bo doesn't notice her enter.

Ally immediately notices that the interior of the house has been completely painted white. She moves into the space slowly, setting down her duffel bag silently. Bo's back is still turned to her. She continues to survey the space for a few more moments, moving closer to Bo. Finally she is right behind him.

A brief silence, then:

ALLY: WHAT THE FUCK HAPPENED TO THE HOUSE?!

(Bo drops the box of tapes, terrified. He spins around.)

BO: *SHHH!* Jesus Christ she finally went to bed!

ALLY: *What the hell happened here?!*

BO: You didn't know about this?

ALLY: No I didn't know about this!

BO: Why the hell did it take you so long to get here? You live three hours away and you show up the night before the funeral? I flew here from *Tel Aviv* and I got here before you.

ALLY: I had shit to do, Bo, I own a business, I can't just— . . . *What happened to the house?!*

BO: I don't know, okay? It was like this when I came in here this afternoon. She said she just wanted to paint everything white, I don't know. She did it after Dad died.

ALLY: Is she drinking?

BO: Some, I don't know. She says not a lot but God knows. *(Pause)* Have you noticed anything weird about her? Has she been off in any way, does she—?

ALLY: I don't know. She's always a little off.

BO: No, but I mean—the last time you were here, was any-thing—off?

(Pause.)

ALLY: God, I don't remember.

BO: How long ago was it?

ALLY: Bo, I'm tired.

BO: *How long was it?*

(Pause.)

ALLY: Like—a couple years ago? Who knows.

BO: A *couple years ago?*

ALLY: WHEN WAS THE LAST TIME YOU WERE HERE?

BO: I LIVE THREE THOUSAND MILES AWAY! *(Catching himself) FUCK. SHHHH.*

ALLY: Bo, I have a life. I can't drive here every weekend / to—

BO: No one's asking you to come every weekend, / but—

ALLY: You think I *enjoy* coming back here for God's sake? Why are you blaming me?!

BO: I'm not—. Okay, okay, enough. We're done now, okay? We're done.

ALLY: Fine. Good.

(Pause.)

BO: Hi, Ally.

ALLY: Yeah, whatever. Hi Bo. *(Pause)* Hi.

(Pause.)

BO: Am I gonna get to meet Max?

ALLY: I don't know. He's—hard to travel with.

BO: Sure. He's what six, seven months?

ALLY: Dammit Bo, he's two. He just turned two.

BO: Oh my God, I'm sorry. He's *two*?

ALLY: Yeah. I haven't seen you in four years, Laura had him two years ago.

(Pause.)

BO: Did you get the book I sent you for him?

ALLY: Yeah, we uh. We got that.

BO: What?

ALLY: It was weird, Bo, it's like a comic book about the Holocaust?

BO: It's a *graphic novel*.

ALLY: Well we started reading it to him, and it got pretty weird pretty fast.

BO: It's not—! I didn't mean for you to give it to him *now*, I just thought he'd like it when he was older, I—. I don't know, I'm sorry. I don't know how to buy things for kids.

(Pause.)

ALLY: It's fine. It was nice.

BO: Anyway I hope I get to meet him.

(Pause.)

ALLY: He's great. He's smart, he loves people, he's—great.

BO: How's Laura?

ALLY: She's fine. Getting a little antsy staying at home all the time, but she's fine.

BO: Good, that's—that's really good.

(Ally moves to the couch, examines it, sits down.)

ALLY: You think this could just be like the way she grieves? Like maybe she just needs to get it out of her system.

BO: I guess.

ALLY: Some people do weird shit when stuff like this happens. Laura's grandpa died two years ago and she went completely nuts for a week and a half. Barely recognized her. Took up *knitting*. She snapped out of it. You wanna smoke?

(Ally opens her duffel bag, pulls out a joint.)

BO: Woah.

ALLY: You think I could come back here *sober*?

BO: I figured you might have calmed down with that since having Max.

ALLY: You kidding? We live on thirty acres. We grow our own.

BO: *Jesus*, Ally, you could go to *prison* for / that—

ALLY: Calm down, the county sheriff is Max's godfather. It's just a few little plants in our greenhouse, anyway. You want some?

(Pause. Ally lights the joint.)

BO: Yeah okay.

(Ally hands the joint to Bo. He lights it, takes a drag. They pass it back and forth.)

ALLY: Why are you looking through this stuff?

BO: I was just—. I don't know. We barely had a relationship after I left. I felt like I didn't even remember what he looked like. Did you know he was sick?

ALLY: He wasn't sick, it was just a heart attack.

(Pause.)

BO: How do you— . . . Are you—sad?

ALLY: Well, yeah, whatever. I guess.

BO: When Mom called me a few days ago, I didn't even answer, just let it go to voicemail. Later that night I actually listened to it, she just said, "Bo, Dad had a heart attack or something, he's gone. You should come home." I just—have no idea how to feel about all of this. After our childhoods, how the hell are we supposed to feel about this? Are we *supposed* to feel sad? Why should we?

ALLY: You don't need to psychoanalyze everything. You'll feel what you feel.

BO: Yeah. I don't know, I guess staring at those photos all day long doesn't help.

(Bo references an iPad sitting in his open duffel.)

ALLY: Hey are your photos on that?

(Ally grabs the iPad.)

BO: Um. Yeah, but—maybe you shouldn't—

(Ally turns on the iPad.)

ALLY: C'mon, I never get to see your stuff.

(She stops, horrified. Pause.)

Oh.

BO: Just put it down.

ALLY: Oh my God.

(Ally looks for a second, then turns off the iPad and hands it back to Bo.)

I—I really wish I wouldn't have seen that.

BO: I told you not to look.

ALLY: You—took those? You were actually there, you saw that? What magazine is gonna print that?

BO: Well, hopefully quite a few. *(Pause)* You okay?

ALLY: Yeah, it's. It's just different now that I have a kid, that stuff gets to me.

BO: Yeah, I bet.

(Carol enters from her bedroom in an old robe.)

CAROL: You know it's almost midnight.

(Ally turns around and faces Carol. They look at one another for a moment.)

ALLY: Hey, Mom.

(Pause.)

You painted the house white. It's pretty fucking crazy.

CAROL: Hi Ally. Don't swear, it's mannish. *(Pause)* It's good to see you.

(Carol sees the box of Super 8 films and the projector.)

What is that?

BO: Oh, I was just—I was looking through some of Dad's old movies—

CAROL: Where did you find that? What are you doing?

BO: Just—the laundry room closet, where they always are. What's the matter?

(Carol grabs the films, goes to the projector and aggressively throws it into the box.)

CAROL: You don't go pawing through people's things, for God's sake.

ALLY: Mom, it's not a big / deal—

CAROL: Oh it's not? You're going to tell me what a big deal is? Just leave things where they are! Don't go destroying my house!

ALLY: You already destroyed it!

BO: Mom, I'm—I'm / sorry—

CAROL: This is already going to be an unpleasant Christmas, so please just— *(Sees the joint)* Drugs! In my house! *(Grabs the joint)* What are you both idiots? You're going to get me arrested! Running a drug house! *(Pause)* Dammit, it's nice to have you both back here. GO TO BED.

(Carol exits with the box while taking a drag of the joint.)

Scene Three

Much later that same night. Ally is sitting at the dining table looking at the photographs on Bo's iPad. After a moment, Carol enters. Ally shuts the iPad.

CAROL: It's almost three in the morning, what are you doing?

ALLY: Couldn't get to sleep.

CAROL: It's too cold, is that it?

ALLY: You painted my bed white. *(Pause)* Why are you still up?

CAROL: Getting used to sleeping alone, I guess.

ALLY: That'd be hard.

CAROL: You kidding? It's great. I spent thirty-nine years sharing a full-size bed with that man.

ALLY: So why aren't you sleeping?

CAROL: I don't know. It's cold.

(Carol goes to a liquor cabinet, takes out a bottle and two glasses.)

You want some?

ALLY: You shouldn't be drinking that.

CAROL: And you shouldn't be smoking pot. I said do you want some?

(Pause.)

ALLY: Yeah, okay.

(Carol sits with Ally, pours them both some drinks.)

Mom, are you okay? You're not going crazy, are you?

CAROL: That's the last time I'm answering that question, you understand? I just wanted to do it, and I know it seems strange, but dammit let me grieve. All right? *(Referring to the iPad)* What were you looking at?

ALLY: It's—nothing. Bo's pictures.

CAROL: Let me see.

ALLY: Mom you don't wanna see these.

CAROL: Oh just give it.

(Ally relents, turns on the iPad, shows it to Carol.)

This is Bo's? Bo took this?

ALLY: Yeah.

(Carol stops, gives the iPad back to Ally.)

CAROL: I don't understand how he came out of me. These interests of his. It's morbid. Why were you looking at that?

ALLY: I just— . . . I don't know, I just felt like looking at it.

367

CAROL: Well you shouldn't. Especially now that you have one of your own, it's gonna scramble your brain. When are Laura and Max coming? The funeral's tomorrow, I told you that, right?

ALLY: Um. I'm not—I'm not sure if they're going to make it, Mom.

CAROL: Not at all? That's crazy, it's your father's funeral! Plus I haven't seen Max since right after he was born.

ALLY: It's hard to travel with a two-year-old. You know. We'll see, maybe they can make it. *(Pause)* Mom, do you— . . .

(Pause.)

CAROL: What?

ALLY: Were you with Dad when he died? You don't have to talk about it if you don't want to.

CAROL: It's okay, I can— . . . Yes, I was with him.

ALLY: So what happened? How did it happen?

CAROL: Well, he was sitting on the couch. I was sitting at the table right here. He was breathing, and then he wasn't. Then I called the police or whatever, they sent the coroner over and he balled him up in a white sheet and took him / to the—

ALLY: But I mean—what happened? What did he do?

CAROL: I told you. He was breathing, then he wasn't.

ALLY: But what did he *look* like?

CAROL: What the hell kind of question is that?

ALLY: Look, I—I don't really know how to feel about this, and I / just—

CAROL: Fine, what happened was a chorus of angels swooped in through the window and pulled him through the ceiling. It was all real magical, all rainbows and—

ALLY: OKAY, MOM.

CAROL: Why do you want to know what it looked like?

ALLY: I don't know, I just—I don't know how to feel about it, okay? I haven't seen him in so long I feel like I can't even picture it, I have no idea what to feel.

CAROL: Listen to me. He was breathing, then he wasn't. He was my husband, then he wasn't. He was your dad, then he wasn't. That's all. It's how I'll go, it's how you'll go.

(Pause.)

ALLY: This is really shitty.

CAROL: I know.

ALLY: Was I a bad daughter?

CAROL: Oh my God.

ALLY: He only got to see Max *once*. I hadn't seen him in two years.

CAROL: He didn't make the effort either, Ally. It's not all on you. You always feel so *responsible*, maybe he should have picked up the phone and called you once in a while. *(Pause)* Here, you know what? I know what will help.

ALLY: What?

(Carol exits momentarily, returning with a cardboard box. She puts it on the ground.)

What is that?

CAROL: I was supposed to do this earlier today. I'm going to have to run it to the funeral home tomorrow morning. You can help me pick it out.

(Carol starts taking men's clothing out of the box.)

ALLY: Oh, God, I don't know if I can do this.

CAROL: Take a deep breath. It'll help you out, seriously.

(Ally picks up a shirt.)

ALLY: Oh my God. I remember this one, he was still wearing this?!

CAROL: He never got new clothes. I bought them for him, he wouldn't even wear them.

(Ally holds up the shirt.)

ALLY: He was wearing this that time I broke my leg in high school. God, he drove me to the hospital and / he—

CAROL: It's too bright, I don't like it. I guess the coffin is like a brownish thing, keep that in mind. It's too expensive. What about this?

(Carol holds up a white dress shirt for Ally to see, but Ally is busy rooting through the box.)

ALLY: Oh my God!

(Ally pulls out a black cape.)

Do you remember this?! He used to put it on for Halloween every year but he wouldn't wear anything else, it was just this stupid cape and like jeans and a T-shirt or something.

CAROL: What are we gonna bury him in a cape?! Put that back.

ALLY *(Laughing)*: No one knew if he was supposed to be a vampire, or a superhero, or Phantom of the Opera—

(Carol grabs the cape out of Ally's hands, throws it back in the box.)

CAROL: You gonna help me with this or are you gonna help me with this?!

ALLY: Geez. Sorry.

CAROL: He looked like an idiot in this thing anyway. Shouldn't have made it for him. *(Rooting through the box)* What is this, *silk*?! When did that man ever wear silk?!

(Pause.)

ALLY: Mom?
CAROL: What?
ALLY: What was he wearing when he— . . . ?

(Carol looks up at her.)

CAROL: Oh for Jeessum sake.
ALLY: Could you just tell me?
CAROL: No, this is weird. You're weird.
ALLY: *Mom.*

(Carol sighs, throwing up her hands, and starts rooting through the box.)

CAROL: Dead man's clothes, *that's* crazy. All I did was paint a house white.

(Carol pulls out a red flannel shirt and a pair of jeans, throws them on the couch.)

There, that was the outfit. And we're not burying him in this, we are *not* burying him in jeans, that's disgusting.

(Ally goes to the couch and clears it of everything except the flannel shirt and the jeans. She starts to lay the shirt and the jeans out on the couch.)

ALLY: Was this where he was sitting?

371

CAROL: What is wrong with you?

ALLY: I just want to know what it looked like!

CAROL: Why?

ALLY: Because my dad died and I don't feel anything, okay?! I just want to know what it looked like so maybe I can—... I don't know, I don't know what I'm doing.

(Pause.)

CAROL: Yes, that's where he was sitting.

(Ally lays out the clothes, placing the shirt on the back of the couch and the jeans on the bottom: the position of a person sitting in the center of the couch. She finishes, stands back, and looks at it.)

ALLY: You were sitting at the table?

CAROL: Yes. What?

ALLY: Go sit down.

CAROL: What is this, a reenactment? We could call the funeral home and have them bring over the body.

ALLY: Just do it.

(Carol, petulant, sits at the table. Ally stands back, looking at the whole stage. Silence.)

He was breathing . . .

(Pause.)

Then he wasn't.

(Pause.)

He was breathing . . .

(Pause.)

Then he wasn't.

(Bo enters from the bedroom, sees Ally. Silence for a moment. Bo watches the two of them.)

CAROL: Get a glass, Bo.

(Pause. Bo considers. He exits to the kitchen, returns with a glass.)

BO: You shouldn't be drinking.
CAROL: Yeah, well.

(Carol pours him a drink, hands it to him. Ally continues to look at the clothes on the couch.)

We're figuring out what to bury him in.
BO: I thought you were having him cremated.
ALLY *(To Carol)*: You were? Dad always said he didn't want to be cremated.
CAROL: You made such a stupid fuss about it, I called the funeral home, I'm having him buried. The stupid coffin is going to cost more than his car, I told that to the idiot funeral director, he just kept saying "these are normal prices, Mrs. Nester" in this little voice, he's such a weenie. *(Takes a drink)* I don't know why your father always had to tell you kids he didn't want to be cremated, what was wrong with him?
BO: He didn't have any suits?
CAROL: What does he need a suit for?

(Bo drinks.)

373

BO: What is this?

CAROL: Oh you know, whatever Dad used to drink. There's a whole box of it in the basement.

BO: It's awful.

CAROL: It's liquor, it's not supposed to taste good.

(Ally gets her glass, joins them.)

ALLY: How was Dad doing this past year or so?

CAROL: What do you mean?

BO: Was he sick?

CAROL: No.

ALLY: Was he drinking a lot?

CAROL: Oh stop. A person dies, that's what a person does. He was fine, he was healthy. He was working fifty hours a week till the day he died.

ALLY: He was a good guy.

CAROL: Okay.

ALLY: Really—special.

CAROL: What was so special about him?

BO: Mom.

CAROL: What? I'm not disrespecting the man, I'm just—. I mean I loved him, I'm not saying I didn't love him. But "special"? Come on. He was a janitor at a hospital for forty-six years.

BO: He had some good stories though.

CAROL: Ugh, all those blood-and-guts stories, I blame him for you running off to these ridiculous countries, you know.

BO: No, I don't know, what do you mean?

CAROL: You used to pull these disgusting stories out of him, severed limbs and car accidents and whatever. You lapped it up. No wonder you're off taking pictures of all that stuff.

BO: It's really not the same thing, Mom. I'm a journalist.

CAROL: Okay Mr. Smarty.

BO: You really think I'm doing what I'm doing because Dad used to tell us gross stories about the hospital? I've won awards.

CAROL: Well then!

BO: No, I mean—. I'm not saying *I'm* all important or whatever, I'm just saying that what I do—it's journalism. If people like me weren't off in these places taking these pictures, Americans could just be complacent about everything going / on in the rest of—

ALLY: Oh boy, here's the speech.

BO: What, you're on her side?

ALLY: No, but you don't need to get up on some liberal high horse about America.

BO: I'm not on any horse, I just want to establish here that what I'm doing doesn't have anything to do with some adolescent fascination with gore.

(Pause. Ally and Carol don't say anything.)

Oh my God.

CAROL: How about we change the subject?

ALLY: Okay, so you would say that what you do is try to wake up America by showing it the "truth" or something, right?

BO: Well it's not printed on my business card that way, but yes, essentially.

ALLY: So there's no part of you that has any morbid fascination with this stuff?

BO: I don't even know what that means—

ALLY: *Do you get a thrill out of it?*

(Pause.)

BO: I mean—. I don't take *pleasure* in it, if that's what you mean. But yeah, I guess there's a thrill.

ALLY: All right, that's all I'm getting at. We're done.

BO: Okay, fine, I don't even know what— . . . *(Pause)* "Liberal high horse"?

ALLY: What?

BO: You said "liberal high horse," why did you qualify it like that?

CAROL: Back and forth, back and forth! Twenty years ago it was about who ate the Easter candy, now it's this nonsense!

ALLY: Forget it.

BO: No, really.

ALLY: You were just getting all down on Americans, it was pissing me off!

BO: But you used the word "liberal" in that way, that annoying way where you say it like you're saying a bad word or something. Like—*liberal.*

ALLY: Oh my God, can we stop?

BO: Are you getting all conservative now?

ALLY: I'm a business owner, Bo, I know for freelancers like you it's easy to believe whatever you want but for business owners like me there are certain economic realities, certain / things that—

BO: But you don't like vote Republican, do you? *(No response)* WHAT?!

CAROL: New topic! New topic!

ALLY: Why is this any of your business?

BO *(Petulant)*: No, I am not sleeping in this house unless she admits to us *right now* who she voted for in the last two presidential elections.

CAROL: New topic! Anything you want! Talk about how batshit crazy Mom painted everything white!

ALLY: I am a *business owner*, Bo, and as a business / owner—

(Carol exits.)

BO: You know, you keep saying this, but I'm not really sure what that means, that doesn't prove your point. "I'm a business owner, therefore we should all be Republicans and let the top one percent live in mansions while poor people starve."

ALLY: Yes, you're right, that's what I'm saying. I just hate poor people! Stupid dirty fucking poor people, I hate them!

CAROL *(From off)*: DON'T USE THAT WORD.

ALLY: YOU SWEAR ALL THE TIME! YOU JUST SAID "BAT-SHIT" LIKE FIVE SECONDS AGO.

CAROL *(From off)*: IT'S DIFFERENT THAN THE F-WORD.

BO: You're a lesbian! You can't be a Republican lesbian, that doesn't exist! You don't even exist!

ALLY: This has nothing to do with me being a lesbian! It's about personal responsibility!

BO: Oh personal responsibility? Even though the Republican Party is controlled completely by hyper-evangelical idiots who believe that the earth is six thousand years old and that women shouldn't be allowed to have an abortion if they were raped by their uncle—

(Carol reenters with Christmas decorations.)

CAROL: CHRISTMASTIME! IT'S CHRISTMASTIME, EVERY-BODY'S HAPPY!

(She begins to sing loudly: "Hark the herald angels sing," etc., continuing over their argument, decorating the room.)

ALLY: I employ eight people, Bo, these are people that I have taken from halfway homes, from prison release programs, because I believe that I can give them the tools to be responsible citizens, to actually contribute something to society without letting them just bounce from welfare check to welfare check—MOM.

BO: Which is great, no one is saying that isn't great! But guess who are the ones putting social programs into place?! LIBERALS! Because Republicans have jammed our prisons with so many nonviolent drug offenders—

ALLY: Oh Republicans did that? *Republicans* did that, single-handedly?

BO: If it was up to them, they'd have us in a fucking caste system, all the fat cats controlling everything and all the poor people and black people shoved into ghettos—

ALLY: OH MY GOD CAN YOU EVEN *HEAR* YOURSELF?! What does this have to do with race?!

BO: MOM.

CAROL *(Switching songs)*: *Deck the halls with boughs of holly, fa la la la la,* etc.

ALLY: There are things about the Republican Party that I don't like, Bo, I'm sure there are things about the Democratic Party that you don't like either. But the point is, I believe in *personal responsibility*.

BO: Oh, personal responsibility, personal responsibility, / blah blah blah—

CAROL: Drinks for everybody! Everybody's happy! / *Silent night, holy night,* etc.

(Carol takes the bottle and pours the remainder into their three glasses.)

ALLY: Yes, personal responsibility, because *that* is how you actually help people, not by handing them checks for nothing, not by shoving them into projects, it's by giving them the tools to help *themselves*.

BO: But Republicans aren't even about that anymore! They're just about making sure that the top one percent continues to control fifty percent of our / economy—

ALLY: You look at me and you ask me how I can be a Republican and a lesbian? The better question is, how can you be a liberal and actually claim to have real compassion for people? Better yet, how can you call yourself a liberal and have ANY CAPACITY FOR CRITICAL THOUGHT?!

BO (*About to explode, unable to compose a thought*): CRITI-CAL—?! YOU HAVE—?! YOU THINK COMPASSION IS—?!

(*Carol smashes the bottle on the floor, shattering it. The room falls silent. A dog is heard barking outside. Everyone is still, Bo and Ally both looking at Carol. The dog continues to bark.*

Finally, Carol exits, returning momentarily with a BB gun. She opens the window and shoots the gun. The dog yips, then is silent.

She closes the window. She looks at them for a few more seconds.)

CAROL: Okay? We're all—? Okay.

(*Carol exits momentarily. She returns with a dustpan and a broom. She bends down and begins to clean up the broken bottle.*)

I know you think it's fine for you to get at one another like this because now you're older and you've read the paper a few times and think you're all smart or something. But it's the same stupid argument. So just cut it out.

(*Silence.*)

BO: Sorry, Mom.

ALLY: Yeah, sorry—

CAROL: Don't be sorry, just don't be idiots.

(Carol finishes cleaning up the glass, then exits with the dustpan and brush. A moment of silence. Ally and Bo don't look at one another.)

BO: Sorry, I—. You're allowed to believe whatever you want. *(Pause)* You didn't vote for Bush *twice*, though, right?

ALLY: Oh my God, Bo, stop.

(Carol returns.)

CAROL: We all better? We get it out of our systems?

BO: Yes, / Mom.

ALLY: Yeah, I think so.

CAROL: Okay then.

(Carol goes back to the table, picks up her drink.)

You two, I swear. One time when you were eight and you were five, I had to spray you with the kitchen-sink hose just to get you to stop. You remember that?

BO AND ALLY: No.

CAROL: Well, it happened. *The kitchen-sink hose*, I'm telling you.

(Carol takes a long drink.)

ALLY: You didn't spray us with a hose, c'mon.

CAROL: Your father video'd the whole thing, I can prove it to you if you want. It's in one of those boxes in there.

(Carol takes another long drink.)

BO: Mom why don't you slow down?

CAROL: Again with the drinking.

(Carol goes to the box, starts taking out some clothes.)

This is what we're burying him in.

(She throws some khakis and a mustard-yellow dress shirt on the couch.)

Executive decision. Done.

ALLY: Mom, we can't bury him in this.

(Ally picks up the shirt.)

CAROL: Why the hell not?

ALLY: C'mon, it's gross, it's stained.

BO: We can go get him a suit tomorrow first thing, don't worry about it.

CAROL: You're going to *buy a suit*? To *bury in the ground*?

BO: It's fine.

ALLY: We'll take care of it, Mom, we can go into Moscow tomorrow and pick up / some—

CAROL: Oh well fine just leave me out then.

BO: You can come, we were just trying / to—

CAROL: You were just trying to what?

(Carol takes another long drink, finishing the glass.)

BO: Okay, that's it. Mom, where's the box of liquor?

CAROL: Why?!

BO: I'm getting rid of it.

CAROL: The hell you are! We bought that case last year at the Costco, it cost us more than two hundred bucks!

ALLY: Mom.

CAROL: *I'm* the adult, you understand?! Me!

ALLY: We're all adults now!

(Bo heads toward the basement, almost out of the room.)

CAROL: OKAY OKAY OKAY.

(Bo stops, looks at Carol.)

Okay. Let's talk about this like adults. We're all adults? We can talk about this like adults. *(Pause)* Please would you take a seat, sir?

(Bo relents, sits down on the couch.)

Now. We are going to have an adult conversation about this alcohol thing because you're both driving me up the wall about it. Shall we begin? Ally, sit down.

ALLY: Mom, I don't—

CAROL: You're an adult, I'm an adult. I guess the fact that I pushed you both out of my own body means nothing to you. Just call me Carol.

BO: Oh my God.

CAROL: Now to the matter of this drinking. When you kids were younger, I may have drank too much. I was never an alcoholic because addiction doesn't exist, but I drank too much. And when Dad asked me to stop, I stopped. Right?

(Pause.)

ALLY: Yes.

CAROL: Now while I was under the influence of this alcohol did I ever hit either of you?

BO: No.

CAROL: Did I ever drink and drive and run over people?

BO: No.

CAROL: All right then.

BO: But you *did* drive Dad's golf cart into the front yard and light it on fire.

CAROL: Exactly, I was a fun person. And besides, I told him I was going to do it if he kept driving it over my tomato plants, he knew it was coming. Point number two! It would be one thing if we had any sort of relationship with each other, but we don't have that, so you have no right to tell me what I can and can't drink.

ALLY: What do you mean we "don't have a relationship"?

CAROL: See now we're talking like adults! The three of us barely know one another anymore. *(To Bo)* You're always off in some stupid country or something— *(To Ally)* and you're a couple hours down the highway but I've barely ever even *met* my grandson. I'm sure you go around telling all your lesbian trucker friends that I some stupid idiot or something—

ALLY: MOM I AM NOT A TRUCKER. I OWN A PRIVATE / TRANSPORTATION—

CAROL: —telling them that it was so wonderful that you got out of stupid little Viola, Idaho, that you're such an enlightened lesbian now, that you don't have time to let your mother see her own grandson.

ALLY: Okay, Mom—

CAROL: We're adults, remember?

ALLY: I know I haven't brought Max over a lot, but—

CAROL: Once. I've seen him—once. Once. *(Pause)* Your father just died and you couldn't even bring him over here.

(Pause.)

ALLY: I'm sorry.

CAROL: Who's sorry? No one's sorry, we're just adults! *(To Bo)* And you, I suppose you think you're all important running off to some war-torn country, you waltz in there with your camera like you own the place—oh look at the American with the camera! He's a journalist, he's so important! God forbid you actually bend down to help these dying kids or whatever, you just stand there snapping pictures of them, and then you come back to little Viola, Idaho with your pictures of dead little boys and you think you're all enlightened, like you're off doing God's work or whatever, I know something you all don't know, I know what's best, *I really think you should stop drinking.*

(Carol goes to the clothes, puts them back in the box.)

We're cremating him, I just decided. I don't care what you think.

(Carol grabs the box of clothes, heads toward the door.)

I'm putting these out for the trash man.
ALLY: Mom—don't, please—
CAROL: What, are you gonna wear them?
ALLY: Look, we get it, okay?! Bo and I are sorry—
BO: No I'm not.

(Carol looks at Bo.)

CAROL: Oh?
BO: I've got nothing to be sorry about. *(Pause)* If you *really* wanna talk, Mom, we can talk, I'm fine with that.
ALLY: C'mon, Bo—
BO: I know that you're having fun getting drunk, telling us off—
CAROL: Oh I'm having a *great time.*

BO: And I know that you get to act like some poor wounded animal because we don't visit you enough—

CAROL: Oh, I'm a poor wounded animal!

BO: But guess what, Mom?! We're not responsible for your happiness!

CAROL: WHO THE HELL SAID YOU WERE RESPONSIBLE FOR MY HAPPINESS?! I JUST DON'T WANT YOU TO GET ON ME ABOUT MY DRINKING!

BO: And guess what?! Maybe my work *is* important, what about that?! Every time I talk to you on the phone you tell me that I need to stop going to these "awful countries," and you act like it's because you *care* about me, but actually it's because you *can't stand* the thought that I'm actually *doing* something with my life.

(Pause.)

CAROL: And why is that? *(Pause)* Go ahead and say it. "Because you never did anything with yours," is that what you were going to say? Because me and your father are just poor little simpletons, is that it?

BO: I didn't say that—

CAROL: But that's what you meant, isn't it?

BO: No, / it's—

CAROL: Yes it is. Yes, it is.

(Silence. Bo and Carol stare at one another.)

ALLY: Okay, guys. It's done, we're done talking.

(Carol continues to stare at Bo for a moment, then exits very briefly. She returns with a video cassette, goes to the camera on top of the television, and puts the tape inside.)

BO: What is that? *(Pause)* Mom. What is that?

(Carol presses play. An image of Martin appears on the screen, as before. He sits facing the camera. Carol exits without looking at Bo or Ally.)

MARTIN *(On video)*: It's—it's December twelfth, I think? Is it?

(No response.)

Carol?

(Ally and Bo stand back, watching the television.)

Are you not even going to talk / to me?
CAROL *(On video, offscreen)*: Oh would you just talk?
MARTIN *(On video)*: What?
CAROL *(On video, offscreen)*: Talk, I said! Talk!
MARTIN *(On video)*: Well what in heck do you think I'm doing?!
CAROL *(On video, offscreen)*: Look in the camera! Don't look at me, look in the camera!

(Martin looks back to the camera.)

MARTIN *(On video)*: Oh geez. Okay, I'm looking into the camera.

(Pause.)

Anyway, your mom wants me to talk so I'm talking. So it's—Nembutal, is what it's called, before I left the hospital yesterday I grabbed these little vials of Nembutal, the internet says it's a very popular method, I guess it's painless, you just drift right off, and / I—
CAROL *(On video, offscreen)*: Who signed for them?

(Carol enters with a fresh bottle of liquor and a full glass. She sips from the glass, watching the video.)

MARTIN *(On video)*: What?

CAROL *(On video, offscreen)*: I said WHO SIGNED FOR THEM.

MARTIN *(On video)*: *I don't know what you mean.*

CAROL *(On video, offscreen)*: You said a doctor had to sign for them or whatever—

MARTIN *(On video)*: No I just took 'em—

CAROL *(On video, offscreen)*: YOU JUST TOOK 'EM?

MARTIN *(On video)*: Yeah I just took 'em, what in the heck else / am I—?

CAROL *(On video, offscreen)*: You said you had to get a doctor to do it!

MARTIN *(On video)*: I didn't say that!

CAROL *(On video, offscreen)*: So you stole them! You just stole them!

MARTIN *(On video)*: ARE WE MAKING A MOVIE OR AREN'T WE?

CAROL *(On video, offscreen)*: THEY'RE GONNA CATCH YOU! YOU'RE AN IDIOT!

MARTIN *(On video)*: THEY'RE NOT GONNA CATCH ME. DON'T CALL ME AN IDIOT.

CAROL *(On video, offscreen)*: YOU'RE AN—

(The shot cuts to static. Ally and Bo stare at the screen. Carol moves in farther, puts the bottle down. Ally and Bo turn to her. Silence, apart from the static on the television.)

CAROL: I wasn't going to tell you, but since we're being all *adult-y.*

(Carol goes to the television, turns it off. The static cuts off.)

Ally I saved the box of clothes, I put it in your room. Keep them if you want, I don't need them. *(Pause)* Well?

(Silence. Bo goes to Carol.)

BO: What the fuck did he do?

CAROL: Oh we're bringing out the F-word, well then.

ALLY: Oh my God.

BO: I don't understand, how would—. How did he—?

CAROL: You heard him, he had some ridiculous drug or something. Took it from the hospital a few weeks ago.

BO: But how did—? You're telling me he just—injected himself with—

ALLY: How could you let him do this?!

CAROL: Oh you know your father, once he gets an idea in his head.

ALLY: But how did—? *(Pause)* No, you're full of shit.

CAROL: Oh am I? I'm full of *shit*?!

ALLY: Dad did *not* just—. He couldn't have!

CAROL: Well since you're the expert—

BO: No she's right, a person can't just—. They would have found out with the autopsy, they would have found needle marks on his arms—

CAROL: Autopsy? What, are we on *Law and Order*? You remember that little skinny kid from your class, what's his name?

BO: What?

CAROL: The little skinny kid from your class.

BO: I don't—? What are you talking about?!

CAROL: WHO WAS THE LITTLE SKINNY KID FROM YOUR CLASS? FROM YOUR CLASS, FROM YOUR CLASS!

BO: *I DON'T KNOW!*

CAROL: Well anyway he's the stupid coroner. Got elected last year, he was the only one who ran. He's gotten himself two DUI's this year already.

ALLY: I can't believe this. I can't believe what I'm hearing.

CAROL: You remember his name?

BO: No, I don't remember his—! *(Short pause)* It's Clive.

CAROL: *Clive.* That's it, little skinny Clive. His parents used to make those god-awful snow cones at the county fair every summer, you remember that?

BO: MOM.

CAROL: Anyway, Clive comes over here with the ambulance or whatever, they look at him for a second and I tell them he just up and died and they were fine with it.

ALLY: But Mom, why did / he—?

CAROL: I rode with them, I asked to ride with them, and they took the body downtown to the funeral chapel but I guess Frank was gone for the weekend or something, and they kept telling me that they wanted to take the body to *Moscow* or whatever until Frank was back on Monday, but I just all-out refused, I have no idea what these funeral chapels are like over in Moscow and I'm not about to—

ALLY: MOM.

CAROL: *Anyway*, Clive said they needed somewhere to put the body and it's not like I could go down to the grocery and ask them to put him in a chest freezer, though we did think about that for a second, but then Clive said that he did all this hunting the week before and he had all these elk carcasses in his garage or whatever, that it was sheltered and cool enough, and so anyway we just stuck him in there with the animals until Monday.

BO: Oh my God.

CAROL: And then Frank came back into town and it all became a little more civilized.

BO: Why are you telling us this?!

CAROL: I guess it's my little attempt at illustrating the reasons why a carefully executed suicide might slip through the cracks around here, I'm just saying.

ALLY: *WHY DID HE DO THIS?*

CAROL: Oh for Jeessum sake.

(Pause. Carol takes a long drink.)

BO: If he was depressed, then why didn't he just—

CAROL: Oh depressed, he was depressed, we should have just given him some pills and he'd be fine, is that it? You're so enlightened Bo, I swear, you're so *enlightened.*

ALLY: Why didn't you call me?! I live three hours away, I could have come down if Dad / was—

CAROL: And what good would you have done? Maybe you could have come down here and guilted him into living a few more years, but what for?

ALLY: What did he say? Did he tell you why?

CAROL: There are a lot of things you two don't understand.

BO: OKAY THAT'S IT.

(Bo stands up, exiting offstage. He returns momentarily with his backpack, shoving his clothes and toiletries into it as he talks.)

CAROL: What do you think you're doing?

BO: I'm leaving.

CAROL: The hell you are!

BO: You can't just—! You can't bring us here, tell us that Dad killed himself, and then just tell us that "we wouldn't understand." It's so fucking *manipulative*—

ALLY: BO.

CAROL: No, he's right. Your brother's right. He's right.

(Bo stops, looking at Carol.)

Bo, you're—. I get it, I see what I'm doing, I can see myself. I'm sorry, okay? I'm sorry.

(Bo looks at her. Carol takes her glass of liquor, holding it up. She looks around, then goes to the Christmas tree, pours the remainder of the glass into the Christmas tree stand. She puts the empty glass down.)

Okay? No more.

(Bo calms down a bit.)

Now if you really want me to try and explain all this—I'll try and explain. I can do that. It may just make things worse, but—we can try it this way. How about that?

(Pause.)

Let's just—sit down. Family time. What's left of us.

(Bo relents, putting his backpack down and finding a place to sit. Ally finds a place to sit as well. Carol remains standing.)

Now the first thing I want you to get out of your heads is any ideas about depression, crazy, whatever. Your father's brain—and mine—was and is doing just fine. All right?

(Carol exits momentarily, continuing to talk.)

(From off) I know that nowadays we all like to explain away everything in life by putting some stupid word next to it—depression, bipolar, schizo-whatever—but we're not talking about that, we are talking about *reason*. All right? *Reason*.

(Carol reenters with two or three of the Costco snack trays. She tosses one to Bo and Ally.)

ALLY: Mom, when someone kills themselves, that means that something *is* wrong with their brain. Someone doesn't / just—

CAROL: Oh shut up with your stupid psychology. Your father *arrived* at this decision, it wasn't something he just came up with last week, he had been thinking about it for years.

BO: *Years?*

CAROL: YES YEARS. LISTEN TO MY MOUTH. YEARS, YEARS.

(Carol opens up a snack tray, eats a bit.)

ALLY: Why?!

CAROL: Well once you kids left I guess he just sorta realized who he was, his place in—. Okay. Listen to me.

(Carol stands up with the snack tray.)

Now I don't know if you even know about this but apparently our entire universe came out of some big explosion or something, and ever since then, all these stars and planets and whatever— *(Grabbing a cracker)* —have just been spiraling out into nothingness—

(Carol throws the cracker to a corner of the room, then grabs more crackers and continues to throw them around the room.)

—and these things that used to be one thing are now just spiraling out into the depths of space or something. And then you've got our little planet—

(Carol takes a cracker, holds it up.)

—that actually has *life* on it.

(Carol takes a piece of salami, puts it on top of the cracker.)

This one special little stupid piece of dirt that has all these people on it, and we're all *very impressed* with ourselves, living on this little planet, but if you actually think about it?

(Carol grabs an unopened snack tray.)

We all just came from the same little stupid speck of whatever. Everything, everything you know about people, time, history, your dirty laundry—it's all just from this same little thing. *The same stupid little snack tray.*

(Carol drops the snack tray on the ground, looking at Bo and Ally.)

Get it?

(Pause.)

BO: You're saying that Dad killed himself because of the big bang?
CAROL: Yeah! Not *just* that, that just sort of—led him to the idea. After you both left we had all this *time* on our hands, and we started reading all these books, and we—
ALLY: What books?
CAROL: *Books*, I don't know. Years ago he saw some program on public television about the big bang and whatever, so he found a few books and we both read them and started getting interested in all that stuff.
ALLY: When did Dad ever read a *book*? Do you guys even *own* any books?

(Pause.)

CAROL: Oh you're right, we didn't go to *college* so I guess we're both as dumb as dirt, is that it?

ALLY: I'm not saying that, I'm just saying—I never even saw him read a *newspaper* let / alone—

CAROL: You sit there barking at me, talking to me like I'm some idiot, like I'm—. I know you'd like to believe that we're just some stupid simpletons, but your father was a real person. A real person who started to understand who he was, his place in—everything. And rather than spending the rest of his life wiping floors at a hospital and wasting away in this house, he released himself into the universe. The most beautiful, meaningful thing he ever did.

(Pause.)

I'm going to bed. Turn out the lights when you're done.

(Carol gets up and exits, taking the bottle of liquor with her. Ally and Bo sit for a moment, silent.)

BO: What are we—? I don't know what we're supposed to do with this. *(Pause) That stupid fucking asshole, why did he do this?!*

ALLY: I have to go to bed, I can't even think. I don't even know what's going on.

BO: And what the hell did Dad ever know about *science*? He never even watched an episode of *Star Trek*, what the hell does he know about science? *(Pause)* I just don't—. After all this time, suddenly the man has an inner life? When the hell did that happen?

(Bo opens up a snack tray, eats a few bites. Silence.)

ALLY: Do you think— . . . ?

BO: What?

ALLY: He didn't do this because of us, did he?

(Pause.)

BO: Because of *us*?

ALLY: You know, because we—. I don't know, we never visited, or—

BO: This is not on us, Ally. I refuse to take any of the blame for this. He was a nonexistent father to us our entire lives.

ALLY: Yeah.

(Pause.)

BO: Ally.

(No response.)

Ally.

(Ally finally looks at him.)

You know this wasn't our fault, right?

ALLY: I know, I know.

BO: He was just—sick, I guess.

(Carol returns with the bottle of liquor and some video tapes in her hands. She stumbles into the room, obviously much drunker than a moment ago.)

Mom.

CAROL: *Well hello.*

ALLY: Mom, c'mon, go to bed, it's late.

BO: Mom you need to stop, give me the bottle.

CAROL: I just had a few little more nightcaps.

(Carol stumbles into the room. Bo takes the bottle from her.)

BO: C'mon, let's go to bed.

CAROL: No I just had something to tell you so quick. Okay? I'll be so quick, I just.

ALLY: Jesus.

CAROL: Now first of all I wanted to give you these to you.

(Carol drops the tapes onto the floor.)

They're tapes of Dad, I had him make you these tapes to try and explain everything, why he did this, whatever. So just watch the tapes and you'll learn so much.

BO: Great.

ALLY: Thank you, Mom.

CAROL: ALSO. I just wanted to let you both know that I'm planning on doing the same thing as your father after the funeral tomorrow just so you know. And I'd like you both to help me with it.

(Pause.)

BO: Wait, what?

CAROL: He saved me some of the drug he used and I'm going take it tomorrow, just like him. So it's good that everything in the house is white, you won't have to worry about selling all of the *stuff*, because it's all white anyway, so after I die you can just throw it all out and just sell the house and be done with it. I've made it very easy for both of you.

(Quick pause.)

YOU'RE WELCOME.

(Black.)

Act Two

Scene One

The television flips on. A shot of Martin appears on the screen.

MARTIN *(On video)*: —which is really just an effort to nego-
tiate ideas of, uh. Relativity, and—you know, Einstein's
relativity—

CAROL *(On video, offscreen)*: Ugh.

MARTIN *(On video)*: —and uh, quantum mechanics, which sort
of seem like they're in opposition / to one another—

CAROL *(On video, offscreen)*: Martin, you don't have to run your
mouth off about whatever, just tell them what string theory
is!

*(Lights rise on the living room, the next morning. Bo sits,
watching the television.)*

MARTIN *(On video)*: You know Carol if *you* wanna do this, I'm fine / with that—

CAROL *(On video, offscreen)*: Talk about the strings! Just get through it!

MARTIN *(On video)*: Okay. So people are thinking that these strings are the basic building block of everything around us—

(Ally enters, holding a book.)

ALLY: Hey.

BO: Hey.

MARTIN *(On video)*: —it's smaller than any other thing we know—smaller than atoms, smaller than quarks—

(Bo turns off the camera and the television shuts off.)

ALLY: Merry Christmas.

BO: Oh my God. It's Christmas morning, isn't it?

ALLY: Yeah. Pretty shitty Christmas, even for this house. You check on Mom?

BO: She's fine. Still asleep. She'll be asleep for a while probably. I looked everywhere for the—whatever.

ALLY: Nembutal.

BO: Yeah. Bathroom, her bedroom—I can't find it. *(Referring to the book)* What's that?

ALLY: I found it in a box outside this morning. Mom left it out for the trash man.

BO: What is it?

ALLY: It's about quantum mechanics. There are notes on almost every page.

(Ally shows the book to Bo.)

There are more out there, too.

(Bo skims through the book, tosses it back down on the couch.)

BO: Hm.
ALLY: So?

(Pause.)

BO: What?

(Ally stares at him.)

What I said?
ALLY: I don't know, Bo, I—. *(Pause)* He didn't seem—sick. Or crazy. Mom doesn't seem sick or crazy.
BO: You're telling me that Mom doesn't seem crazy? After last night?
ALLY: She was drunk.
BO: I think a double suicide counts as crazy, Ally. Should we call the—police? I don't know, who do you call when someone is crazy? The hospital?
ALLY: Wait—what do you mean?
BO: Well I don't know, I don't know how you—commit someone, I don't know how to do that. Do I call the, like—asylum? Is that what it's called?

(Bo goes to an end table, taking out a phone book.)

ALLY: What are you doing?
BO: I'm just—I'm just looking.
ALLY: You're looking up "asylums" in the fucking phone book?!
BO: Well I don't know! At least I'm doing something!
ALLY: You're a retard!
BO: *You're* a re—! *(Catching himself)* Oh my God, how old are we?

(Bo throws the phone book back into the end table.)

ALLY: You can't just—. You can't just *commit* her, Bo. It's not the nineteenth century.

BO: She's threatening to kill herself.

ALLY: Okay so, say we make her go to the hospital, and she gets interviewed by a psychiatrist or whatever—you really think she's dumb enough to actually *tell* them that she's planning on killing herself? All she has to say is that we're lying.

BO: What, so you want to just *wait around* until she kills herself?!

ALLY: No I'm not *okay* with it, I'm just—. What, are we gonna strap her down at night, pump her full of Thorazine during the day?

BO: *Dear God, every time I come home.* I walk into this house and it's like every bit of reason, every shred of rationality just flies right out the window. At least being in a country at war, you know what the hell is going on, you understand people's motivations, but in this house?!

ALLY: Well maybe if you'd get off of your high horse for a / second—

BO: My *liberal* high horse.

ALLY: Maybe if you just got off it, you'd realize that some people just feel completely—*alone*, some people really don't have any reason to move from day to day, some people don't—

(Ally stops, looks at Bo, red-faced. She suddenly looks down, putting her face in her hands. Bo stares at her. Silence.)

BO: What are you—? What are you doing?

(Ally doesn't move.)

Are you crying? *(Pause)* Holy shit. You're crying.

(Silence. Bo is motionless. Ally continues to cry into her hands silently.)

Do you want like—a hug?

(Bo, not knowing what to do, gets up, moves to Ally. He awkwardly puts his arms around her. As soon as his arms touch her:)

ALLY: GET THE FUCK OFF.
BO: *Sorry*, I don't know what to— . . . ! *(Pause)* Sorry.

(Ally starts to regain herself.)

Are you—sad about Mom?
ALLY: Shut up.
BO: Is it Dad?
ALLY: No, it's— . . . *(Pause)* Laura and Max left.

(Pause.)

BO: What do you mean?
ALLY: Me. They left me. Laura left and she took Max with her. I'm not even sure where she went. I think she might be with her cousin in Seattle.
BO: What happened?
ALLY: *That's just the thing, nothing happened, nothing—. (Pause)* She just kept saying that I don't spend enough time at home, that I don't spend enough time around Max, or—. I don't know. She's just—crazy, that's what it is. She's crazy.
BO: She left the state and took your kid with her because she doesn't feel like you spend enough time at home?

ALLY: I know! She's crazy! *(Pause)* I mean I work a lot, but it's for them! I do it for them!

BO: How much do you work?

ALLY: I don't know.

BO: You get weekends off though, right?

ALLY: Yeah right, I wish. Weekends. We have double the amount of runs to the airport on weekends, I'm usually doing some of the driving myself, not to mention all the courier deliveries we have / for the—

BO: You don't take *any* days off?

ALLY: I own a business! Every day I'm directing thirty-six twelve-passenger vans and—

BO: What time do you get home usually?

ALLY: I don't know—eleven? Midnight, I guess?

BO: Are you serious?

ALLY: *I own the second-largest fleet of passenger vehicles in Northern / Idaho—*

BO: OKAY okay. You just sound—busy. That's a long work week.

ALLY: I mean I get Thanksgiving and Christmas off, and—. Goddammit.

(Ally buries her head in her hands.)

I just don't get it. We have money, a two-story house on thirty acres. She has her own organic garden. Max has anything he could ever want. I don't know when this— stopped working.

BO: Look, business is good, right?

ALLY: Yeah.

BO: So hire a manager or something. You can delegate some of this stuff, can't you?

ALLY: Bo this thing took me *ten years* to build, I'm not hiring some idiot who's gonna screw it all up.

BO: But you do realize that most people don't have that kind of work week. Especially people with a one-year-old.

ALLY: HE'S TWO, BO. MY SON IS TWO YEARS OLD.

BO: SORRY. Sorry.

(Pause.)

ALLY: It's also that— . . .

(Ally trails off.)

BO: What?

ALLY: Look don't get all weird when I say this, but *maybe*, *sometimes* I feel a little like—we shouldn't have had a kid.

(Silence.)

BO: Woah.

ALLY: Not like—*all the time*, I just.

(Pause.)

Look it's not like I don't love him, I love him more than anything, that's *why* I feel like maybe we should have—. I mean, look at what this kid is being born into. Global warming, a collapsing economy, countries exploding, Islamic fanatics trying to take over the country—

BO: Okay you can't actually believe that Muslims are trying to / take over—

ALLY: SHUT UP I DON'T CARE IF YOU THINK I'M RACIST SHUT UP.

(Pause.)

Anyway. I'm just saying, that we seem to have brought a new life into this world at a pretty screwed-up time, and—. Do you realize that by the time he's my age, it's going to be the year 2042? Are we even going to *make* it that far? Who the fuck are *we* to bring another life into the world, right now? What are we even thinking?

(Pause.)

And so I get to thinking about all of this stuff, and it just seems like I should *prepare* in some way, that if I'm a responsible parent I really should have some sort of plan if—whatever happens, you know? So I get some money together to build a shelter, just in case something were to happen, and Laura got all angry at me because I didn't tell her about it, but I / was just—

BO: What do you mean a "shelter"? What does that mean?

ALLY: You know, like—in case anything happens. Like an underground shelter, like a bunker. I know it sounds crazy, but when you really consider what could happen in the next twenty years it's really / not—

BO: How much is it costing you?

ALLY: There's a company in Eastern Washington that does this stuff, they get really good prices, I did my homework. And I'm taking care of a lot of the installation myself, they just send the basic structure and / I'm—

BO: How much will it cost?

ALLY: I have a payment plan, I just—. *(Pause)* A little under fifty thousand, okay?

BO: Holy *shit*, Ally.

ALLY: *Shut up.*

BO: You spent fifty thousand dollars and you didn't tell your *wife*?

ALLY: She would've gotten all weird about it!

BO: Yeah because it's crazy!

ALLY: Do you know how much shit is going on right now?! How many different ways this whole fucking country could just blow up right in our / faces—

BO: Oh right, because things have *never* been this bad, right? Ally, terrible things have always happened. Economic meltdowns, epidemics, war, genocide, whatever—it's been going on since forever, and will continue to go on forever, and the world isn't gonna blow up anytime soon. God, everyone in this country is so fucking obsessed with themselves that they have to manufacture this apocalypse bullshit because their lives are so boring / that they—

ALLY: OH MY GOD I DON'T NEED THE SPEECH. *(Pause)* Just forget it, never mind.

(Pause.)

BO: You want some coffee?

(Pause.)

ALLY: Yeah.

(Bo exits momentarily.)

BO *(From the kitchen)*: Have you tried just giving her a call?

(Ally doesn't respond.)

(From off) I SAID—

ALLY: I HEARD YOU SHUT UP.

(Bo reenters with two cups of coffee, hands one to Ally.)

BO: So?

(Silence.)

ALLY: Maybe I shouldn't.

(Pause.)

BO: What do you mean?
ALLY: Just, I don't know. Maybe I shouldn't.

(Carol enters in her pajamas, obviously hungover.)

CAROL: There's coffee?
BO: Yeah.
CAROL: Okay. Good morning, Merry Christmas, Merry Christmas.

(Carol exits to the kitchen.)

ALLY: Don't say anything to her about Laura and Max.
BO: Of course I'm not going to say anything. We've got enough to deal with. *(Pause)* What did you mean, "maybe I shouldn't"? Why *wouldn't* you call her?

(Pause.)

ALLY: Forget it.

(Pause.)

BO: You should call her.
ALLY: I know.
BO: *You should call her.*
ALLY: *I know.*

(Carol reenters with coffee. She goes to the stereo, presses play. Christmas carols begin.)

CAROL: Remind me not to drink that stuff anymore. Your dad was crazy, that stuff is terrible, gives me hangovers. I'm sticking to my Crème de Menthe.

ALLY: How about *not* drinking, Mom, how about that?

CAROL: You kids, I swear to God. I have one drink too many and it's the Spanish Inquisition! String her up! Guillotine! *(Pause)* I won't drink anymore, not while you're here. But it's not because I have a problem, it's because you two are irritating. *(Referring to the music)* Oh I like this one.

BO: Mom?

(Carol doesn't respond. She's listening to the music.)

Mom.

CAROL: Ugh. What?

(Bo goes to the music, turns it off.)

Do you have to turn that off?

BO: Yes.

CAROL: Right, I forgot that it's your job to make sure I don't get any of the things in life that make me feel good. Continue.

(Pause. Bo goes to her.)

BO: We want you to check yourself into the hospital.

CAROL: What?

BO: We think it'd be best, and we don't want to force you, so we want you to check yourself in.

CAROL: What do I need to go to the hospital for?

BO: We don't want you to hurt yourself. We care about you—

CAROL: Ugh.

BO: —and we don't want you to hurt yourself.

CAROL: Who's hurting herself? I'm not hurting myself! I'm drinking coffee!

BO: Where is the drug?

CAROL: What drug?

BO: The drug that Dad used? Where is it?

CAROL: Damn your father's terrible liquor, I never should have told you that. If I just would've stuck to my Crème de Menthe I never would have blabbed.

BO: I already took all of the knives out of the kitchen—

CAROL: What did you do that for?! What did you do with my knives?!

BO: I took them out.

CAROL: Those are expensive knives! They're Swedish or something!

BO: I just—. I just put them somewhere, they're fine. And I hid Dad's old hunting rifles, and took all of the medicine out of the bathroom, but I can't make this house totally safe for you, which is why we really think that you / should—

CAROL: Where did you put my knives?

BO: I'm not telling you.

CAROL: I'll call the police! Where did you put them?!

BO: Mom it's—they're fine!

CAROL: If you gave them to the Goodwill I'm going to buy them back right now and stab you with them.

BO: THIS ISN'T—Mom, I'm trying to have a serious conversation right now, I just hid them because I didn't want you to hurt yourself with them, but this isn't about that, it's—

CAROL: Where did you hide them?!

BO: THEY'RE JUST IN THE BASEMENT SOMEWHERE, OKAY?!

CAROL: THEY'RE GONNA GET RUSTED IN THE BASEMENT!

BO: DEAR GOD PLEASE STOP TALKING ABOUT THE KNIVES! WE JUST WANT YOU TO GO TO THE HOSPITAL, ALL RIGHT?! WE WANT YOU TO CHECK YOURSELF INTO THE HOSPITAL!

ALLY: Bo, could you just—? You don't have to *scream* at her—

BO: Look are you going to help me, or not?

ALLY: Why can't we just sit down and talk like rational human beings?!

BO: Because she isn't rational! Nothing about this is rational!

ALLY: Oh right because you're so superior and / we're just—

BO: When did I say I was "superior"?!

CAROL: WHAT IN THE HELL DID I SAY TO YOU KIDS LAST NIGHT?!

(Pause.)

BO: You don't remember what you said to us?

CAROL: I remember spilling the beans about Dad, but what did— . . . *(Pause, remembering)* Oh. *(Pause) GAH* your father's liquor.

(Carol goes to the stereo, turns the Christmas carols back on.)

I wasn't planning on telling you kids until after the funeral, I thought we could at least get through that first, but— might as well get it over with anyway.

BO: Do you have the drug? The thing that Dad used?

CAROL: Well of course I have it. It's very peaceful, I guess it's the most popular method among doctors who are suiciders, so it's kinda classy. And it's very peaceful, it won't look ugly or anything. I have it all planned out for you.

(Carol goes to a drawer, takes out a piece of paper.)

I wrote down all the instructions. I'd like you kids to be around when it actually happens but then you have to leave right away and just go shopping or something, then you come back and you call the police and tell them you found me. It's really simple, I've made it easy.

409

BO: Mom you realize—we're not going to let you do this. There's no way that we would let you do this.

(Pause.)

CAROL: Did you watch the videos I gave you?

ALLY: We watched some of them.

CAROL: Then I don't know what else you kids want from me, I don't—. *(Pause)* Okay, how about this? Let's walk through it. I'll walk through it and I'll show you kids that it's not bad at all.

BO: What?

(Carol goes to the couch, reaching inside of a cushion. She takes out a vial of Nembutal and a syringe.)

ALLY: Oh my God—

BO: *Mom, give that to me right now.*

CAROL: What?! Why should I?!

BO: I don't want you hurting yourself!

CAROL: Are you listening to me?! I'm just going to walk you through it! I'm not doing anything!

ALLY: Mom just give us the—. Just give it to us, please.

CAROL: I'm not giving it to you kids, you'll just drop it or lose it. I'll put it away, okay?

(Carol puts the vial into her pocket.)

Okay, so here's how it'll happen. I'll be sitting right here, just like your dad.

(Carol sits on the couch.)

And I want my Christmas carols to be playing but not this tape, I want the Bing Crosby. Remember that, okay? Write it down on that paper.

ALLY: It's fine—

CAROL: WRITE IT DOWN. YOU'RE GONNA FORGET.

ALLY: I'LL REMEMBER.

CAROL: Anyhoo, I'll be sitting right here like this. And we'll say our good-byes or whatever and then I'll go like this.

(Carol puts the syringe up to her arm.)

And I'll inject the stuff into me, and then I'll die. Okay? I'm dying right now, this is me dying.

(Carol slumps over. Pause.)

Okay so then I'm dead and then you two have to get out of here, you need to just leave for an hour or two. Maybe just an hour, you don't want me smelling up the place. Martin smelled a little bit, I think he may have pooped himself, but I won't do that.

BO: Okay, Mom, we don't need to—

CAROL: I SAID I WON'T POOP MYSELF. *Jeessum Crow.* Okay then when you come back here and you have to call the police, you say you just found me like this—and then Clive will come in and he's gonna ask you what happened, and you're gonna tell him that you just found me like this.

(Pause. Carol looks at Bo and Ally.)

Well?

ALLY: What?

411

CAROL: Say it. Pretend I'm Clive, tell me what happened. I just want to hear how you'll say it.

BO: No, we are / not—

CAROL: Ally, just say it. Just say "we walked in and found her like this."

(Pause. Bo glares at Ally. Ally relents.)

ALLY *(Awkward, annoyed)*: We walked in and found her like this.

CAROL: THAT'S HOW YOU'RE GONNA SAY IT?

BO: OKAY ENOUGH. *(Pause)* This isn't happening. We are not going to do this.

CAROL: Bo, it's really not that bad, you only have a few things that you need to do—

BO: You're not hearing me, Mom—we are not going to help you do this. Neither of us are going to participate in this.

(Pause.)

Do you know how many dead bodies I've seen, bodies of people who *didn't* want to die, who were *forced* into these situations, and—? There are a lot of people who would love to have your life right now, and you just giving up, it's—. It's vulgar.

CAROL: Bo I've been thinking this through for years now, nothing you can possibly come up with right now is anything I haven't thought of before. It's not sad, it's not immoral, it's just—what it is. I'm done. Nothing left for me to do. I'm sorry that it seems vulgar to you, but it's—my life. The last thing I have control over. It's not about depression, or pain, or whatever. It's about *my choice*.

(Pause.)

I helped your dad, and now—I'd like you to help me.

(Bo and Ally are silent.)

Please.

(No response. Carol thinks.)

You kids watch the rest of the tapes from your dad, think about it, and if you still think I'm just stupid—you can just go. You don't have to be here if you don't want to. Up to you.

(Carol exits. The lights snap to black. The TV flickers and begins to play.)

Home Video

Martin appears on the television, as before.

MARTIN: You kids remember when Grandpa was in the hospital, right before he died? And I didn't let you see him, I didn't allow you to go to visit with him. And you thought that I was so cruel for doing that, you thought that I was a monster, that I was— . . . Carol, you remember that?

CAROL *(Offscreen)*: Yeah. I remember.

(Lights slowly rise on the living room. Bo sits, watching the television.)

MARTIN: He was real thin toward the end. Tubes hooked up to him, barely recognized me. Cancer had gone to his brain, his eyes turned this milky blue and he'd just stare forward, right through you. This guy who fought in World War II, who started his own business from the ground up,

413

and— . . . Every day I'd go to work. I'd be mopping the floor right outside his room. I'd pass by it around three forty-five in the morning, and I'd open the door and look at him. Started bringing the camera with me to work, taping him, so I wouldn't forget what he looked like.

(Pause.)

Yesterday I pulled out some of those tapes to remind myself what he looked like. Thing is, these tapes—they don't last forever. Eventually, they just turn to static. You watch them enough, let them sit in a box long enough, they lose the signal. I hadn't watched the thing for years, but I guess I had watched it so many times—the tape was just static.

(Pause.)

I watched it for a while. The whole thing is—just static.

Scene Two

A few hours later.
Ally enters, sees Bo. A bottle of the liquor sits out. Bo is drinking from a glass.

ALLY: Hey. Where were you?

(Bo stops the tape, not looking at Ally.)

HELLO?
BO: I didn't feel like going, okay?
ALLY: It was really shitty of you to miss this. There are certain things that people *do* when their parent dies.

BO: Look I'll participate in what I want to participate in, all right? *(Pause)* Where's Mom?

ALLY: She's downtown.

BO: Downtown?

ALLY: She just dropped me off. She's getting the flowers for the funeral.

(Bo gets up.)

BO: And you just—*let her go*?

ALLY: *Yeah*, so what?

BO: So right at this moment, she could be out in the middle of the forest hanging herself from some tree, that's what you're telling me?

ALLY: A TREE? WHAT THE HELL ARE YOU TALKING ABOUT?

BO: Fine. Just let her do whatever she wants, who cares?!

ALLY: She's an adult! I'm not her babysitter!

(Bo drinks.)

And you're fucking *drinking*?

BO: Yeah, so what?

ALLY: Fine, whatever. Sit back and be totally fucking useless. I'll take care of *everything*, because for some reason it's my responsibility to cart Mom around and make / sure—

BO: You know, you're sort of— . . .

(Bo trails off.)

ALLY: What?

BO: Nothing.

ALLY: No really, what? What big stupid speech do you have for me now?

415

BO: You're sort of pathetic sometimes, you know that?

(Silence. Ally stares at him.)

ALLY: I'm sorry, what was that?

BO: I said *you're sort of pathetic sometimes*. And I'm not even talking about you spending tens of thousands of dollars on some underground crazy-tank, or voting for Bush. Those things *aside*, you're still sort of just—pathetic. You always just side with Mom and Dad, no matter what. Dad killed himself? Fine with you. Mom wants to do the same thing? Ally has no problem with it! You were always just so fuck-ing—*spineless* with them, I just— . . .

(Silence.)

ALLY: No, that's great, keep going. *(No response)* Oh you're done? You can keep going. Because I'll just stand here and listen to you spew your self-righteous bullshit because I'm so *spineless* and *pathetic*. Right? *(Pause)* And since I'm so *spineless* and *pathetic*, I won't tell you that when you up and left when you were seventeen, believe it or not you were actually leaving a fourteen-year-old girl in this house *alone with them*. For three years, all their crazy shit that *had* been equally distributed between the two of us was suddenly directed *entirely* at me. Suddenly Dad only had one kid and he had to make sure that every movement I made was on tape—

BO: OKAY.

ALLY: But it's okay because you're some big important pho-tographer, you *really matter*. I however stuck it out here, I waited until college to actually leave—

BO: And then you did exactly what I did, you stopped coming here.

ALLY: I know it's convenient for you to believe that, but I *was* coming back here. For years after I left I still came home for Thanksgiving, Christmas, called Mom every week, all the while building a business with an annual operating budget of over a million dollars.

BO: Oh I'm very impressed, Ally. You live in one of the wealthiest capitalist economies in the world and you managed to create a *business*, it's so impressive. Too bad you don't spend half as much time thinking about your family as you do thinking about your business.

ALLY: What the fuck did you just say to me?

BO: You heard me.

ALLY: Are you saying I'm a bad parent?

BO: No, all good parents spend their kid's college money building apocalypse bunkers and working until midnight every night—

(Ally punches Bo in the shoulder.)

Did you just *hit* me?

ALLY: Don't talk to me about my family. I'll kick your ass.

BO: Oh you'll "kick my ass"?

ALLY: I will *break you.*

BO: Oh sure.

ALLY: What, you think I'm fragile? Go ahead.

(Ally punches Bo again.)

BO: All right, you need to stop touching me *right now.*

ALLY: You've spent your whole life in third-world countries exploiting other people's misery. How about that?

BO: Oh is that what I've been doing?

ALLY: You're ignorant, childish, self-righteous, *immoral*—

417

(Bo pushes Ally.)

BO: How about that?
ALLY: That's great, I like it.

(Ally pushes Bo back, harder.)

BO: I said don't fucking touch me, Ally. I don't want to hurt you.
ALLY: Oh, you don't want to *hurt* me?
BO: Shut up.
ALLY: Oh big strong man, I'm just a poor widdle / woman!
BO: SHUT UP.
ALLY: Please don't hurt me!

(Bo goes at her. They begin to wrestle for a bit. Ally manages to get the upper hand, pins Bo down on the ground.)

OH BIG STRONG MAN WHAT JUST HAPPENED?
BO: YOU'RE REALLY HURTING MY ARM. YOU ARE ACTUALLY HURTING MY ARM.

(Ally twists his arm, Bo screams in pain. Just then, Carol enters, holding a huge potted bouquet of white carnations accented with pink ribbons. She looks at Bo and Ally, who don't notice her.)

ALLY: SAY "I'M A RETARD"! SAY IT!
BO: FUCK YOU!

(Ally twists his arm, Bo cries out in pain. Carol puts down the carnations and exits.)

OKAY OKAY I'M A RETARD! GET OFF ME!
ALLY: NOW SAY "OBAMA'S A RETARD"!

BO: WHAT?!

ALLY: SAY IT!

(Bo manages to wrestle his way out of her grip and pins her down onto the ground.)

BO: SAY "I'M A STUPID LITTLE GIRL"!

ALLY: GET OFF ME!

BO: I'M A STUPID LITTLE GIRL!

(Just then Carol enters with a garden hose trailing behind her. She sprays Bo and Ally. They immediately break up, rolling off one another. Carol continues to spray them for a moment, then stops. Ally and Bo have begun to laugh uncontrollably on the floor, unable to talk.)

CAROL: What, you're *laughing* now? *(Pause)* You're both crazy.

(Ally and Bo continue to laugh. Bo notices the white carnations.)

BO: What—? What are those?

(Ally looks at the flowers.)

ALLY: Oh my God, what are those?

CAROL: They're for the funeral.

(Ally and Bo continue to laugh.)

ALLY: Why—? Why are they *white*? They have *pink ribbons*!

CAROL: Glenn the florist made it for some wedding, but the bride didn't want it or something.

BO: That's—? That's for the *funeral*?

CAROL: It was fifty percent off! What do you want from me?!

(Bo and Ally break into another fit of laughter.)

You two are both crazy.

(Carol exits with the hose. Ally and Bo start to calm down. Their laughter subsides.)

BO: I didn't hurt you, did I?
ALLY: No, did I hurt *you*?
BO: No, I'm—I'm fine.

(They get up. Carol reenters.)

CAROL: All right idiots, are you done with whatever that was?
BO AND ALLY: Yeah.
CAROL: All right then. *(Pause)* You two make a decision yet? Either of you sticking around?

(Pause. Bo and Ally don't respond.)

Well you'll have to decide soon, because I'm doing this right after the funeral.

(Carol exits into the kitchen. Pause.)

BO: What are you gonna do?
ALLY: I'm not going to leave her alone, I'm not gonna . . . *(Pause)* What are you gonna do?
CAROL *(From off)*: If you don't want to be here, then all I ask is that you take care of selling the house. You won't make much money off it but you can split it down the middle, or whatever you want.

(Carol reenters with a Christmas-themed tablecloth, four Christmas-themed plates, and a rag. She cleans the water off the dining table as she speaks.)

I don't know where the deed is but Dad says where it is in one of those videos. Like I said, it's all nice and easy. Ally, help me with this?

(Carol unfolds the tablecloth.)

ALLY: What are we doing?
CAROL: It's Christmas.
ALLY: Mom, I / don't—
CAROL: Let's have a Christmas.

(Ally looks at Bo, then helps Carol spread the tablecloth out. Carol sets the plates.)

We only have a few hours left together, and it's Christmas, so let's have something to eat. Okay?

(Carol goes to the stereo, turns on the Christmas carols, then exits again to the kitchen. Ally sits down, looks at Bo.)

ALLY: Bo, c'mon. Just sit down.

(Bo doesn't move.)

This is the last time we're gonna be with her, let's just—. C'mon.

(Carol reenters with a large box full of the Costco snack trays. She places a snack tray on each plate.)

CAROL: It's not much, but it's what we have left.

(Carol sits down at the table.)

(To Bo) C'mon, Bo. Christmas dinner.

(Bo doesn't sit down. Silence. Finally, Bo leaves the room. Ally and Carol watch him go.)

ALLY *(Calling out)*: Bo. C'mon, just—

(Bo reenters with his bag, shoving clothes into it.)

Bo, *please*—

BO: I'm not—. I'm not staying here for this. *(Pause)* I don't know why you need us here, why you need us to watch you—. But I'm not going to.

(Bo heads toward the door.)

CAROL: Bo.

(Bo, at the door, stops. He doesn't look at Carol. Pause.)

You know, I didn't have control over a lot of things in my life. I know your dad and I weren't perfect, but try growing up with my parents. If I'd have tried to leave when I was seventeen and move to New York City, become a *lesbian* . . . They'd've shot me dead, I'll tell you that much.

(Pause.)

I have had very little say in how my life has played out, and I just want this *one last thing*. And I want to have you both here, with me.

(Pause.)

Please.

(Silence. Then finally, without looking at Carol or Ally, Bo exits. The lights snap to black. The television begins to play.)

Home Video

Carol appears on the television.

CAROL *(On video)*: All right, well. Your dad wants me to say something too, but I don't—. Oh, Martin, I don't know, I—

MARTIN *(On video, offscreen)*: It's fine, keep going.

(Ally sits on the couch, watching the video.)

CAROL *(On video)*: Lately I've been watching his old videos of you two more than he has. The Christmas videos mostly. Fights, lots of fights. Bo being angry. Ally being distant. Tapes are starting to fade. Dad watched them so much, some of them are just completely static.

(Pause.)

Martin brought this book over the other day that had a picture from this telescope out in space, a picture of all these galaxies, hundreds of them. Nowadays we know exactly where we are, exactly what we are. I think about what my grandparents knew, what their parents knew, their parents and their parents . . . They must have felt such a responsibility to do things, have kids, move forward, whatever. But now, we know just what and where we are. And it's sort of beautiful, I don't know. Thinking of our place within that—Martin and me, you kids, all these videos of our Christmases fading into static.

(Pause.)

I hope you kids will watch these, I hope you'll understand what we're doing, I hope—.

(Pause, looking away.)

Martin I don't want to do this anymore, I don't—. Just stop taping me, please just tape over this, I don't want them to—

(The shot cuts out, lights rise on:)

Scene Three

That evening.
    Ally, in funeral black, enters with the potted carnations. She puts the pot down on the floor, then plops down onto the couch.
    Carol trails behind Ally, wearing black denim and a black blouse.
    Carol sits down on the couch next to Ally.
    Pause.

CAROL: It was nice.
ALLY: Fifteen minutes long.
CAROL: Exactly, it was nice. No use in making a big fuss out of anything. The pastor barely knew him anyway. *(Pause)* Well, I suppose if Bo didn't go to the funeral, then he probably won't be coming back. Will he?

(Pause.)

ALLY: I don't—. I'm not sure, Mom.

(Pause.)

CAROL: But you're staying?

ALLY: Yeah. I'm staying. *(Pause)* Mom, why don't—? *(Pause)* I think we should probably—talk.

CAROL: About what?

ALLY: I don't know, just—. We need to like—talk about stuff, right?! This is the last time we're ever going to talk! We need to have big stupid emotional conversations about—stuff!

CAROL: I have no idea what you're saying to me right now.

ALLY: Well you're about to kill yourself, and we barely even talk anymore / and we—!

CAROL: Oh here we go, it's time to have this discussion. All right, let's get this over with. Number one, we were bad parents.

ALLY: No, that's not what / I mean—

CAROL: Well maybe not *bad* parents, but we could have been better. Two, Dad was filming you all the time. Three, I may have drank too much. And four, after Bo left, we were terrible to you. *But*, you should have brought Max over more. Done! Big issues resolved!

ALLY: *Godammit* why can't we just talk?!

CAROL: Ally, do you think any amount of talking is going to make you feel like we've said everything we needed to say?

(Pause.)

ALLY: No, probably not.

CAROL: So there we go! Let's just have a pleasant conversation while we still can, all right?

ALLY: Everyone in my life is leaving me, Mom. *(Pause)* Laura left me. She took Max. That's why they aren't here.

425

CAROL: What happened?

ALLY: I—screwed up? I've been working eighty-hour weeks ever since Max was born, I just put down fifty thousand dollars on this bunker on our property without telling her—

CAROL: HOW MUCH MONEY? WHAT'S A BUNKER?

ALLY: Never mind, it's—. I just messed up, I've been messing things up for a while.

CAROL: Where did she go?

ALLY: Pretty sure she's in Seattle with her cousin.

CAROL: Have you called her?

(Pause.)

ALLY: Mom, what if I'm not up to this? I've been screwing up the first two years of his life, what's to say I'm not gonna screw up the next sixteen? What if I— . . .

CAROL: What? "What if I'm like Dad?" Is that what you were going to say?

(Carol looks at her, considers for a second.)

Well, I don't know, maybe you're right. Maybe you shouldn't call them.

(Pause.)

ALLY: Really?

CAROL: Maybe you *would* just screw him up. Maybe you should cut your losses, let them go while he's still young enough to forget about you.

ALLY: Mom—

CAROL: Better yet why don't you just have some of that Nembutal with me? A nice old-fashioned mother-daughter suicide, how about that?

ALLY: OKAY. Okay.

(Pause.)

CAROL: Ally, you—.

(Pause.)

I know what it's like to live in fear of becoming your parents, believe me I get it. So I'm gonna tell you something my parents never told me.

(Pause.)

You're not me. You're not your father. You're thoughtful, driven, and you could be a great parent if you let yourself be. You feel like you spend too much time working? Hire someone. You spent a whole bunch of money on something without telling Laura? Apologize. You're smart enough to fix this.

(Pause.)

ALLY: Yeah.

(Pause.)

CAROL: So you'll call her?
ALLY: Yeah. I'll call her.
CAROL: Good. That's—good.

(Pause.)

ALLY: Thank you, Mom.

CAROL: Well, no need to get all sentimental about it.

(Pause. Carol smiles at her, then gets up.)

Okay, well. You still have the piece of paper, right? The instructions?

(Pause.)

ALLY: Are we—? We're doing it now?
CAROL: No reason to wait. You still have the instructions I gave you?
ALLY: Yeah, I—. Yeah. *(Pause)* I don't—. I don't know where the Bing Crosby tape is.
CAROL: Oh, don't worry about it.
ALLY: Mom, maybe we should wait, maybe Bo will come back—
CAROL: Honey, if he wanted to be here, he'd be here. *(Pause)* You sure you want this? I wouldn't blame you for leaving.
ALLY: I want to be here. Really.

(Pause.)

CAROL: Okay.

(Carol exits into her bedroom. Ally sits down on the couch. Bo enters, in funeral black. Ally looks at him.)

ALLY: Hey. You're here.
BO: Yeah. *(Pause)* I was on my way to the airport.
ALLY: Why'd you come back?

(Carol reenters with the Nembutal and syringe. She stops when she sees Bo.)

CAROL: Well hello. *(Pause)* Are you—here?

BO: Mom, were you supposed to do this with Dad? Were you supposed to do this together?

(Pause.)

CAROL: Bo, why is it so important for / you to—?

BO: Why do you need us to be here?

(Pause.)

CAROL: I was going to take it right after he did. Make sure it worked. Then I'd go.

(Pause.)

ALLY: Why didn't you?

(Pause. Carol begins to pace the room, turning on the lights on the Christmas tree, turning on other Christmas decorations, turning on the Christmas carols.)

CAROL: Dad didn't want you kids involved. But I guess when I saw him sitting there, not breathing, I just—. Still felt like I didn't want to leave. So I painted everything white, thought maybe that would make me feel better, erasing everything or whatever. But I—realized I wanted you both back here. Every Christmas we always forced you kids to act like you were happy and whatever, and—. I just wanted to have you both here for the holidays one last time. Talk to one another for real. We didn't have many truthful moments with one another, and I thought maybe I could—.

(Pause.)

Thank you, both of you. For being here.

(Carol has finished setting up the Christmas decorations. She dims the lights. For the first time the room feels cozy, warm, set up for Christmas.

Carol moves to a shelf, picking up a small ceramic vase. She reaches inside and pulls out a video tape.

She goes to Bo, offering him the tape.)

It's the last video. The last one we made for you kids. He wanted you to see what it was like, to see that it wasn't scary or sad. I started filming right after he— . . .

(Pause.)

Watch it.

(Pause. Bo takes the tape. He moves to the television, putting the tape in the camera.

Carol moves to the couch and sits, picking up the Nembutal and syringe.

Bo presses play on the camera, the stage transforms into:)

Last Home Video

The lights go out and a projection immediately fills the entire space: the old living room, before it was painted white, projected on top of the present living room. The effect should be that the entire room suddenly returns to what it looked like before it was painted white; for the first time, the room has gained color.

A video of Martin is projected on the couch; Martin (on video) and Carol (live) both hold the syringe and Nembutal in their hand. They are rolling up their sleeves, looking for a vein. We hear Carol's recorded voice from the past, talking to Martin.

CAROL *(On video, offscreen)*: Do you want me to—bring you anything?

MARTIN *(On video)*: Oh it's fine.

CAROL *(On video, offscreen)*: Do you / want—?

MARTIN *(On video)*: Honey, it's fine. I'm doing fine. Thanks.

ALLY: How long is to going to take?

CAROL: Not long, I think.

BO: I don't really—. Should we—say something?

CAROL *(On video, offscreen)*: Should I say something? Read you something?

CAROL: No.

MARTIN *(On video)*: It's fine.

(Carol and Martin fill their syringes with Nembutal.)

CAROL: Now I don't want you making a fuss over my funeral. Just keep it simple. Have me cremated.

BO: Okay.

ALLY: You sure it won't hurt?

CAROL: No, not at all. Just drift off to sleep.

MARTIN *(On video)*: I actually feel sort of—optimistic. Like in a few minutes, time and space aren't going to matter. It's almost like I can feel it.

CAROL *(On video, offscreen)*: Oh you're full of it.

MARTIN *(On video)*: Seriously. You'll feel it too. It's—freeing. In a few days, I'll be cremated, and I'll just be energy spreading out into the universe. Feels pretty good.

(Martin and Carol inject the Nembutal into their arms.)

CAROL *(On video, offscreen)*: Martin?

MARTIN *(On video)*: Yeah?

CAROL *(On video, offscreen)*: Are you going?

BO: You feel okay?

CAROL: Yeah, I feel—good. I feel really good.

MARTIN *(On video)*: I think so.

ALLY: I just wish we knew each other. I wish we all knew each other better.

CAROL: That doesn't matter now.

MARTIN AND CAROL: Soon I'll just be energy spreading out into the universe.

(Pause.)

It really feels sort of—beautiful.

(The lights fade out around Bo, Ally, and the rest of the room; the only light on stage is a small pool of light around Carol and the projection of Martin.
Carol and Martin breathe in, then out.
They breathe in, then out.
They breathe in, then out.
They breathe in, then are still.
A brief moment of silence.
Black.)

END OF PLAY

Acknowledgments

The author would like to thank Playwrights Horizons, Boise Contemporary Theater, The Old Globe, Rattlestick Playwrights Theater, Seattle Repertory Theatre, South Coast Repertory, Williamstown Theatre Festival, and Victory Gardens. The author would also like to thank the following people who supported the development of these plays: Davis McCallum, Braden Abraham, Eric Ting, Joanie Schultz, Martin Benson, Stella Powell-Jones, Portia Krieger, Casey Stangl, Adam Rapp, Jerry Manning, Jenny Gersten, Chay Yew, Matthew Cameron Clark, Marc Masterson, David Van Asselt, Tim Sanford, Adam Greenfield, Barry Edelstein, and especially John M. Baker, who was instrumental in the creation of all five plays.

SAMUEL D. HUNTER's plays include *The Whale* (Drama Desk Award, Lucille Lortel Award for Outstanding Play, GLAAD Media Award, Drama League and Outer Critics Circle nominations for Best Play), *A Bright New Boise* (Obie Award, Drama Desk nomination for Best Play), *The Few*, *A Great Wilderness*, *Rest*, *A Permanent Image*, *Pocatello*, *Lewiston*, *Clarkston*, and most recently, *The Healing* and *The Harvest*. He is the recipient of a 2014 MacArthur "Genius Grant" Fellowship, a 2012 Whiting Writers Award, the 2013 Otis Guernsey New Voices Award, the 2011 Sky Cooper Prize, the 2008 PoNY/Lark Fellowship, and an honorary doctorate from the University of Idaho. His plays have been produced in New York at Playwrights Horizons, LCT3, Rattlestick Playwrights Theater, Clubbed Thumb, and Page 73, and around the country at Seattle Rep, South Coast Rep, Victory Gardens Theater, Williamstown Theatre Festival, The Old Globe, Woolly Mammoth Theatre Company, Denver Center Theatre Company, the Dallas Theater Center, Long Wharf Theatre, and elsewhere. His work has been developed at the O'Neill National Playwrights Conference, the Ojai Playwrights Conference, Seven Devils Playwrights

Conference, and PlayPenn. He is a member of New Dramatists, an Ensemble Playwright at Victory Gardens, and was a 2013 resident playwright at Arena Stage. A native of northern Idaho, Sam lives in New York City. He holds degrees in playwriting from NYU, The Iowa Playwrights Workshop, and Juilliard.